THE LIVES OF COMMUNITY HEALTH WORKERS

The importance of community health workers is increasingly recognized within many of today's most high-profile global health programs, including campaigns focused on specific diseases and broader efforts to strengthen health systems and achieve universal health care. Based on ethnographic work with Ethiopian women and men who provided home-based care in Addis Ababa during the early rollout of antiretroviral therapies, this book explores what it actually means to become a community health worker in today's global health industry.

Drawing on the author's interviews with community health workers, as well as observations of their daily interactions with patients and supervisors, this volume considers what motivates them to improve the quality of life and death of marginalized people. *The Lives of Community Health Workers* also illuminates how their contributions at a micro level are intricately linked to policymaking and practice at higher levels in the field of global health. It shows us that many of the challenges that community health workers face in their daily lives are embedded in larger social, economic, and political problems, and raises a resounding call for further research into their labor and the health systems they inhabit.

Kenneth Maes is Assistant Professor of Anthropology at Oregon State University, USA.

Anthropology and Global Public Health

Global Mental Health
Anthropological Perspectives
Edited by Brandon A. Kohrt and Emily Mendenhall

Pesticides and Global Health
Understanding Agrochemical Dependence and Investing in
Sustainable Solutions
Courtney Marie Dowdall and Ryan J. Klotz

THE LIVES OF COMMUNITY HEALTH WORKERS

Local Labor and Global Health in Urban Ethiopia

Kenneth Maes

Routledge
Taylor & Francis Group

NEW YORK AND LONDON

First published 2017
by Routledge
711 Third Avenue, New York, NY 10017

and by Routledge
2 Park Square, Milton Park, Abingdon, Oxon OX14 4RN

Routledge is an imprint of the Taylor & Francis Group, an informa business

Library of Congress Cataloging in Publication Data
Names: Maes, Kenneth, author.
Title: The lives of community health workers : local labor and global
    health in urban Ethiopia / Kenneth Maes.
Other titles: Anthropology and global public health.
Description: New York : Routledge, 2016. | Series: Anthropology and
    global public health | Includes bibliographical references and index.
Identifiers: LCCN 2016025353 | ISBN 9781611323603 (hardback : alk.
    paper) | ISBN 9781611323610 (pbk. : alk. paper)
Subjects: LCSH: Caregivers—Ethiopia—Addis Ababa. | Public health
    personnel—Ethiopia—Addis Ababa. | Home care services—Ethiopia—
    Addis Ababa. | HIV-positive persons—Services for—Ethiopia—Addis
    Ababa.
Classification: LCC RA645.37.E8 M34 2016 | DDC 362.1409633—dc23
LC record available at https://lccn.loc.gov/2016025353

ISBN: 978-1-61132-360-3 (hbk)
ISBN: 978-1-61132-361-0 (pbk)
ISBN: 978-1-315-40078-5 (ebk)

Typeset in Bembo
by Apex CoVantage, LLC

For Doris, Mark, Karen, and Dick

CONTENTS

FIGURES

ACKNOWLEDGMENTS

This book is made possible, first and foremost, by the extraordinary openness and generosity of the community health workers and nurses whom I encountered in Addis Ababa. These women and men were welcoming and sympathetic to my attempts to understand intimate aspects of their lives. They also provided uplifting models of compassion and equanimity.

The directors and staff at the Hiwot HIV/AIDS Prevention, Control and Support Organization, the Medhen Social Center, and the HIV/AIDS Department at ALERT Hospital in Addis Ababa generously granted me access to conduct research and facilitated so many of my efforts to collect data and understand their programs. I am forever grateful in particular to Sister Regat Tesfamariam, Sister Tibebe Maco, Dr. Yigeremu Abebe, Dr. Berhanu Gebremichael, Dr. Bisrat Taye, Tenagne Kebede, Shimeles Girma, and Michael Hailu.

The research on which this book is based would not have been possible without funding from multiple sources. A dissertation award from the National Science Foundation (BCS-67062516) supported much of the fieldwork in Addis Ababa. A senior NSF award (BCS-1155271/1153926) has funded my more recent efforts to understand the role of community health workers in Ethiopia's national health system, as have fellowships and awards from the National Institutes of Health (D43 TW01042 and T32 HD007338–23), Emory University's Global Health Institute, and Emory's AIDS International Training and Research Program. Most recently, an award from Oregon State University's Center for the Humanities provided crucial support that allowed me to develop this book manuscript. To all of these sponsors, I am deeply grateful.

Dr. Fikru Tesfaye (then at the Addis Ababa University School of Public Health), Professor Yemane Berhane at the Addis Continental Institute of Public Health, and Hailom Banteyerga and Aklilu Kidanu at the Miz-Hasab Research

Center provided essential mentoring and institutional support during my fieldwork in Addis Ababa. Charlotte Hanlon, Atalay Alem, Georges Reniers, Sister Takebash Araya, and Yilma Melkamu also provided helpful guidance during the early stages of my research. Selamawit Shifferaw, Yihenew Alemu Tesfaye, and Meseret Meressa provided both friendship and exceptional assistance in data collection and research design. Yihenew has continued to be an invaluable source of insight into so many spheres of economic, political, and social life in Ethiopia. Meli, Tamrat, and Wintana provided a home and incredible moral support for more than a year in Addis Ababa, as well as a window into their day-to-day lives. I could not have asked for a better host family. Meli also provided crucial research assistance, not to mention great care when I fell ill. My deep gratitude also goes to Melkam Hailom, whose kindness, humor, and spirit have been truly precious to me. She is the first reason I always look forward to returning to Addis Ababa. I would also think twice about repeating my fieldwork experience in Addis Ababa without Jed Stevenson, whose camaraderie was always just an eight-hour bus ride or phone call away. Through the years, I have benefited in countless ways from our friendship.

At Emory University, I received advice and support from many mentors, teachers, students, and staff. These people include Bradd Shore, Joseph Henrich, Dan Sellen, Chikako Ozawa-de Silva, Carol Worthman, Mel Konner, Dorothy Fitzmaurice, Lynn Sibley, Pamela Scully, Sita Ranchod-Nilsson, Ulf Nilsson, Debra Keyes, Sybil Bridges, Sally Pattison-Cisna, Dredge Kang, Sarah Barks, Sarah Davis, Michelle Parsons, Julie Solomon, Brandie Littlefield, Dan Hruschka, Dan Lende, Ryan Brown, Ben Junge, Eric Lindland, Erin Finley, Sarah Willen, Amanda Thompson, Bethany Turner, Jennifer Kuzara, Brandon Kohrt, James Broesch, Tanya Macgillivray, Leonardo Marques, Tyralynn Frazier, Amanda Seider, Kwame Phillips, Bonnie Kaiser, Jennifer Sweeney Tookes, Amber Campbell, Molly Zuckerman, Jo Weaver, Michelle Dynes, and Jenny Mascaro. I cannot imagine better advisors than Craig Hadley, Peter Brown, Ron Barrett, and Joyce Murray—exceedingly generous with their wisdom, energy, and time. Long live the legacy and our memories of George Armelagos, friend and mentor to many students and colleagues at Emory and beyond.

Brown University's Population Studies and Training Center (PSTC) provided invaluable postdoctoral support during my early attempts to formulate this manuscript. At Brown, thanks are due especially to Daniel Jordan Smith, Michael White, Andrew Foster, Stephen McGarvey, David Lindstrom, Catherine Lutz, Mark Lurie, Abigail Harrison, Bianca Dahl, Megan Hattori-Klein, Kelley Alison Smith, Nicola Hawley, Tom Alarie, Susan Silveira, Priscilla Terry, and Shauna Mecartea.

Wendy Madar, David Robinson, and Joy Futrell at Oregon State University's Center for the Humanities; Chunhuei Chi in the Center for Global Health; and Mehra Shirazi, Daniel Lopez-Cevallos, Liddy Detar, Bradley Boovy, Adam Schwartz, Charlene Martinez, Natchee Barnd, and Karen Mills in the School of

Language, Culture, and Society provided generous moral and material support as I wrote this book. I am forever grateful for the outstanding leadership of Susan Shaw. It is a massive privilege to work with such inspiring colleagues in a school that values engaged and applied research examining culture, power, and social justice. In the Department of Anthropology, Bryan Tilt, David McMurray, Joan Gross, Nancy Rosenberger, Leah Minc, Lisa Price, Drew Gerkey, and Loretta Wardrip have been exceptional colleagues. I'm also grateful to Larry Becker and Badege Bishaw for their leadership of OSU's Africa Initiative. I owe a big debt to Melissa Cheyney and Andy Meskil, who have done so much to help my family balance work and life. Great thanks are also due to my many students, including graduate students in my 2015 Cross-Cultural Health and Healing class, who provided very helpful comments on an earlier draft of this book: Araya Assfaw, Eileen Celentano, Sean Dalton, Chris McFarland, Erin Presby, McKenna Pullen, Megan Richardson, Jessica Seifert, Jason Skipton, and Callie Walsh-Bailey.

Numerous others have provided valuable intellectual feedback as I developed this book, including Daniel Mains, Teferi Abate Adem, Yared Amare, Bruck Fikru, Christopher Colvin, Alison Swartz, Noelle Wiggins, Jennifer Johnson-Hanks, James McCann, Susan Cotts Watkins, John Brett, Alexander Rödlach, Barrett Brenton, John Mazzeo, Catherine Panter-Brick, João Biehl, James Pfeiffer, Ippolytos Kalofonos, Josh Snodgrass, Rebecca Warne-Peters, Claire Wendland, Aunchalee Loscalzo-Palmquist, Marit Østebø, and Lovise Aalen. Special thanks are due to Kristin Harper, who provided outstanding and detailed feedback on an earlier version of the entire manuscript, and to Svea Closser, whose collaboration has provided me with a constant source of intellectual rigor, curiosity, and enjoyment.

Emily Mendenhall and Peter Brown were very patient and provided exceptionally helpful guidance with the manuscript. Jack Meinhardt and Jennifer Collier at Left Coast Press and Katherine Ong at Routledge also provided valuable editorial assistance. I am sincerely grateful to two anonymous reviewers for insightful and constructive suggestions, which I tried hard to address during the final revisions.

Finally, I want to thank all my family and friends for their love, support, humor, and patience, including Mom, Dad, Kristine, Julie, Miles, and Georgia. My deepest thanks go to Cari, whose name became my mantra in Addis Ababa. Every step of the way, she has given countless hours of her time to provide me with laughter, affirmation, reality checks, and time to write and travel, all while maintaining her own scholarship on the history of 20th century public health initiatives, from which I have also benefited. Thank you.

All the remaining shortcomings of this book, of course, are solely my responsibility.

ABBREVIATIONS USED IN THE TEXT

ALERT	All Africa Leprosy and Tuberculosis Rehabilitation and Training Centre
ART	Antiretroviral therapy
ARVs	Antiretrovirals
BINGO	Big International NGO
CHBC	Community Home-Based Care
CHWs	Community Health Workers
CMD	Common Mental Disorder
DFID	Department for International Development
EMA	Ethiopian Medical Association
EPRDF	Ethiopian People's Revolutionary Democratic Front
EPHA	Ethiopian Public Health Association
EPRP	Ethiopian People's Revolutionary Party
FCHV	Female Community Health Volunteer
FHI	Family Health International
FMOH	Federal Ministry of Health of Ethiopia
GFATM	Global Fund to Fight AIDS, Tuberculosis and Malaria, or Global Fund
GPEI	Global Polio Eradication Initiative
GWOT	Global war on terror
HAART	Highly active antiretroviral therapy
HAPCO	HIV/AIDS Prevention and Control Office
HEP	Health Extension Program
HEWs	Health Extension Workers
HBC	Home-based care
IMF	International Monetary Fund
ITUC	International Trade Union Confederation

L10K	Last 10 Kilometers Program
LHW	Lady Health Worker
MACHW	Massachusetts Association of Community Health Workers
MAP	World Bank's Multisector AIDS Program
MDGs	Millennium Development Goals
MDPH	Massachusetts Department of Public Health
MEISON	All-Ethiopia Socialist Movement
MPHA	Massachusetts Public Health Association
NCHWAS	National Community Health Workers Advocacy Study (US)
NGO	Non-governmental organization
OPEC	Organization of Petroleum-Exporting Countries
ORCHWA	Oregon Community Health Workers Association
PEPFAR	US President's Emergency Plan for AIDS Relief
PIH	Partners in Health
PLWHA	Person/People living with HIV/AIDS
PMTCT	Prevention of mother-to-child transmission
RCT	Randomized controlled trial
SIM	Sudan Interior Mission
UNAIDS	Joint United National Programme on HIV/AIDS
UNDP	United Nations Development Programme
UNFPA	United Nations Population Fund
UNICEF	United Nations Children's Fund
UNV	UN Volunteers
USAID	United States Agency for International Development
WFP	World Food Program
WHO	World Health Organization
WPE	Workers Party of Ethiopia

INTRODUCTION

In 2007, the Ethiopian government placed a bronze rectangular plaque in the center of an unimpressive traffic circle on the southwest leg of Addis Ababa's ring road, thereby creating the capital city's first "Volunteers Circle." The circle is miles away from the monumental and historical squares located in Addis Ababa's city center. There are no big buildings around, and much of the immediate surroundings consist of dirt lots littered with trash. Yet on a sunny Saturday morning in May 2008, the second annual Ethiopian Volunteers Day, Volunteers Circle became a ceremonial space packed with people and temporary canopies colored red, green, and yellow—the colors of Ethiopia's flag. Police were positioned to keep the unusual quantity of pedestrians safe from the minibuses, dump trucks, and SUVs that made their way through the roundabout. A few state and private news reporters were also on the scene, cameras in hand. Though Addis Ababa's landfill was nearby, it was downwind that morning, and the pleasant highland air competed only with truck fumes to fill the noses and lungs of the people who assembled.

In 2008, the Ethiopian Volunteers Day event was planned by the staff of a local non-governmental organization (NGO) named Hiwot, who wanted to celebrate their large workforce of volunteer community health workers.[1] The Hiwot NGO had emerged in Addis Ababa in the 1990s to prevent and provide care for people with HIV/AIDS and had since grown to become one of the largest NGOs in the country, with over six hundred community health workers or CHWs on its rosters.[2] Their CHWs were trained and supervised primarily to support the provision of free antiretroviral therapies (ART) to a rapidly expanding number of new patients—a national program initiated in 2005. Thus the NGO expected its volunteer CHWs to spend anywhere from 15 to 40 hours a week visiting the homes of a dozen or so people living with HIV/AIDS, providing them with

FIGURE 0.1 Ethiopian Volunteers Day, 2008.

Photo courtesy of the author.

counseling, treatment support, and routine care, as well as accompanying them as they sought resources from clinics, NGOs, and government welfare offices.

Though Hiwot trained and supervised CHWs working throughout the capital, it focused much of its attention on the ART program housed at ALERT Hospital, one of the country's biggest and best-resourced ART programs, located near the southwest city limits. At the beginning of ALERT's ART program, which was intended to cover two of Addis Ababa's ten districts, 8,000 out of a total population of 760,000 people were estimated to be in need of ART (FMOH/HAPCO 2006b). At the helm of the program was a respected Ethiopian medical doctor, who managed a staff of ART-specialist physicians, nurses, pharmacists, and data clerks. During a presentation he gave in 2006 to visiting Canadian donors, he impressed upon his audience that his relatively small staff was seeing between 180 and 200 patients a day. Nurses were doing some of the doctors' work, data entry and patient intake clerks were doing some of the nurses' work, and cleaners and records filers were doing some of the patient intake clerks' work. It seemed everyone in the clinic was working well beyond his or her official job description, as the number of people accessing ART at ALERT went from zero at the end of 2004 to nearly three thousand by mid-2006 and then kept on growing.[3]

ALERT's ART staff relied upon the daily efforts of several hundred CHWs, who walked and bussed around some of Addis Ababa's dense and sprawling peripheral neighborhoods, locating and accompanying patients who needed ART but were scared, uninformed, or unable to access clinical treatment and care. The vast majority—up to 90%—of these CHWs were women. As I came to learn, most were currently unemployed and had been unemployed before becoming NGO volunteers. In many other respects, however, they were a diverse group. Some of them had worked in various low-level, insecure jobs at factories and schools, or as migrant housekeepers in the Middle East. Some made small amounts of money by selling vegetables on the street or serving as part-time parking attendants. They ranged in age from 18 to 45 years, and had varying levels of education. Several had not finished secondary school, while the majority of them had, and a few had taken courses in local colleges or universities. They identified with various ethnic groups, mostly Amhara or Oromo, but also Tigre and Gurage. While the vast majority were Orthodox Christians, several identified as Protestants and a few as Muslim.[4] About 17% of the CHWs were HIV-positive, against a background prevalence of about 10% in the capital. Many more knew close relatives and friends who were living with the virus.

In 2002, the World Health Organization (WHO) emphasized the expediency of honoring and recognizing volunteer CHWs in ceremonies and providing them with "badges, uniforms, T-shirts, umbrellas" and the like (WHO 2002).[5] For the Ethiopian Volunteers Day event, the NGO mustered up at least two hundred of its volunteers and gave all who showed up that morning matching white T-shirts and paper visors, on which had been printed (in Amharic, the lingua franca of Addis Ababa), "Let us protect children from HIV/AIDS and spread volunteer service" and "Everyone should give volunteer service in order to improve the country and fellow people!"

Their apparel also displayed the logos of the Hiwot NGO and its major international partner in the new age of free ART: Family Health International or FHI, a well-known BINGO or "Big International NGO" based in the USA.[6] In their T-shirts and visors, packed into the circle and milling about the surrounding area, the volunteers waited for the arrival of the invited guests—officials from various local and international NGOs and government health offices. The officials eventually arrived and took their seats, and the event unfolded with synthesizer-accompanied performances by professional Ethiopian dancers, interspersed with a series of speeches, jokes, and poems delivered by the invited officials.

The various NGO officials who delivered speeches bestowed immense praise upon the volunteers and thanked them for their daily care for people with a stigmatized and life-threatening illness. They also reiterated a series of messages about how the kinds of sacrifices that the CHWs made generated a sense of happiness and fulfillment. An Ethiopian man representing a new start-up NGO called the Ethiopian Association for Voluntary Service said that the benefits of volunteering "begin with mental satisfaction." A Ugandan woman representing

FIGURE 0.2 Visor and T-shirt given to community health workers at Ethiopian Volunteers Day, 2008.

Photo courtesy of the author.

UN Volunteers (UNV), whose speech title was listed in the event's program as "The Need to Promote Voluntarism," proclaimed, "The joy that comes from volunteering is the biggest reward." The director of the Hiwot NGO, dressed in the same T-shirt and visor as the volunteers, bestowed praise on her large cadre of hardworking CHWs and compared them to candles giving light and hope to their patients while melting away in self-sacrifice.

An Ethiopian official representing FHI delivered a speech in which she claimed that she even felt envious of the volunteers and the happiness they derived through caring for others.

> When we [i.e., officers] go to see what the volunteers are doing, we see that they walk through the back alleys—even if there is rain, mud, or bad smells. . . . And yet they are happy with what they are doing. We want to look after ourselves when it is raining . . . But these volunteers are giving their time for the patients instead of taking care of themselves. I would be pleased if all of us could do their job—I believe that it would be an important opportunity to learn a lesson. For the future, I wish you the strength and the interest to continue your good work for your country and society. God will help you. Thank you.

Ethiopian Volunteers Day coincided with the 2007–2008 global food price crisis, which led to the loss of food aid, skyrocketing food prices, and substantial psychological and social suffering for residents of Addis Ababa, including the volunteer CHWs and their patients, who both spent large proportions of their tiny incomes on their daily bread. Getting paid for their work—from the government, FHI, Hiwot, or whoever—could have been very helpful for these CHWs. But creating paid CHW jobs along with the rollout of ART was not the aim of these institutions. Instead, they maintained a policy of encouraging volunteerism. The Hiwot NGO had for some time provided its volunteer CHWs with a monthly food package, not unlike the food packages targeted at the volunteers' own patients. But by the time of the Volunteers Day celebration in mid-2008, high global food prices coupled with historically low World Food Program donations had interrupted the food package stream that ended with the Hiwot NGO and its CHWs and patients. As a result, CHWs and some of their patients—those whose body mass indexes fell above a newly instituted cutoff—no longer received food packages. All the NGO could offer (with funding support from FHI) was to reimburse the bus fares and mobile phone expenses that the CHWs incurred during their daily work. Thus the officials who spoke at Ethiopian Volunteers Day in 2008 made concerted efforts to focus on the uplifting aspects of working as an unpaid CHW and to express their thanks and admiration.

The CHWs present listened carefully, applauded in response to the officials' speeches, and ululated and clapped along with the song and dance. Not once

FIGURE 0.3 An NGO official makes a prepared speech at Ethiopian Volunteers Day, 2008.

Photo courtesy of the author.

FIGURE 0.4 Community Health Workers applauding at Ethiopian Volunteers Day, 2008. Photo courtesy of the author.

during the event, however, was one of them invited to provide a candid testimony. The ceremony put the CHWs and their labor center stage without involving them as active participants. The event, to borrow a phrase from the BINGO official, was an important opportunity—not to learn a lesson, but to communicate to the CHWs, the media, and the public about the need to promote volunteerism and about how to imagine volunteerism: as a sacrifice that brings mental satisfaction a valuable return.

The Labor and Lives of Community Health Workers

After many years of waning interest and investment in CHWs, many stakeholders in the field of global health are now reaffirming their importance within many of today's most high-profile global health interventions, including campaigns focused on specific diseases and broader efforts to strengthen health systems and achieve universal health care. Global health action today is led by partnerships between wealthy and needy governments, NGOs of various sizes, pharmaceutical and medical technology corporations, and international health institutions, a category that includes WHO, UNICEF, and World Bank (Cueto 2013). Commonly referred to as public-private partnerships, their actions are funded by multiple donors and guided by various goals, including economic development and health systems strengthening, homeland security, reduced mortality rates, and population adherence to beliefs and behaviors deemed healthy. Scores of these high-level institutions—including WHO, UNICEF, GlaxoSmithKline, USAID, Johnson & Johnson, the Gates Foundation, and many more—have signed on to a global health initiative devoted to financing the addition of at least one million CHWs to the health systems of low-income countries in sub-Saharan Africa, and have called for innovative and evidence-based policies that improve recruitment, retention, and performance of community health workforces (Bhutta et al. 2010; Dahn et al. 2015; Earth Institute 2011; Perry and Crigler 2014; Singh and Chokshi 2013; Singh and Sachs 2013; Watt et al. 2011). Where there is no doctor or other health professional, or where there are not enough of them to provide for universal access to primary health care, leaders of these institutions envision CHWs filling the gaps. They envisage, furthermore, that CHWs will take health care into homes and reduce the burden borne by hospitals and health centers. Even where there are doctors and health professionals, people see CHWs as useful, because they meet people "on their level" and provide intimate, personalized primary health care even to marginalized people.

CHWs might be as important, if not more, than the handful of high-profile global health leaders whom we might be able to name. Too often, however, representations of CHWs in government documents, NGO reports, and the media are little more than caricatures, often based on a desire to portray them as happy, heroic, and self-sacrificing savers of lives.[7] Based on ethnographic work with a group of Ethiopian women and men who served as CHWs providing home-based care in Addis Ababa during the early rollout of antiretroviral therapies, this book illustrates what it actually means to become a CHW in today's global health industry.

The following chapters provide glimpses into the intimate work that CHWs do to improve the quality of life and death of the most marginalized people in their own communities. CHWs—women and men with voices, names, faces, families, and histories—were drawn to this unpaid work out of a mix of desires: to see people with AIDS become healthy, to decrease the stigmatization surrounding HIV, and to link up with NGOs that might provide them with some form of economic support or opportunities for future employment. Hearing from CHWs in their own words is increasingly important, as these workers appear poised to take on numerically bigger roles in the global health industry. But this ethnography will go beyond exploring their motivations and work with patients. It will examine the intertwined histories that produced the epidemics, health institutions, and populations of underemployed people that comprised this particular CHW program in Addis Ababa in the early 21st century. It will show how and why a web of donors, officials, and supervisors attempted to implement a problematic policy of volunteerism that was in many ways inappropriate in a setting of high unemployment, poverty, and food insecurity, and how these actors attempted to produce a workforce willing—to some extent—to work for free. It will explain why these AIDS-focused volunteer CHWs in the capital of Ethiopia were far from becoming autonomous forces of health equity and social justice, with seats at policy tables and the power to make government and non-governmental institutions bend to their will. And it will examine the extent to which community health work generated both satisfaction and distress for these workers, as they strove to find and create ways to improve their own lives.

Overall, this book illuminates the intricate links between CHW contributions at a micro level and policymaking and practice at higher levels in the field of global health, and demonstrates that a more intimate understanding of the former can improve our understanding of the latter, and vice versa. It shows us that many of the challenges that CHWs face in their daily lives and work are embedded in much bigger social, economic, and political problems—including unemployment, poorly regulated and unfairly governed health systems, warfare, inequality, and other human rights violations. And it raises a resounding call for much more social science research into the labor and lives of CHWs and the health systems they inhabit.

Morality, Power, and Policy-Relevant Research

The issue of CHW payment has driven much debate in recent years, since in many places CHWs are either unpaid or paid very little. Many argue that the use of unpaid and underpaid CHW labor in health programs is unfair: the people who donate their labor as CHWs so often want decent, paid jobs in order to meet their daily needs and escape poverty, and they *deserve* better payment for their important work. Physician-anthropologist Paul Farmer raises this issue:

> Imagine that it has become a radical notion to suggest that you actually pay poor people for their labor. . . . Of course you should pay poor people for their work. . . . You notice that [volunteer] models [of community health work] almost always come from non-poor people. . . . And I think we should be a little bit suspicious when people who don't have to worry about food and shelter . . . [argue] that we shouldn't pay poor people to help us do a project . . .[8]

In other words, relying on unpaid CHW labor is exploitative and unfair, given the fact that billions of dollars poured into the new field of global health in the early 21st century have managed to create plenty of well-paid jobs for non-poor professionals in the global north and south. A just and equitable global health industry must pursue not only the improvement of health-care delivery systems but also protect the right of poor people—not just highly educated professionals—to fair and regular remuneration for their labor as a means to basic economic security.

Many stakeholders in global community health interventions further argue that providing adequate salaries and benefits for CHWs will bring broader social and economic gains. In fact, several recent and influential publications regarding CHWs are virtually unanimous: CHWs should be paid a living wage, if not as a fundamental right, then as an economic stimulus that favors women and their social networks, since CHWs around the world are so often women living amid high levels of unemployment and insecure employment. For example, a widely cited WHO policy guideline from 2008 asserts, "Wages for community health workers may contribute to broader human development and poverty reduction strategies" (WHO 2008: 36). Likewise, the authors of a recently published CHW Investment Case (Dahn et al. 2015) claim that strong, formalized CHW systems can deliver "a positive economic return, reducing unemployment, and empowering women" (p. 8).[9]

Payment is not the only matter that has driven debate in the CHW arena. Another fundamental issue is the question of how exactly CHWs should participate in health programs and systems. For decades, the idea of *local participation* has occupied a central position in discourses about community health workers and primary health care. Yet different actors maintain divergent visions of CHW participation (Colvin and Swartz 2015; Leban et al. 2014; Lehmann and Sanders 2007; Standing et al. 2008). Many scholars and public health professionals articulate a model of CHWs as potentially cost-effective health-care delivery mechanisms—apolitical human resources who work for relatively low wages, saving lives, and averting disease with smartphones, medical technologies, health education, and referrals to services offered by states, NGOs, and donors. Others have long wished to see CHWs become more effective agents of social and political change, who not only provide empathic care but also organize and mobilize communities to address inequalities and social determinants of health through changing policies and holding powerful institutions accountable for their actions (Werner 1981). Many continue to criticize the reduction of community health workers to "mere delivery mechanisms" for health programs; that is, the expectation and encouragement among funders, policy makers, program directors, and medical staff that CHWs work with their heads down to prevent and treat illness, and the lack of encouragement and support for CHWs to take more control over the design and implementation of social policies or to speak up about social injustices that underlie health inequalities (Arvey and Fernandez 2012: 1634; Ingram et al. 2014; Manchanda 2015; Pérez and Martinez 2008; Sabo et al. 2013). When CHWs do not directly participate in the governance of the programs they serve, many see this as contrary to principles of good governance for health systems, including affirmations that decision makers in the health sector should be accountable to the public and that all people should have a voice in decision making for health (Lewin and Lehmann 2014; Siddiqi et al. 2009).

These two issues—CHW payment and the forms of participation in which they engage—clearly garner public expressions of moral convictions from an array of global health leaders. Such expressions are important in bringing about key changes in CHW policy and practice. Yet targeted change in the design and operation of CHW programs around the globe cannot rely on them alone. There is also great need for research into what is actually happening in the day-to-day functioning of CHW programs: how various stakeholders, including CHWs themselves, experience and deal with these issues as moral and political actors, and how current and historical policies and political-economic contexts shape what happens at the ground level.

How do CHWs, their supervisors, and health officials—working within the unique political economy of the global health industry—attempt to shape public understandings and forms of participation of CHWs? How do CHWs go along with or resist attempts to extract their labor, and how do other stakeholders respond? In what ways are CHWs at least attempting to exercise control over policy decisions that deeply affect them and their neighbors? How do donors, development professionals, and CHWs negotiate, share power, and hold each other accountable? Whose moral sentiments and demands are being heard, and whose are being ignored? What alliances and antagonistic relationships are unfolding? How do historical political and cultural legacies shape CHW policies and practice? How might wider health-system goals and political objectives influence the ways CHW programs are governed and how they evolve?

These are and will likely remain crucial questions for the conduct of CHW programs in the 21st century. Unfortunately, there is not enough research asking and answering these kinds of questions. In recent years, much CHW research has adopted what can be called a human resources mentality. This growing body of research, conducted by public health professionals and economists in partnership with employers of CHWs, including ministries of health and NGOs, uses surveys, interviews, and administrative data (on, for example, number of referrals or births in facilities) to determine the extent to which worker retention, performance, and health indicators improve in response to specific interventions—for instance, a new CHW training program or a new CHW incentive structure (e.g., Alam and Oliveras 2014; Ashraf et al. 2015; Bhutta et al. 2011; Schwarz et al. 2014). The relative abundance of this kind of research likely reflects that many (but not all) global health leaders and practitioners construct the pursuit of global health as a set of primarily technical and economic problems involving cost-effective "product delivery." From this perspective, CHWs are the low-level laborers deemed necessary for primary health-care delivery, akin to tools to be manipulated by supervisors and technicians skilled in economic, psychological, and management theories, as well as evaluations of intervention success.

This kind of research has brought much needed attention to CHWs and the programs they serve. It has produced a considerable body of knowledge that many policy makers and CHW employers find useful. But CHW programs involve much more than technical and financial questions; they also depend upon the relationships, values, and goals of a variety of actors, including supervisors, health officials, donors, researchers, and community health workers, all political and moral actors empowered and constrained in different ways by structural inequality and prevailing policies and norms in the global health industry. These various actors struggle and in some instances cooperate for control—over their own lives, workforce performance, local work and living conditions, health system functioning, and global policies—as much as they wrestle with technical challenges in the delivery of health care. In many places around the world, CHWs have organized their own labor movements, associations, and political action groups, engaging other power holders and policy makers with an aim toward improving their own job conditions and livelihoods and bringing about various other social, political, and economic changes. And in many places around the world, governments, NGOs, and donors are likely concerned about the future of CHW associations and power, and are interested in assembling workforces that are responsive to incentives and directives. As this book will show, even in places without CHW labor movements or associations, CHWs still participate in interactions with supervisors and officials, seeking out changes in their lives and the policies and structures that constrain them, alongside their efforts to forge relationships with and improve the lives of others in their care. Despite having major implications for the functioning of current and future CHW programs and health systems, these kinds of interactions do not get studied enough.

Ethnography emanating from the tradition of critical medical anthropology, which tends to focus on explaining relationships among population health, social, economic, and health-related experiences and desires of individuals, and structures of power and inequality (Kleinman 2006; Singer 1995; Singer and Castro 2004), can illuminate the complex social histories and cultural politics involved when people are recruited, trained, and deployed as CHWs. The last several years have seen a fair level of this kind of insightful and policy-relevant research, marking an important step in the evolution of knowledge about health systems and the field of global health. In the future, more researchers will pursue work in the arena of community health worker programs, drawing inspiration from previous studies as well as other influential publications (e.g., Perry and Crigler 2014). But in order to ensure that designers, financers, and directors of CHW programs around the world are critically aware of what is happening in the inherently social, political, and context-specific health systems they are trying to govern, there is need for much more intensive work in countless contexts around the globe. Thus this book aims not only to advance understanding of the plights and victories of CHWs but also to encourage current and future generations of public health-focused researchers, practitioners, and activists to produce more research in this rapidly evolving area.

In Chapter 1, I examine the political, economic, and policy context for the work that CHWs do in Addis Ababa and describe the path that Ethiopia has taken with regards to CHW labor. Chapter 2 then charts the intertwined histories of the global movement to treat AIDS, the ART program designated as Addis Ababa's center of excellence, the neighborhoods that fell into that program's catchment area, and the life of one of the CHWs who fell into the labor pool targeted by that program. This historical narrative helps us see just where CHWs are coming from socially, economically, and spiritually, and how their lives have intersected with those of the transnational institutions, epidemics, health-care movements, economic policies, and pharmaceuticals that co-constructed the great need for CHW labor in the early 21st century. Chapter 3 then turns to the production of CHWs through processes of recruitment, initiation, and training carried out by a mix of non-governmental, government, and neighborhood organizations. Recruitment stories reveal the nature of initial interactions between "management" and labor in which a cast of NGO supervisors, government officials, and medical professionals attempt to assemble and produce their ideal workforce. Here we begin to understand the politics and acts of care in which Ethiopian volunteer CHWs participate. Instead of actively participating in the design of their program, work conditions, and rallies, CHWs in Addis passively participated in interactive rituals largely shaped by NGO and government actors. Like the Ethiopian Volunteers Day ceremony recounted earlier, these ceremonies and rituals connected CHWs' socio-emotional and physical labors to notions of *sacrificing* to save and improve the lives of other people in need and to related ideas of *deriving spiritual merit and mental satisfaction* through this kind of sacrifice. These sentiments may actually be common across diverse CHW contexts and expressed in local idioms rooted in particular social, religious, and political histories. In Addis Ababa, they became normative by being repeatedly circulated within ceremonies such as Ethiopian Volunteers Day, as well as in day-to-day rituals—recruitment interviews, trainings, and other interactions—that brought together donors, program managers, health officials, supervisors, CHWs' care recipients, and CHWs themselves.

I argue that moral sentiments such as sacrifice and satisfaction play an important role in shaping the participation of many CHWs. Sentiments of sacrifice and spiritual satisfaction are proclaimed and reinforced by CHW supervisors and health officials to encourage intimate forms of care and anti-discrimination that are crucial for improving the quality of life of people living with otherwise debilitating and stigmatized illnesses. From another, more critical perspective, however, the emphasis that health officials give to sacrifice and spiritual satisfaction—on the part of underemployed, poor CHWs—points to how the global health industry can exploit human capacities for empathy, solidarity, care, spirituality, and moral passion in pursuit of the goals of saving lives and extending health care, while neglecting peoples' lack of employment, political freedom, and power. The emphasis on sacrifice and satisfaction is further troubling because it may obscure the psychological distress that is a common and important aspect of CHWs' participation in today's global health industry, emanating largely from the frustrations and shame of joblessness that they experience along with many of their own neighbors and care recipients. Chapter 4 thus follows CHWs after they are deployed and examines their capacities for building close and supportive relationships with stigmatized patients, and explains the complex ways in which CHWs respond emotionally to their difficult work.

Moral sentiments of sacrifice and spiritual satisfaction may also keep CHWs from gaining a place at policy tables by keeping the focus on their role as emotional and physical laborers rather than as people who are very capable of developing policies and partially controlling the implementation of policies. Yet despite these particular attempts at governing and socializing CHWs, CHWs still form opinions on the fairness of various inequalities and exchanges that they encounter as underpaid, relatively powerless, low-level workers. Sometimes, carefully, they voice their experiences of distress and dissatisfaction and perceptions of unfairness, adding them to the circulation of moral sentiments surrounding community health work. As I show in Chapter 5, they participate in negotiations and arguments with supervisors over job conditions, as well as express their intentions to drop out of the CHW role. Because of dominant notions of sacrifice and satisfaction, and their own concern for the suffering of others, they are often compelled to find ways of expressing their distress and desires that do not make them look too self-interested—that is, overly interested in better pay and security for themselves, and not interested enough in the health problems of their intended beneficiaries. I discuss these observations in relation to CHW labor relations in other parts of the globe where CHWs have organized themselves and launched labor movements. This is a crucial discussion to have at this point in time, for there is too little attention in the CHW literature to the existence and evolution of CHW labor relations, and there is much room for improvement in our understanding of the unique and familiar moral sentiments and power inequalities involved in such relations in different contexts. In a concluding chapter, I summarize a series of recommendations for future research into CHW programs and goals for policy makers and other stakeholders to consider.

Studying a CHW Program: A Methodological Overview

To generate a rich data set with which to analyze CHWs' emotional experiences, socioeconomic statuses, motivations, and relationships with patients, supervisors, and evolving health systems, I used a mix of methods, including participant observation, in-depth interviews, document review, and a longitudinal survey of a random cohort of CHWs.[10] The antiretroviral therapy program that I studied was one of the largest in Ethiopia. It involved a partnership among various institutions that will be discussed in later chapters, including a public hospital on the outskirts of Addis Ababa, a handful of local NGOs, international NGOs, donors, technical support agencies, and local civil society organizations. My introduction to this program came from the Ethiopian physician who directed the public hospital's HIV/AIDS treatment clinic, whom I met at Emory University in Atlanta. When I made my first visit to the clinic in June 2006, I came with a simple research plan aimed at understanding the social and clinical circumstances surrounding the deaths of people who had recently gained access to antiretroviral medications. I also aimed to simply familiarize myself with the landscape so as to prepare for a longer, larger, and more in-depth study.

During my first summer in Addis Ababa, I studied Amharic and worked with a translator to conduct verbal autopsies (that is, post-mortem interviews) for about 30 patients who had died during 2005 and 2006 while receiving treatment at the clinic run by my physician host. Through this short research project, I learned that, often times, the volunteer CHW who had cared for and supported the treatment of the deceased was the person most informed and prepared to speak about both clinical and social aspects of the patient's death. As I learned about these volunteer CHWs, my research interests drifted toward their own labors and lives.

In May 2007, I returned to Addis Ababa to begin 20 months of fieldwork. One of the data clerks in the public ART program, whom I had befriended in 2006, invited me to live with her and her husband and their young daughter in their modest home, not far from the hospital. I ended up living with them for over a year before moving to a nearby neighborhood and a room I rented from another Ethiopian family seeking rental income. Over those 20 months, I focused on what motivated these CHWs to confront death and discrimination, how they formed relationships with patients, and what roles they played in Ethiopia's internationally funded ART programs. I wanted to understand CHWs' experiences of poverty, distress, and fulfillment, as well as their desires for change in their lives and job conditions. I also wanted to understand how supervisors and officials attempted to produce an effective, cooperative, and unpaid workforce. I thus designed my study while thinking deeply about the CHWs' relationships with patients and within the hierarchy of medical and bureaucratic staff who interacted with them.

From May 2007 through the end of 2008, I conducted participant observation, informal interviews with CHWs and government and NGO officials, and an extensive review of government and NGO documents. I visited patients' homes with CHWs and several of the CHWs' own homes, spending time with them in the absence of supervisors. To assess further the actions and discourses of people in positions of relative power, I sought out various governmental officials, local NGO officials, and international NGO officials for informal interviews and discussions. I attended a month-long CHW training session as well as other meetings and events (such as Ethiopian Volunteers Day) that brought together CHWs, supervisors, and higher-level officials. Each day, while making observations and participating in conversations with various informants, I jotted field notes in a handheld notebook. At the end of the day, I typed up my field notes—elaborating on my jottings and reflecting further on what I had learned that day. Being a white male PhD candidate from the US helped me gain access to higher-level staff, including NGO directors and doctors. My identity also distanced me from many of the CHWs, though several—especially the CHWs who were, like me, in their twenties—were very interested to get to know me. In general, I went about building rapport with CHWs by emphasizing that I was a student and not an NGO employee, consistently showing up at CHW venues, and learning to speak Amharic.

After ten months of participant observation, document review, and informal interviewing, I began a yearlong, longitudinal survey with 110 CHWs randomly selected from the rosters of NGOs that cooperated with the public hospital's ART program. Each respondent participated in three waves of surveys over the course of 2008, contributing self-reported data on household demographics, socioeconomic status, food insecurity, and psychological distress. Part of the sample comprised newcomers, who had just been trained and deployed at the time of the first survey wave in February 2008. The other part of the CHW sample had been actively serving for about 12 months on average at the time of the first survey wave. The survey thus followed a cohort of newcomers as they progressed through their first ten months in the role, alongside a cohort of "veterans" who were in their final 10 months of the 18-month service period expected of them.

I was particularly interested in the levels of food insecurity and psychological distress experienced by the CHWs. Food security, defined by the UN's Food and Agriculture Organization (FAO) as access to a diet of sufficient quantity and quality for all household members at all times, through socially acceptable ways, to maximize the likelihood of healthy and active living (FAO 2004), has received a high level of attention from policy makers and researchers in the last decade. Given that there is more than enough food production to feed the world, and given the fundamental biological and sociocultural importance of food, food insecurity is a meaningful measure of the deprivation that results in part from the failures of markets, governments, and other institutions to provide basic sustenance to billions of people around the world.[11] Also, in the past decade, a number of studies have demonstrated close links between food insecurity and psychological distress, suggesting that high levels of distress can often make it even more difficult to access food and that food insecurity causes distress by creating feelings of frustration and shame and by contributing to the erosion of social ties that depend on sharing and exchanging food (Hadley and Crooks 2012; Hadley et al. 2012). A focus on the links between poverty, food insecurity, and distress was and is a compelling way to draw attention and understanding to the economic, social, and emotional challenges facing CHWs in settings of poverty.

Multiple advisors and assistants helped me develop, adapt, and pre-test the survey. To measure food insecurity, I used a version of the Household Food Insecurity Access Scale (HFIAS), which had recently been proposed as a universal scale for international use (Swindale and Bilinsky 2006). An instructor at Addis Ababa University (AAU) who specialized in public health nutrition translated the HFIAS from English into Amharic and told me his impressions of its applicability. He felt that each of the items would be interpreted more or less as intended by the survey developers, and our pre-tests with CHW respondents confirmed this. We went a couple steps further to check that the Amharic version of the HFIAS was a valid measure of food insecurity by collecting data on the CHWs' household income and personal consumption of various foods in the previous 24 hours, and showing that these varied between less food-insecure and more food-insecure CHW households in the expected direction (Maes et al. 2009).

To decide upon a measure of psychological distress (there are many used in epidemiological studies), I consulted with Dr. Atalay Alem, a leading psychiatrist at AAU who had extensive experience conducting mental health–related research in Ethiopia. He informed me of the existence of an Amharic version of the WHO's Self-Reporting Questionnaire (SRQ), a checklist of common symptoms related to disorders of depression and anxiety. The Amharic translation of the SRQ had already been used several times in previous research in urban Ethiopia (e.g., Mogga et al. 2006). It had also undergone a fairly extensive protocol of adaptation and validation, carried out by a team of social science researchers and psychiatrists (Zilber et al. 2004). Through a mix of qualitative and quantitative work, previous researchers had added a handful of locally expressed idioms of distress to the checklist, determined the statistically optimal number of self-reported symptoms to use as a cutoff for screening probable cases of emotional disorder, and carefully compared what the checklist said about respondents' distress levels to independent diagnoses generated through a "gold standard" psychiatric assessment (Zilber et al. 2004). For these reasons, it made sense to pre-test and use the Amharic SRQ in the survey to assess the psychological distress of CHWs.

In addition to these measures of food insecurity and psychological distress, the survey included several questions that interested me: about CHWs' desires and preferences in regards to future work, the quality of their relationships with their closest patients, and their workloads (e.g., the number of ambulatory and bedridden patients assigned to their care, and the number of hours per week they spent volunteering). When it came time to conduct the survey, I trained and closely supervised four Ethiopian research assistants to collect the data at each of the three survey waves. We appointed our randomly sampled respondents to meet us in private rooms provided by their respective NGOs on specific days and times. All of the surveys were conducted face-to-face between respondents and the interviewers, with the latter marking answers in pencil or pen on the paper pages of the questionnaire. The research assistants worked in pairs in order to maximize data quality (while one did the questioning, the other could double-check that the questions were being asked and answered as intended). This approach had an added impact of making the survey interviews more comfortable for the respondents: having three people increased the level of banter in what can otherwise be overly rigid interview situations. At the end of each day, my research assistants and I met to look over each survey for data entry errors and inconsistencies, and to discuss the context of each survey interview. I entered all of the survey data myself, typically on the same day it was collected or the day after. Though I conducted some preliminary descriptive analyses while in the field, full analysis of the three waves of data—including multivariate regressions and multilevel models—began after I left the field.[12]

To generate detailed narratives of CHWs' lives, including their daily interactions with their patients and superiors, I turned to in-depth interviews that were semi-structured—in other words, interviews guided by a list of questions that also took on conversational and open-ended qualities. I used the first wave of survey data collected from the random sample of CHWs to select, purposively, 13 CHWs to participate in a series of up to six semi-structured interviews, each lasting from about 30 minutes to 2 hours. In drawing this purposive sample, I aimed to account for the preponderance of women in the CHW population yet also over-sampled men to capture a range of experiences (thus I interviewed ten women and three men). I also selected participants with varied lengths of service, ages, marital statuses, years of schooling, socioeconomic statuses, and HIV status. In conducting the interviews, I again benefited greatly from training and working closely with exceptional Ethiopian research assistants, who were empathic, skillful, and able to make up for my admittedly limited command of the Amharic language. We took pains to make these interviews private by meeting in the CHWs' own homes or, when conducted on the premises of the NGO, by obtaining a private room. Conducting multiple interviews with the same respondents every few weeks contributed to the establishment of rapport and trust between us and the respondents, which is desirable in and of itself and helpful in encouraging veritable strangers to talk more openly about their lives, work, and desires.

I digitally recorded all of the interviews. Then, within approximately two weeks of conducting each interview, I sat down with one of my Amharic-speaking research assistants to listen to the audio recordings and to transcribe and translate our interviews verbatim. This helped me improve my own Amharic skills while ensuring that the nuances of my respondents' intended meanings were faithfully captured. While still in the field, I coded both my field notes and interview transcripts, using a single codebook combining both a priori codes and "in vivo" codes that emerged during data collection and review.

In the future, ethnography will hopefully play bigger roles in mixed methods studies of the production and consequences of health programs, policies, and systems. While this methodological overview points to some useful considerations for researchers designing ethnographic studies focusing on CHWs and CHW-related programs, certainly there is no one ideal way to mix methods. As I argue in this book, when it comes to conducting CHW-related research, the most important thing is to point our attention and instruments of data collection not only at CHWs and the people for whom they provide care and services but also at the local, national, and global health systems of which CHWs are a part, and at people in positions of relative power within these systems.[13] As in all areas of scientific inquiry, it is also fundamental to describe clearly the methods used, including their strengths and limitations and the roles played by various actors in shaping those methods, to enable others to evaluate the findings and develop new research protocols.

Researchers cannot separate the research they do from their own values and their own participation in processes of political and social change. The relatively close relationships I developed with CHWs in Ethiopia have strongly influenced my opinions of their positions within the global health industry. I believe CHWs deserve and have a right to at least a living wage, better job conditions, and upward social and economic mobility. The last ten years have seen the emergence of the Global Health Workforce Alliance, the Frontline Health Workers Coalition, and the One Million Community Health Workers Campaign, each of which have had important impacts on global health policy and practice. Despite the connotations of terms such as worker "coalition," "alliance," and "campaign," these institutions emerged not from CHWs seeking to improve their job conditions; rather, they were formed by health professionals and policy experts based mainly in North American and European institutions seeking to promote an enhanced role for CHWs in extending primary health care, in part through fundraising, awareness raising, and building an expanded body of evidence on best practices in CHW programs. While these institutions have much to offer to the development of CHW policy and practice, I want CHWs to have the freedom to autonomously organize, to help shape their own work conditions according to their needs and desires, and to partner with allies and broader social movements seeking to reduce inequalities in power, wealth, and health. I believe that if CHWs have such freedoms, then they can more effectively address structural and social determinants of health, in cooperation with partners in various political and social sectors, thereby making goals of health equity and social justice more achievable.

My hope is that ethnographic research that carefully attends to the evolving ways in which CHWs cooperate and contend with those who deploy them, while maintaining focus on CHW successes in reducing inequality and improving quality of life and social solidarity, will help in the development of evidence-based as well as equitable and social justice-based health programs that truly value the power, skills, and knowledge of community health workers. In the concluding chapters of this book, I offer further considerations and recommendations for future research into the labor, lives, and relationships of CHWs and the health systems they serve.

Notes

1. Hiwot means "life" in Amharic, the lingua franca of Addis Ababa and much of urban Ethiopia. This is not a pseudonym. This book uses the actual names of NGOs and government offices, as well as of the officers leading or holding high positions in these institutions. The identities of other individuals featured in this book, including CHWs, their supervisors, and other low-level workers and interlocutors, are disguised with pseudonyms.

2. There are many definitions of community health workers (CHWs) in the literature. Wiggins and colleagues (2013) define CHWs as "skilled community members who work with communities to improve holistic health and well-being through a variety of strategies," which equates CHWs with a broad category of people who have existed in human groups throughout history and even prehistory. In the 20th century, CHWs became formalized in the United States and many other parts of the world (Wiggins et al. 2013). Generally speaking, community health workers are one of a variety of health workers who work within the realm of primary or community health care, spending different proportions of their time in clinical facilities, community outreach locations, and the homes of people who, despite struggling with various illnesses, have long lacked dependable access to primary health care. In general, CHWs receive less formal training than nurses and spend more of their time performing house visits and community outreach in comparison to other health professionals (see Earth Institute 2011: 11–12).

3. This made ALERT second only to one other public hospital in Ethiopia, located in Addis Ababa's city center, as a provider of ART (FMOH/HAPCO 2006b).

4. Ethnicity and religion are much more complex and shifting than categories and statistics suggest (Abbink 2011a; 2011b). People of different ethnicities often marry in Ethiopia and have for a long time, and some people may choose to report their mother or father's ethnic identity in different situations. Others may be able to take on a different ethnic identity at some point in their lives. Religious identity, too, is somewhat fluid in an international capital such as Addis Ababa. One CHW, for instance, told me that he was interested in the Protestant religion, but that he was also "afraid to go and join a Protestant church," reflecting a lingering tendency among Orthodox Ethiopians to marginalize and disparage Pentecostalism. A couple of CHWs were even interested in Buddhism.

5. These recommendations were included in WHO's influential "framework for action" on the organization of community home-based care for people with HIV/AIDS in "resource-limited settings" (WHO 2002).

6. Family Health International has more recently been renamed "FHI 360." At the time, FHI was a major recipient of funding from the United States Agency for International Development (USAID).

7. See, for instance, https://www.youtube.com/watch?v=3hA1kzU4m8s&list=PLUR5 KGQKa4M4co_0ahK36ImiVZsgKTl4F (accessed April 28, 2014).

8. See http://www.pbs.org/now/shows/537/ (accessed June 1, 2014). The WHO's Draft Global Strategy on HRH (2015) also proposes that ministries of health, civil service commissions, and employers should "ensure fair terms for health workers, including favorable employment conditions and remuneration, as well as job security, a manageable workload, continuing education, professional development opportunities, enhanced career development pathways, family and lifestyle incentives, hardship allowances, housing and education allowances, and grants" (p. 8).

9. Drobac and colleagues, in the textbook *Reimagining Global Health*, similarly reason that compensating community health workers can benefit "not only the individuals but also their families, communities, and local economies" (Drobac et al. 2013: 176). And the WHO's Draft Global Strategy on Human Resources for Health (2015) states that part of the overall goal is "promoting equitable socio-economic development

through decent employment opportunities." As we will see in a later chapter, payment for CHWs is also framed as a sustainability issue.

10. The research reported here was funded by the United States National Science Foundation's Cultural Anthropology program (#0752966). I obtained ethical approval from Emory University, Addis Ababa University's Faculty of Medicine, and ALERT Hospital.

11. In the past three decades, international researchers have sought to develop tools for measuring food insecurity that directly assess the experience of the phenomenon at the household level, and measuring food insecurity has become a part of much anthropological and nutritional research as well as monitoring the effectiveness of pro-poor programs (Hadley and Crooks 2012). Although a standard food insecurity measurement tool has been available for use in the United States for several years, a standard scale proposed for international use—the Household Food Insecurity Access Scale (HFIAS)—was published only as recently as 2006 (Swindale et al. 2006).

12. See Maes et al. (2010a; 2011) for further details on analyses of survey data.

13. Emily Mendenhall and Brandon Kohrt (2015) make a similar point—about the need for ethnographic and mixed methods research that examines not only relatively powerless and suffering people but also people in positions of power—in regard to global mental health-related research. They also provide a very useful overview of the roles that various quantitative, qualitative, and ethnographic methods can play in global health research.

1

COMMUNITY HEALTH WORKER PAYMENT AND PARTICIPATION IN ADDIS ABABA'S ALICHA MILLENNIUM

There is a roughly seven-and-a-half year gap between the Ethiopian and Gregorian calendars. So when I returned to Addis Ababa to begin fieldwork in April 2007, Ethiopia was just a few months away from the year 2000. The turn of the Ethiopian millennium was accompanied by government discourses about an Ethiopian economic and cultural "renaissance." Residents in Addis Ababa were less optimistic. In early September, a few days before New Year's Eve, some Ethiopian friends told me over dinner that it had become popular to refer to the new era as "*ye'alicha millennium*." The term *alicha* refers to a "bland" stew lacking spice, particularly the mix of red pepper, salt, garlic, ginger, and other herbs known as *berbere*. Since the prices of these key ingredients in Ethiopian cuisine had skyrocketed along with other staples, people in the capital were settling for blander dishes, if they could afford food at all. In rural folk experience, being deprived of spice is a sign of impending famine or declining household economic status and food security (Amare 1999; 2010).

Unfortunately, the Ethiopian Y2K coincided with the global food crisis of 2007 and 2008, the largest shock to the global economy since the early 1970s when a similar food price crisis rocked the world. In mid-2008, global food prices escalated rapidly to 150% of their 2006 prices, driven by a "perfect storm" of increased global demand for food and biofuel crops, harvest shortfalls, rising petroleum costs, climate change, depreciation of the US dollar, and food price speculation (Dawe 2008, 2009; Headey and Fan 2008; Robles et al. 2009). While price increases were seen globally, the impact was predicted to be greater in low-income countries where poverty was combined with high spending on food as a proportion of total household expenditures (Ivanic and Martin 2008; Zezza et al. 2008). This was particularly true for Ethiopia, where food prices had been increasing since 2004—the same year that free ART became widely available. Available data showed that beginning in August 2004, Ethiopia's food price index had been even higher than the world index (International Monetary Fund 2008; Loening et al. 2009; Ulimwengu et al. 2009).

Food price inflation in Ethiopia, furthermore, was closely tracking global oil prices. Ethiopia imports the majority of its petroleum from Saudi Arabia and other countries in the Middle East. Faced with a surge in oil prices on top of food prices, the Ethiopian government decided in early 2008 to end government fuel subsidies. Virtually overnight, the price at the gas pump climbed from 7.77 Ethiopian birr (about 0.75 USD) to 9.60 birr (about 1 USD) per liter. Along with the resulting surge in public transportation prices, long waits at fill stations generated plenty of frustration.[1]

Skyrocketing rents were another important and despised fact of life in 2007 in Addis Ababa. Several factors were driving this surge, including food price inflation, an influx of diaspora members who returned to Addis Ababa from North America and Europe in anticipation of the millennium celebrations, and a general failure of the supply of housing in Addis Ababa to keep up with rapid population growth driven by rural-to-urban migrations. The year 2007 saw newspaper reports and public discussions about the increasing number of "moon houses" (*chereka bet*), shanties constructed under the cover of night in vacant lots and fields dotting the capital city.[2] Renters generally had little protection from landlords who decided to raise their rent, and many faced either paying ever-higher rents month to month or moving out to make way for someone else who would. The synergy of hikes in the cost of food, transportation, and housing was astounding to people in Addis Ababa.

Ethiopia's prime minister at the time, Meles Zenawi, blamed merchants and landlords for artificially inflating prices and rents. Many people in Addis blamed the government, however, for not doing enough to control inflation.[3] In mid-2008, after several months of contemplating policies, the Ethiopian government decided to begin purchasing wheat on the world market and provide it to urban households and millers at subsidized prices. Addis Ababa's city government also began to sell thousands of public "condominium" style housing units at low cost to citizens. The government dispersed the condos across several massive complexes and rationed them through a lottery system. After an initial registration, the government randomly chose several waves of winners and offered low down payments (about 2,000 USD) and cheap home loans to complete the purchase. The lottery favored women: the policy was that seven out of every ten "winners" would be women.[4]

While these moves perhaps helped to quell dissent and reduce some of the food and housing insecurity rampant in the capital, they did nothing to address the concurrent rationing of water and electricity that was also testing the patience of Addis Ababa residents. In 2007 and 2008, when water flowed perhaps once in a week or for a couple of hours in the middle of the night, access was easier in households that had private water sources. Women and children from poorer households who got water from collective faucets could expect to wait several hours in line to fill up a couple of 20-liter jerry cans. Recurrent electricity outages were yet another feature of daily life in Addis in 2007 and 2008.[5] At night, eerie darkness shrouded the scores of people walking the streets, only visible when lit by the headlights of passing cars. Sometimes the outages followed a somewhat regular schedule—for instance, every Monday and Wednesday from 8:00 a.m. to 8:00 p.m. But they often struck without warning. For businesses without access to generators or fuel, the blackouts were crippling.

The irony of the conditions of the new millennium was not lost on residents of Addis Ababa: a "renaissance" into a world characterized by skyrocketing food prices as well as rationing of housing, water, electricity, and gas. This is the economic context in which the CHWs in this book lived and worked.

Nearly all of the 110 volunteer CHWs that we randomly surveyed during 2008 could be labeled poor, with per capita household incomes of 0.40 USD per day on average. This level of income actually falls below standard international cutoffs of "extreme" and even "ultra" poverty. When I sorted the CHWs' incomes into ordinal categories, the cutoffs had to be set incredibly low and close together: under 16 cents, 16 to 33 cents, 33 to 66 cents, and above 66 cents. Only 11% of the sample was in the "least poor" category, in which they might still be earning less than one USD per day.[6]

The data on food insecurity were just as astonishing, though understandable in light of the obvious difficulties people in Addis Ababa faced in finding work and making money. Twenty-five percent of the sample reported "mild" food insecurity, meaning they had at least worried about their household food access in the previous month or ate foods that were less preferred and even unwanted. About 35% reported "moderate" food insecurity, meaning they had reduced the quantity of the food that they ate in the previous month. Another 20% reported *severe* food insecurity, meaning that at least once in the previous month, they or someone in their household had gone a whole day without eating or had gone to bed hungry because of a lack of food. In total, 80% experienced some form of food insecurity. Eskinder, a middle-aged man and one of the volunteer CHWs I followed closely (and about whom we'll learn much more in the next chapter), summed up the feeling of many of his peers: "Nowadays, it is only that life is expensive and there is no employment." These conditions, in turn, led many people as well as me to ask the following question: Why didn't the ARV program create paid jobs that could have helped address the widespread unemployment and food insecurity that Eskinder lamented?

The Global Sustainability Doctrine Meets Ethiopia

Answering this question requires examining factors that shape funding levels and patterns in contemporary CHW programs. Perhaps one of the most important factors is what's called the sustainability doctrine: the idea that health development projects are sustainable only when local organizations can take over a project and sustain it with local initiative and labor when the donors who originally financed it pack up and leave (Swidler and Watkins 2009; Watkins and Swidler 2013). In this approach to sustainability, which is commonly adopted by global health donors and thus by the institutions they give money to, creating jobs and paying local labor with international donor funds is considered a bad idea, because these expenditures cannot be sustained by cash-strapped local organizations and governments when international funding is pulled out. With the sustainability doctrine in effect, "volunteerism"—calling on local people to donate their time and energy to a health or development program—becomes the best policy option (Swidler and Watkins 2009).

To get a sense of how the sustainability doctrine works, one can look to a study published in 2014 by Marie-Renée B-Lajoie and colleagues, which sought to investigate how global NGO officials conceptualize the question of CHW motivation and incentivization. The study targeted NGO officials in the CORE Group, a US-based network of influential NGO and government partners that "generate collaborative action and learning to improve and expand community-focused public health practices for underserved populations around the world."[7] The CORE Group is thus an important locus of knowledge and power in the global health field today, one that strongly promotes a reliance on CHWs. In interviews, some CORE Group NGO officials expressed the belief that paying CHWs can economically empower them and lead to superior performance. Some also recognized that problematic inequalities exist between underpaid CHWs (who tend to be women) and well-paid, high-level officials (who more often tend to be men). The fact that viewpoints like this exist within the CORE Group is encouraging. The comments of these \ NGO officials, however, point\ to the ultimate influence of international donors and their notions of sustainability: "Donor practices and what other organizations and governments were offering CHWs had the biggest influence on NGO practices, particularly in defining what is 'sustainable' beyond the duration of the programme" (B-Lajoie et al. 2014: 7). CORE Group program managers described an "inherent tension" between their objectives and the priorities of donors. Some described resistance from donor agencies to incorporate financial incentives if they could not be sustained. Not surprisingly, this pushed programs to move away from paid job creation. The NGO officials also identified competition between programs over short-term grants as a major barrier to effective capacity building within their CHW programs. These comments from officials and managers in some of the most prominent and active global health NGOs highlight the influence that donors have over norms and policies that deeply impact the lives of poor people.

An unwillingness to pay for local labor and create jobs on the part of donors is partly a result of the macroeconomic concerns of the World Bank and IMF and the legacies of structural adjustment, which involved slashing government payrolls in order to reduce wage bills (Cometto et al. 2013; Goldsbrough 2007; Ooms et al. 2007; Pfeiffer and Chapman 2010; Rowden 2009).[8] Structural adjustment was thus identified in the WHO's 2006 World Health Report as a "driving force" of a global human resources for health crisis (WHO 2006). The IMF and World Bank may no longer continue to openly discourage governments from raising public sector payroll expenditures, encourage NGOs to take over public health services, and simultaneously discourage donors from funding NGO payroll expenditures. Nevertheless, the damage has been done. In the wake of structural adjustment, paying for essential labor became widely *imagined* as financially unsustainable, and promoting unpaid community-based health care thus became economically imperative (Campbell et al. 2008; Dräger et al. 2006; Farmer 2008; Pfeiffer 2013). In following this entrenched set of values, expectations, and policies, community health programs in low-resource areas have had to rely on local people's willingness to donate their labor. Since global donors have simultaneously been motivated to pay for high-level "expert" labor (i.e., NGO officers, consultants, and auditors), the sustainability doctrine exacerbated a salient inequality between local, underpaid laborers and salaried, transnational professionals in many African health programs.

The sustainability doctrine has, of course, been questioned and criticized. Interestingly, the Ethiopian government joined this cast of critics in the first decade of the 21st century. In 2003, Ethiopia's Federal Ministry of Health initiated a national Health Extension Program (HEP) that has since played a big role in putting Ethiopia on the global health map. The HEP is commonly called the Ministry's "flagship" initiative and the "bedrock" of Ethiopia's attempt to accelerate the expansion of primary health-care coverage, particularly for people who live in rural areas where access to services is often highly limited (FMOH 2007). The HEP involved the construction of thousands of new health posts throughout the countryside as well as the creation of full-time, *salaried* CHW jobs for roughly 34,000 young Ethiopian women. Health Extension Workers or HEWs have at least six and in many cases ten years of schooling, and then receive one year of health education before being deployed to a health post in one of Ethiopia's approximately 15,000 *kebeles*, the lowest level of government administration in the country. As CHWs, HEWs are responsible for a large number of primary health-care services, including prevention and treatment of some infectious diseases (e.g., malaria); improvement of water sources and nutrition; family planning; routine vaccinations and supplementary vaccination campaigns; facility-based pre-, peri-, and postnatal care for mothers and newborns; surveillance of illnesses; and collecting and reporting data on health-services utilization and population health indicators.

In return for their work, HEWs receive a monthly salary, about $112 as of mid-2014, which puts them near the bottom of the public worker pay scale but nevertheless fundamentally distinguishes them from the "volunteer" CHWs deemed "sustainable" within the sustainability doctrine. Ethiopia's previous minister of health, Dr. Tedros Adhanom, highlighted this policy decision by calling the sustainability doctrine into question in the pages of the *WHO Bulletin*. In an interview published in 2009, he identified the key to the success and sustainability of the HEP as "engaging health extension workers as full-time salaried civil servants" and thereby "moving away from volunteerism" (WHO 2009).[9] Ethiopia's Fourth National Health Accounts also asserts that job creation and the engagement of HEWs as "full-time government-salaried civil servants" marked "an important shift away from volunteerism—a feature viewed as key to HEP's early success and long-term sustainability" (FMOH 2010: v).

In voicing this sustainability heterodoxy, the Ethiopian minister of health had an important partner: the World Health Organization. In 2008, WHO asserted that "essential health services cannot be provided by people working on a voluntary basis if they are to be sustainable" (WHO 2008):

> While volunteers can make a valuable contribution on a short term or part time basis, trained health workers who are providing essential health services, including community health workers, should receive adequate wages and/or other appropriate and commensurate incentives. . . . [T]he burden of evidence indicates that stipends, travel allowances and other non-financial incentives are not enough to ensure the livelihood of health workers and that the absence of adequate wages will threaten the effectiveness and long-term sustainability of community health worker programmes.
>
> *(WHO 2008: 35–36)*

In short, poor people do not want to simply donate their labor, and unpaid workers will eventually seek other opportunities or perform poorly, thus imperiling public health programs. Others have voiced this commonsense view. Based on his extensive experience working with Mozambique's public health system, anthropologist James Pfeiffer argues that paying CHWs helps guarantee that a health-care program will be sustainable (as well as more universal and equitable in its coverage of populations in need) (Pfeiffer 2013: 178). And in the Public Broadcasting Service (PBS) documentary *House Calls and Health Care*, which showcases the work of the well-known international NGO Partners in Health (PIH) in Rwanda and deals explicitly with the question of whether or not to pay CHWs, physician-anthropologist and PIH co-founder Paul Farmer claims that he had never seen a project be effective for long without compensating its community health workers.[10]

These statements, uttered by actors as varied as Ethiopia's minister of health, WHO, and anthropologists deeply engaged in the field of global health, mobilize alternative conceptualizations of sustainability and development, emphasizing a need for governments and their donors to commit to sustained funding for community health worker salaries in order to improve and sustain health-care delivery systems. They challenge the sustainability doctrine by suggesting that the widespread reliance on unpaid labor creates programs that are *unsustainable*.

When I conducted research on CHWs focusing on HIV/AIDS in Addis Ababa in 2006–2008, however, there was no movement away from volunteerism. The government did not attempt to deploy its own salaried workforce of caregivers and treatment supporters. Instead, as in other African countries, large numbers of people continued to be recruited solely for unpaid "volunteer" positions (Maes and Kalofonos 2013). A brief examination of the HEP makes it clear that the Ethiopian government had given serious thought to whether or not CHWs should be expected to donate their labor. Given that the government rhetorically and practically "moved away from volunteerism" with the HEP in the countryside, the government's willingness to accept the involvement of thousands of unpaid "volunteer" CHWs organized by multiple NGOs in the urban AIDS sector demands explanation.

One factor behind why job creation was never an explicit goal in this particular arena is that the amounts of labor deemed necessary to ensure the success of ART for millions of Ethiopians and Africans was massive. International organizations knew from experience that successful treatment with high adherence rates was possible as long as CHWs closely followed and supported patients (Farmer et al. 2001). At the time, the price of paying for all of this labor probably seemed gargantuan, even though cost exercises performed later by PIH, the Clinton Foundation, and the Earth Institute showed that the costs could actually be quite low (Drobac et al. 2013; McCord et al. 2013; see also Dahn et al. 2015).[11] The Ethiopian government likely could not fathom creating the number of CHW jobs needed for ART support in the cities on top of their job creation plans for the rural HEP.

Aside from budget constraints, it is important to remember that NGOs had already proliferated in Addis Ababa and across urban Africa by the time free ART arrived (see Chapter 2). In the pre-ART era, NGOs like the ones I encountered in Addis Ababa provided much of the care for HIV-infected and AIDS-affected individuals, families, and orphans, and did so with local volunteer labor (Iliffe 2006). Thus when combination ARV drugs became more widely available in sub-Saharan Africa, generating a sharp increase in the demand for treatment support and care, volunteers had already been organized by local NGOs and community organizations for years. International NGOs and donors forged partnerships with these NGOs and community organizations, providing them with donor funding and training, and helping them to continue recruiting and supervising unpaid "volunteer" CHWs (Kalofonos 2014). Take, for example, Family Health International, the PEPFAR-funded, US-based NGO that supported the Hiwot NGO (introduced at the beginning of this book) and many other NGOs in urban Ethiopia. In 2006, FHI-Ethiopia's program evaluations director explained to me that because FHI is a "technical assistance organization," it did not "practice implementation" and instead relied on "local implementing partners"—in other words, local NGOs, many of which had existed and relied on volunteer labor for years, developing more and more local knowledge about social, clinical, and other aspects of the epidemic.

Job creation was not an explicit goal in the arena of ART scale-up in urban Ethiopia, furthermore, because other goals—of saving lives through pharmaceutical therapies and preventing the emergence of drug-resistant HIV strains—generally took precedence. In Ethiopia, as in many other places in sub-Saharan Africa, the government constructed HIV/AIDS as a disaster threatening to derail the country's development progress and deepen the poverty of the body politic. Ethiopia's National AIDS Council thus officially declared HIV/AIDS a national emergency in 2000. At the same time, many advocates of global ART equity envisioned the provision of medicines not as the ultimate goal, but as a "wedge issue" that would create space and leverage for broader poverty reduction, health systems strengthening, and social justice, particularly in the wake of structural adjustment programs that helped drive up unemployment and poverty and weaken health systems in Africa in the 1980s and '90s (Irwin and Scali 2007; Kim and Farmer 2006; Ooms et al. 2008; Pfeiffer et al. 2008). Unfortunately, across the world, many governments, donors, and activists settled into a pursuit of the narrow goals of quickly getting ARV drugs to the millions of people in need. Anthropologist João Biehl refers to this as the "pharmaceuticalization" of public health and humanitarianism, which took shape throughout the world with the rollout of ART in low-income countries (Biehl 2006). The rollout of ART was also accompanied by fears of epidemics of drug-resistant HIV among public health and biomedical experts (Vella and Palmisano 2005; Wainberg et al. 2011). Allaying these fears depended upon assurances of strong systems capable of ensuring high levels of drug adherence and of monitoring and appropriately responding to the virtually inevitable emergence of drug-resistant strains. Paying for CHW labor would mean having much less money to spend on the medicines, biomedical technologies, and other service delivery and monitoring components needed to save lives and prevent epidemics of drug-resistant HIV. Faced with limited resources, donors and governments across Africa likely figured that if CHWs would do the work for free, then they should do the work for free, since then the number of lives saved could be maximized and the threat of drug-resistance minimized.

This taken-for-granted logic behind a reliance on unpaid CHWs is illustrated in a short film documenting ALERT Hospital's ART program, the program that is central to this book. Produced by FHI in 2005, the short documentary opens on a well-known Ethiopian proverb: "When spider webs unite, they can tie up a lion." The metaphor here is clear: the HIV epidemic (not to mention a potential epidemic of drug-resistant HIV) is a threatening beast, but this beast can be overcome through a tightly spun, cooperative web of government- and donor-backed clinics, NGOs, and CHWs. In the documentary, various leaders involved in ALERT's ART program testify to the rationality and necessity of making volunteer CHWs—who comb the surrounding neighborhoods searching for and checking up on patients—a part of the web needed to tie up the lion. Dr. Yigeremu Abebe, director of ALERT's ART program, says,

> [The system] is very capable, because we are working very closely with these NGOs that are heavily engaged in home-based care, and they recruit [patients] together with local government agencies [i.e. *kebeles*], and send patients to us. [. . .] Since recruitment [of patients for antiretroviral therapy] is initiated by volunteers, the most forgotten patients are brought here. And the best system—especially in the urban centers—is the home-based care system. Without linking with that, it is not possible to achieve [antiretroviral] therapy.

Sister Tibebe Maco, director of Hiwot, a.k.a. FHI's "local implementing partner" in Addis Ababa, further emphasizes the efficacy of the hundreds of drug adherence-supporting volunteers her organization had come to deploy:

> If you give [antiretroviral] treatment without home-based care, you just dump the treatment on the floor or in the garbage. You don't know whether the patient took it or not, whether he sold it or not—you don't know! You cannot follow. You cannot supervise. It's beyond your control. But if it is home-based care, you know where the treatment is. Even if he vomits after taking the treatment, you know whether the tablets go out or not. The [volunteer] caregivers even register that. They are responsible!

Other government and NGO officials with whom I spoke made similar comments about how volunteer CHWs were a means to an end: a successful ART program, one that saves lives and prevents epidemics of drug-resistant HIV. The program evaluation director at FHI-Ethiopia's headquarters, for instance, told me, "You can call these volunteer caregivers our 'tools' for achieving care of the patients." Likewise, when the head of health programs at the federal HIV/ AIDS Prevention and Control Office (HAPCO) and I discussed the role of volunteerism in the rollout of ART, and I asked him if relying on unpaid labor was a problematic policy, he replied that volunteers need care, but that "at the end of the day," the goal is improving patient adherence, which translated to both survival and the suppression of drug-resistant HIV. Considering the human resource crisis in Ethiopia and Africa more generally, he said, "Volunteerism is critical." The HAPCO official also expressed a desire for research that would generate direct evidence of the efficacy of unpaid CHWs. The indicators he had in mind were drug adherence and morbidity and mortality rates, and he envisioned a comparison of ART patients with volunteer caregivers to those without.

These comments reveal how paid professionals in the global health industry elide the question of whether relying on volunteer labor is socially and morally acceptable, by emphasizing that this policy is mandatory, given the gravity of the HIV/AIDS epidemic, a lack of human resources and funding, and the "ultimate goal" of saving lives through pharmaceutical adherence and biomedical efficacy. The AIDS emergencies in Ethiopia and sub-Saharan Africa more generally were exacerbated by decades of underinvestment in health systems, conflict, poverty, and the structural violence of colonialism and deregulated postcolonial capitalism (Iliffe 2006). Yet these deeper problems of social, political, and economic injustice took a back seat to problems of ART provision and adherence. Due to a narrow humanitarian focus on life-saving drug access and adherence, and a failure to raise and allocate money for CHW job creation and other interventions aimed at poverty reduction, many patients gained access to sophisticated drugs but not to basics such as food, employment, and high-quality primary health care (Kalofonos 2010). Moreover, many unemployed and food-insecure people were met with opportunities to *donate* their labor to ART programs.

Medical and cultural anthropologists in recent years have provided critical and constructive examinations of how concerns over biosecurity as well as the humanitarian sentiments of actors within governments and non-governmental organizations end up rationalizing policies and practices that perpetuate and create inequalities (Biehl 2007; Bornstein and Redfield 2011; Fassin 2005; Fassin 2012; Feldman and Ticktin 2010; Ticktin 2011). The issue of ART is a key case in point. Using unpaid volunteers to put people on ART became a case of humanitarian and biomedical ends both justifying the means and obscuring other important problems.

By using a metaphorical spider web to describe the multisectoral nature of AIDS care and treatment support in Addis Ababa's age of ART, the FHI documentary implied that each of the silk strands in a spider's web—the NGOs, the government, the various donors, etc.—is more or less equal in size and power and hence value. In reality, the CHWs in the program provided incredible amounts of valuable resources to the web, in forms of emotional and social labor, in ways unlike any of the other strands. And yet they were not paid, in contrast to the other strands. Perhaps a spider web metaphor would be more useful in getting us to see the CHWs as comprising a web of unpaid caregivers, spun by local and international NGOs, donors, and government agencies, or to see both the CHWs and the people for whom they cared as stuck in a spider's web of widespread unemployment, a rapidly rising cost of living, and the narrow humanitarian and biomedical goals of health officials and donors.

Pushing for Change or Following Directions?

The issue of payment for CHWs is clearly an important one, given the levels of unemployment and food insecurity they often face. But for many CHWs and

CHW allies around the world, issues of power and participation in processes of social change are just as fundamental. From this perspective, the metaphorical spider web linked up experts, officials, and professionals *with decision-making power* and CHWs who were expected to not only volunteer their time and energy but also be absent from policy tables and adhere to decisions handed down to them. This arrangement counters a principle that CHWs and other community representatives should participate meaningfully in the control and design of their health-care system, a principle that has motivated and inspired many CHWs and public health actors since the first half of the 20th century (Lewin and Lehmann 2014).

Attendees of the Alma Ata Conference of 1978, which convened roughly three thousand international health stakeholders to address the need for a primary health-care revolution, officially declared the importance of this principle (Cueto 2004; Newell 1975; Standing and Chowdhury 2008; Werner 1981).[12] The Declaration of Alma Ata (WHO 1978) affirmed that health—"a state of complete physical, mental and social wellbeing, and not merely the absence of disease or infirmity"—is a fundamental human right and that governments the world over have a responsibility to provision adequate resources to secure the health and the social determinants of health of their people. The Declaration also played an important role in defining the role of local participation within health development programs. For example, Article VI of the Declaration defined primary health care as "essential health care based on practical, scientifically sound and socially acceptable methods and technology made universally accessible to individuals and families in the community through their full participation." Article VII emphasizes that primary health care "requires and promotes maximum community and individual self-reliance and participation in the planning, organization, operation and control of primary health care." Article IV, the most succinct, simply says, "The people have the right and duty to participate individually and collectively in the planning and implementation of their health care."

These articles—with their language of "full" and "maximum" participation in not just the implementation but also the planning and control of health programs—connect local participation in primary health care to a pursuit of *social justice* and a more equal distribution of power, resources, and well-being (Muller 1983). The primary actor behind the Alma Ata Declaration, WHO Director General Halfdan Mahler, likened the very idea of primary health care—with its ultimate goal of health equity—to social justice, which he considered a "holy phrase" (Basilico et al. 2013; Cueto 2004). The emphasis on this particular conceptualization of participation in the 1970s was partly a reaction to the tendency to channel the lion's share of health resources to doctors in urban hospitals and the top-down and sometimes heavy-handed tactics of international public health campaigns—namely, the WHO's controversial malaria and smallpox eradication campaigns of the '50s, '60s, and '70s. The Declaration's emphasis on participation sent the message that health equity requires not just appropriate methods and technologies but also the ability of previously socially and politically marginalized people to exercise control over their health-care system and hold accountable other actors, including state officials, donors, and development foundations (Basilico et al. 2013; Cueto 2013).

After the Alma Ata Conference, several countries institutionalized CHW programs as a strategy to extend primary health care to impoverished populations and to address the relationships between poverty, inequality, and community health (Perry et al. 2014). CHWs in many parts of the globe played roles in larger movements for social justice, including the political empowerment of marginalized rural and urban populations. In the early period of Nicaragua's revolution (1979–1990), for instance, CHWs—known locally as *brigadistas*—"banded together to teach their neighbors about health problems and the relationship of these problems to underdevelopment," hoping that their demands for better care "would emanate from the grassroots to the centers of political power" (Nading 2013: 90; cf. Morgan 2001; Rifkin 1996). Similarly, CHWs in the United States became vehicles for social justice in socially and politically charged contexts during the 1960s and later in the '80s and '90s. Their roles have involved publicly attesting to the realities of exclusion and marginalization lived by people in their communities (including themselves) and proposing and working toward remedies at *multiple levels* to ensure "that individuals and communities share equally in the benefits society has to offer" (Pérez and Martinez 2008).[13] Acting at multiple levels meant improving interpersonal relationships, connecting underserved persons and families to existing services and available resources, and pursuing changes in government and public policy that would lead to greater equality in the distribution of power, services, and resources.[14]

Scholars and public health practitioners have noted, however, that many CHW programs in the 1970s and '80s were actually statist and top-down rather than autonomous movements seeking health equity and social justice (Basilico et al. 2013; Berman et al. 1987; Gilson et al. 1989; Maupin 2011; Walt 1988). For instance, India's mid-1970s implementation of community health worker programs were supposed to give CHWs the power to "develop culturally sensitive health education messages responsive to local resources and health practices," but ended up doing little more than creating "another cadre of paraprofessional health workers responsible to the health center, not the community" (Nichter 1999: 303). According to anthropologist Mark Nichter, higher-level health staff wanted to control the CHWs rather than allow them to control the health system, illustrating "the tendency of the health care bureaucracy to resist innovations which undermine preexisting power structures" (p. 303; cf. Werner 1981; Standing and Chowdhury 2008).

This tension—between encouraging CHWs to participate powerfully in health programs and attempting to control their every move—continues today. According to Lehmann and Sanders (2007), debates among donors and health officials over the roles of CHWs rarely use the Alma Ata–connected discourse and tend to be "much more pragmatic and technical" (Lehmann and Sanders 2007: 21). Meanwhile, many critical scholars and practitioners within the field of global health are concerned that social justice orientations remain at the margins and that CHWs have been reduced to serving as "a mere delivery mechanism for health programs"—engaging in top-down monitoring of health behaviors, mediating discipline and health technologies, and producing and reporting large quantities of data for program auditors, policy makers, and donors (Arvey and Fernandez 2012: 1634; Kalofonos 2014; Nading 2013).

Why are so many CHWs today working as "mere delivery mechanisms" and not as "agents of change"? Lehmann and Sanders (2007: 22) propose that the latter forms of local participation are more likely to occur and be sustained under conditions of "popular mobilization, such as in the aftermath of a liberation struggle or after the replacement of military or repressive regimes by popular governments."[15] In short, broad popular mobilization for social justice is crucial in generating more politically active CHWs, but is lacking in many contexts in both the global north and south.

The case of Ethiopia appears to provide support for this view. In Ethiopia, CHWs in the 21st century are not considered to be agents of structural change and social justice—not in urban HIV/AIDS treatment support or in rural primary health care.[16] In the run-up to the Ethiopian millennium and in subsequent years, conditions have not been conducive to "grassroots" or bottom-up popular mobilization for equity and social justice. Far from it: Addis Ababa's *alicha* millennium was marred not only by economic woes of unemployment, extreme inflation, and scarcity of electricity, water, and housing. It was also tainted by widespread unease and unhappiness with state violence and repression.

The political strife that darkened the turn of the Ethiopian millennium has a long history, but national elections in May 2005 played a key role in bringing Ethiopian politics to a point of crisis (Abbink 2006). At first, the elections of 2005 saw a remarkable level of open opposition to the ruling party. Leaders of opposition parties were given space to speak their criticisms and debate with ruling party leaders on nationally broadcast, state-run TV and radio. On the streets of Addis, opposition parties hung posters and communicated with voters via PA systems, and a growing number of people greeted each other with the opposition party sign of fingers held up in a "V." A few days before the elections, public rallies for both the ruling party and the opposition were held in the center of the city. Massive numbers of citizens, as well as a large contingent of police, turned out for the opposition party rally—and it passed peacefully. According to Burgess (2013: 106), "the sense of optimism and hope for democracy . . . was tangible" (see also Abbink 2006).

Almost immediately after voting closed in May 2005, however, things took a turn. Meles Zenawi, Ethiopia's prime minister (and head of the party that had ruled Ethiopia since 1991), banned public gathering and demonstrating. He conceded that the opposition had won a majority in the Addis Ababa elections as well as dozens of parliament seats at the federal level. Yet he also claimed that his party had achieved overall electoral victory, despite the fact that vote counting was at an early stage. As vote counting proceeded, citizens and independent observers reported wide voting irregularities, intimidation, harassment, and fraud. Opposition parties claimed the ruling party's vote rigging had denied them several victories, and they called for peaceful public demonstrations. Students, taxi drivers, street children, teachers, and many more responded vociferously with sit-ins and demonstrations.

To the dismay of many in Ethiopia and around the world, government police forces violently quelled the public protests, leaving dozens of people dead with tens of thousands more arrested and incarcerated (Burgess 2013: 106; Abbink 2006). "Political deadlock followed and disillusion came to reign in the mind of the public," according to political anthropologist and Ethiopia observer Jon Abbink (2006: 176). Over the next several months and years, the ruling party grew increasingly authoritarian and protective of its hold on power, killing more protestors and locking up more journalists.

At ALERT Hospital, in between a laboratory and physiotherapy building, six emergency tents were set up a few days before Ethiopian New Year's Eve. Hospital personnel told me they were there to triage and treat potential victims of mass violence in the form of terrorism, popular uprising, state-perpetrated violence, or a combination of these. Many connected the tents to the violence that occurred after the 2005 elections, when those killed and injured by state police were rushed to the massively overloaded *Tikur Anbessa* (Black Lion) Hospital in the center of the city. Thankfully, the tents at ALERT Hospital went unused, as the millennium celebrations passed without widespread violence in the capital. Yet people were still uneasy at the time and feared to talk publicly about their unhappiness at the fact that the government was holding many political prisoners and actively attempting to silence what many viewed as legitimate political opposition.

While Ethiopia's ruling party has garnered serious criticism from global human rights organizations, the European Union, and even some members of the US Congress, Ethiopian leaders have generally been able to obtain the support of western donors.[17] This is partially explained by geopolitics that link the Horn of Africa with the rest of the globe. Ethiopia is a crucial ally in the US/UK-led war on terror. As Feyissa (2011) explains, the global war on terror has included substantial investments in the Horn of Africa, targeting the rise of political Islam in the Sudan. The US policy of "encircling" the Sudan involved establishing a category of what it called Frontline States, which included Ethiopia in the 1990s. In the 2000s, as attention shifted to Ethiopia's other neighbors, the country was categorized as an "anchor state" in the war on terror and has remained a strategic ally to the United States (Feyissa 2011: 793–794).

The US government has received a great deal from this arrangement: intelligence sharing, bases from which to launch regional drone missions, a "black site" for interrogating prisoners, and a relatively secure state in the Horn of Africa, with a strong military that can potentially be mobilized to help battle enemies of the United States in the region (Feyissa 2011). And not just potentially: in 2006, amid international criticism over Ethiopia's human rights abuses, the Ethiopian army, backed by the United States, invaded Somalia and quickly defeated the Union of Islamic Courts, which had gained power in Somalia and appeared poised to take control away from the internationally backed Transitional Federal Government of Somalia (Barnes and Hassan 2007).

In return, the Ethiopian state receives substantial US military and development aid, despite its attempts to control its population and economy (Feyissa 2011). Partnering with the United States thus helps the ruling party achieve its multiple goals of staying in power, maintaining security, controlling the population, and developing the nation. Ultimately, despite threats of reduced funding from some donors, most international donors and NGOs have refrained from publicly criticizing government practices and policies, and Ethiopia's ruling party has been able to avoid a reduction in international aid channeled through the central government and to pursue its social, economic, and political agendas.[18]

Such politics are not conducive to CHW programs that firmly uphold the importance of CHW participation in processes of social change and political action intended to shape their health-care systems and living environments. Many of the hospital and NGO staff who directly supervised the CHWs I encountered in Addis Ababa took a critical stance toward the Ethiopian government's authoritarianism. At the same time, they were not about to express their criticisms publicly or use their organization as a way to upset the status quo. Sister Selamawit, for instance, a supervisor nurse employed by the Hiwot NGO, expressed to me in private her disapproval of the government's crackdown on political freedoms. We discussed Mesfin Woldemariam, a septuagenarian professor from Addis Ababa University, human rights advocate, and opposition leader, who at the time was being held as a political prisoner. Selamawit was upset that he was still in prison along with other intellectuals, students, and opposition leaders. She was also well aware of and disheartened by the barriers to community organization in Addis Ababa. In 2007, she was invited to meet with a women's club at Addis Ababa University to talk about how to strengthen it. The meeting, however, was cancelled—for political reasons, according to her. She explained that the government was cracking down on educated and politicized youth, still a vanguard of social justice movements in Ethiopia. Even if Selamawit and her colleagues felt strongly that the Ethiopian public ought to have the freedom to shape their health system, living conditions, and government, they knew that publicly pursuing such change through the organization and its CHWs was a recipe for disaster. If local Ethiopian NGOs wanted to stay on the good side of government officials and maintain cooperation with their international NGO and donor partners, and thus remain viable organizations, then their staff had to work with the status quo, treating CHWs as apolitical "tools" for achieving adequate care for patients and prevention of (drug-resistant) HIV.

This brings us back to the dominance of humanitarian goals and fears of drug resistance. The kinds of political troubles reviewed earlier tend to be ignored in the development and global health industries in order to focus on humanitarian and biomedical goals (Fassin 2013; Ferguson 1994). Such goals thus not only eclipse questions of adequate payment for low-level workforces. They also help draw attention away from questions about international alliances, warfare, inequality, and heavy-handed ways of governing and controlling populations, all of which have important implications for the well-being of individuals, communities, and populations, and for the functioning of CHW programs.

Conclusion

In Ethiopia, the global sustainability doctrine's preference for drawing on unpaid volunteer CHWs was simultaneously upheld and challenged in largely disconnected contexts. In the arena of rural primary health care, the creation of salaried CHW jobs was central to the mission. In the arena of urban AIDS care and treatment support, creating salaried CHW jobs was not on the agenda. A focus on life-saving drug access, drug adherence, and prevention of drug-resistant HIV, moreover, meant that the global movement to treat HIV/AIDS in Ethiopia and other low-income countries ushered in access to new pharmaceuticals and expanded opportunities to donate one's time and energy to supporting the rollout of ART, but largely left out food security and employment. Meanwhile, residents in Addis Ababa were lamenting an *alicha* millennium characterized by unemployment and insecure access to food, water, electricity, fuel, and housing.

As in many places around the world, CHWs in Addis Ababa were not invited to health-policy tables, or expected to be political forces seeking social and health system change. This goes against a vision of CHWs that many uphold, which sees the organized pursuit of structural changes as a role that CHWs can and should play, in addition to their roles in extending and delivering health care (Colvin and Swartz 2015). CHWs were not playing these roles in part because they and Ethiopians generally were living in fear under an authoritarian ruling party that had become highly intolerant of political and ideological opposition (Bach 2011; Burgess 2013).

Examining the national and transnational context of community health work is important, for it obviously shapes and limits the forms that such work takes. With knowledge of political and economic contexts, it is also difficult to ignore that there are fundamental political and economic problems confronting CHWs and their fellow citizens, involving global power imbalances and the account-ability of states and donors to people living in poverty, which lie at the root of the poverty and synergistic epidemics (or syndemics) of infectious and non-infectious diseases that are devastating populations throughout the world (Singer 2011). These problems will require much more than distributing and managing medical technologies and human resources, and they are problems that CHWs cannot solve on their own. There is a great need for research into CHWs' evolving relation-ships with these larger problems and with other actors who are responsible for, harmed by, or seeking to solve these problems. Such research can better prepare us to discuss alternative approaches to the challenges that lie ahead. The following chapter thus continues to explore the historical processes that shaped the context of community health work in Addis Ababa, while also tracing the life of a CHW.

Notes

1. At the time, 9.60 birr per liter was the equivalent of about $3.80/gallon. At the time of this writing (Oct 2013), gas costs about 20 birr per liter, which was the equivalent of approximately $4.20/gallon.
2. The city administration deemed such houses illegal and often tore them down with little warning. See, for example, the "Top Story" in Addis Ababa's English newspaper *Fortune* on May 27, 2007 (Volume 8 No 369), entitled "Out in the Cold," which cov-ered the city administration's controversial campaign of demolishing "moon houses" in the city in the run-up to the turn of the millennium. An op-ed entitled "Do It. But Do It Right and Just" followed in the June 3, 2007, edition of *Fortune* (V. 8 No. 370).
3. See *Fortune* (newspaper) Vol. 8 No. 370, June 3 2007, "Edible Oil: Not to Taste."
4. The condos were constructed quickly and, from the perspective of many inhabitants, poorly, with leaky plumbing, crumbling concrete, troublesome electric wiring, and misaligned windows. This large-scale housing project is a massive social experiment, furthermore, with unclear impacts on social networks, community trust, and solidar-ity among previous and new neighbors. (See "More Ambitious Planning for Capital's Housing Shortages" *Fortune* V. 8 No. 374 July 1, 2007; "City Auctions Apartments for 7,000 Br/Sqm" *Capital* V. 9 No. 446 July 1, 2007; "Condo Metropolis—Construc-tion of Condominiums Accelerated" *Capital* V. 10 No. 473 January 6, 2008; and "Condos Pushed to Peripheries" *Fortune* V. 8 No. 411 March 16, 2008.) Ultimately, it appears that government-subsidized condos have reinforced existing class and status inequalities; several friends have complained to me that the distribution has favored the middle and upper classes, as well as people with patrons in government.
5. Water and electricity shortages in Addis Ababa bring up the politics and socioen-vironmental impacts of hydroelectric dam construction and the roles of competi-tor international donors—namely, the US/IMF bloc and China. On electricity and hydroelectric projects in Ethiopia, see Abbink (2012) and Matthews et al. (2013).
6. The levels of poverty we were able to document make it clear how different these "volunteers" are from volunteers in the United States and other wealthy settings. One study of volunteers in the United States, which used data collected from a nationally representative sample in 2000, found that the majority of volunteers had household annual incomes between $30,000 and $100,000; about 30% had incomes under $30,000, while 12% had incomes over $100,000 (Borgonovi 2008). These income figures would be higher if they were corrected for current USD values.

7. See http://www.coregroup.org/about-us/who-we-are-and-what-we-do (accessed January 10, 2016).
8. Reduced public expenditures in health including human resources for health (HRH) led to poorer quality and often nonexistent public health care, while private sector care remained inaccessible because of the inability of many people to pay for care (Pfeiffer and Chapman 2010).
9. The HEP has been heralded as a success and a model for other countries: within a few years of deploying all those women to villages throughout the country, Ethiopia witnessed significant gains in multiple population health indicators (CNHDE 2011; FMOH 2011; Global Health Workforce Alliance 2010b; Teklehaimanot and Teklehaimanot 2013). In the *Lancet*, Donnelly (2010) described the significance of the HEP: "The number of women dying in childbirth decreased. The number of children immunized increased. And the number of families gaining access to clean water soared. Ethiopia had created a model to improve primary health care for others to follow" (p. 1907).
10. The WHO's statement has met with criticism. Glenton et al. (2010), for example, suggest that the WHO based its recommendation to stop relying on unpaid and underpaid CHWs on little empirical research, despite the rhetoric used in the policy document ("the burden of evidence indicates . . ."). Their claim appears to be based in part on a problematic tendency in 21st-century global public health to count only randomized control trials (RCTs) as "empirical research" and only their results as "evidence" (Adams 2013; Cohen and Easterly 2009). There are not any RCTs, to my knowledge, that have been used to test the impact of CHW payment on program sustainability, perhaps in part because this would necessitate a fairly lengthy longitudinal study, and RCTs tend to involve "before-and-after" protocols with relatively short time frames.
11. Advocates for paying CHWs and "moving away from volunteerism" have recently used formal cost exercises to show that paying CHWs would be a smaller expenditure than widely believed. One cost exercise carried out by PIH and the Clinton Foundation estimated that paying a CHW to accompany every AIDS patient in Rwanda to ART would cost $3 to $5 per capita per year, a small proportion of the country's overall health budget (Drobac et al. 2013: 175–6). Health economists from the Earth Institute's One Million CHW Campaign recently conducted their own cost analysis and came up with a similar figure: $6.86 per "inhabitant covered by the CHW subsystem" per year, or an annual average of $3,750 to train, equip, support, and manage each CHW (McCord et al. 2013). Drobac and colleagues emphasize that their cost exercise did not take into account the long-term savings embodied in a healthier population and stronger health system. Global health donors and institutions that focus on up-front costs, including low-level labor costs, often discount such savings. On the one hand, these costing exercises may be considered helpful in countering the belief that creating CHW jobs is simply too expensive. On the other hand, we have to question how those who perform these cost analyses decide upon the amounts allocated to CHW salaries and benefits. Further, we have to ask the following question: Why should CHW salaries be settled by health economists who are interested primarily in cost-effectiveness and who probably want to have or enjoy having the power to negotiate their own salaries with their employers?
12. Early models of local participation in health care include China's "barefoot doctors" as well as village health teams organized by Christian missionaries in Africa and elsewhere (Basilico et al. 2013; Cueto 2004; Maupin 2015).
13. Ingram and colleagues (2012) note that CHWs have existed in multiple forms in the United States since the 1960s and currently are employed by a number of private and public agencies at the local level. Typically focused on communities and individuals marginalized through structural and interpersonal racism, classism, sexism, ableism,

and heteronormativity, CHWs in the United States address a number of health concerns, including environmental health, maternal health, HIV/AIDS, alcohol use, interpersonal violence, and, increasingly, chronic diseases (Ingram et al. 2012). It was not until 1998 that a comprehensive Community Health Advisory Study attempted to identify the core competencies of CHWs in the United States through CHW surveys and organizational case studies (Ingram et al. 2012: 530).

14. It is helpful to be clear about what "the pursuit of social justice" means in general and in the realm of community health in particular localities. Researchers at the CDC-funded Arizona Prevention Research Center (Sabo et al. 2013) relate CHWs' pursuit of social justice to their community organizing and advocacy efforts and divide CHW advocacy into three levels or domains: (1) advocacy within a CHW's own agency; (2) civic advocacy directed at health and social service agencies, clinics, hospitals, businesses, and law enforcement agencies; and (3) political advocacy directed at school boards, city councils, county boards of supervisors, state representatives, and governors. Examples of advocacy directed toward CHWs' own agencies include promoting the status of CHWs within the organization, obtaining resources needed by CHWs, and working to correct the ways in which one's own agency communicates and delivers services to beneficiaries. Examples of civic advocacy include engaging civic leaders or governing bodies to improve community infrastructure, health, and social service policy. Examples of political advocacy include collecting signatures for ballot measures, contacting elected officials, including governing and legislative bodies, and drafting and pushing for specific legislative changes. Qualitative data collected for the 2010 US National Community Health Workers Advocacy Study (NCHWAS) provide examples of these various kinds of advocacy and organizing (Sabo et al. 2013).

15. One example of a "supportive political context" cited commonly in the literature is that provided by the Sandinistas in Nicaragua (Nading 2013; Wiggins 2012). Lehmann and Sanders (2007) suggest that even in the context of the Sandinistas in Nicaragua, CHWs, or "brigadistas" as they were locally known, did not all necessarily approach some ideal of political participation.

16. Compare Maes et al. 2015; Banteyerga 2014.

17. In response to the 2005 election violence and the crackdown on dissent, members of the US Congress, the EU, and other international donors threatened to defund the central government and to direct money instead to NGOs and to Ethiopia's district bureaucracies.

18. For Ethiopia's ruling party, having strong, authoritarian control over the economy and over citizens' beliefs and behaviors—as opposed to having an autonomous civil society that attempts to hold the state accountable and change policies and practices—is deemed necessary to ensure economic growth, poverty reduction, and an eventual Ethiopian "renaissance" amid highly unfavorable international terms of trade as well as domestic opposition (De Waal 2012; Little 2014; Maes et al. 2015).

2

BECOMING A COMMUNITY HEALTH WORKER

A Biosocial and Historical Perspective

Eskinder did not know his exact age. He estimated it at 35 in 2008, yet based on his life narrative he was likely closer to 40, born perhaps around 1967. Among his fellow volunteers and NGO supervisors, Eskinder had a reputation as an outstanding and compassionate CHW. The story of how he arrived at this position involves some twists and turns.

The rise of the HIV/AIDS epidemic features prominently in this story. Yet another stigmatized infectious disease with a deeper history had in fact shaped Eskinder's life. His mother, born in southern Ethiopia, had contracted leprosy at the age of five. She and her parents then set off on a seven-year quest in search of a cure from various indigenous healers and Orthodox churches in southern and central Ethiopia. After several years, they met an Islamic scholar in *Gurage*, a couple hundred kilometers south of Ethiopia's capital, who told her parents: "There is no medication here. But there is a cure in Addis Ababa, in a place called *Zennabawarq*." At 12 years of age, Eskinder's mom then trekked to the Princess Zennabawarq Leprosarium, where she started treatment and became a resident of the surrounding village of Gebre Kristos. It was around the end of the 1950s.

The Princess Zennabawarq Leprosarium dates back to 1930, when Ras Tafari Makonnen ascended to Ethiopia's highest throne as Haile Selassie I. One of his early acts as the Ethiopian *negus negist*, or king of kings, was asking the United Presbyterian Protestant missionary and field director of the Sudan Interior Mission (SIM) in Ethiopia, Dr. Thomas Lambie, to found and run a leprosarium on the outskirts of Addis Ababa.[1] Lambie, whose aim was to extend Presbyterian work into the south of Ethiopia, saw the value of a hospital as an entry point (Donham 1999). When the Emperor requested that he build a leprosarium in Addis Ababa, he agreed.[2] The American Leprosy Mission provided a grant of 20,000 USD to fund construction, and a 5,000 USD annual budget (Terecha

2005). In return, the Emperor granted Lambie permission to establish SIM head-quarters in Addis Ababa (Terecha 2005).

The Leprosarium was constructed on the southwest outskirts of the capital city, where the road to Jimma crosses the Akaki River. After initially bestowing his own name upon the new internationally financed leprosarium, the Emperor decided to dedicate it to his daughter. Today, the leprosarium that attracted Eskinder's mother and grandparents is a more general hospital and research facility targeting a number of diseases, including AIDS. It is now known as ALERT Hospital to the doctors and nurses who staff it and the national and international officials who run and finance it. Yet many residents of Addis Ababa still refer to the facility and its adjacent bus stop as *Zennabawarq.* Eskinder, who spent some time bedridden in one of the hospital's wards, knew it by both its names.

This chapter examines the histories of Eskinder's life, the institutions that comprised the health program he and his fellow CHWs served, the cycles of poverty and infection they confronted, and the neighborhoods in which they lived and worked. Becoming a CHW is not just about being exposed to a recruitment call, deciding to join up, and going through basic training. In Addis Ababa and in multiple parts of the world, becoming a CHW involves processes and structural determinants that extend into the past and span the globe. Examining these intertwined biosocial histories also drives home the complexity and dignity of

FIGURE 2.1   A sign at ALERT Hospital's main gate, 2007.

Photo courtesy of the author.

FIGURE 2.2 Murals above the main gates at the St. Gebre Kristos church, located adjacent to ALERT Hospital, 2007.

Photo courtesy of the author.

CHWs' lives, and shows us where CHWs are coming from. Understanding these histories is crucial to understanding the actions and goals of CHWs as they confront evolving and intertwined epidemiological, political, and economic problems.

Transformations

In 1935, just two years after the Princess Zennabawarq Leprosarium was inaugurated, Italian fascist forces overthrew Haile Selassie. They occupied Ethiopia until 1941, when Ethiopian troops, aided by British and US forces, expelled the Italians and Haile Selassie returned from exile in England and Khartoum. After the return of the Emperor to his throne, the Princess Zennabawarq Leprosarium expanded to accommodate a multitude of new patients.[3] From various corners of Ethiopia came men, women, and children, some unwillingly, compelled by government authorities, and others voluntarily, in search of better medical treatment—particularly after the introduction of dapsone injections in the 1950s (Terecha 2005). Eskinder's narrative puts his mother into the latter category.

Eskinder's mother eventually met and married a man employed by the Leprosarium to make shoes for patients with leprosy. He did not have a "skin disease," Eskinder pointed out. But he did have a life-altering encounter with another infectious disease: malaria. Shortly after getting married, Eskinder's father was transferred by the Princess Zennabawarq Leprosarium to work at a newly established leprosarium located in Awash, some 200 kilometers away and 1,400 meters below Addis Ababa. In the lowlands of Awash, however, he soon came down with a strong bout of fever, prompting him to leave his job and return to the capital city—and his new wife.

According to historian Mesele Terecha, life in and around Gebre Kristos village had deteriorated in the 1940s and '50s. Theft and interpersonal violence were common features of daily life (Terecha 2005: 107–8, 160–74). Not far from the village was located the city's primary dump for solid and liquid waste. The Ministry of Public Health and Addis Ababa's municipal government tried to segregate Gebre Kristos from the rest of the city because of its association with leprosy and destitution, labeling the village as a site of "no visitors." Thus there was limited socioeconomic interaction between residents of Gebre Kristos and the rest of city. Unable to get his old job back or to move out of Gebre Kristos, Eskinder's father had few options. He started sewing mattresses—a job that brought little income or prestige.

A few years later, Eskinder was born, the eldest of five siblings raised in Gebre Kristos. His birth roughly coincided with an important turn of events for the Princess Zennabawarq Leprosarium. In 1963, the same year that the Organization of African Unity was established in Addis Ababa, a committee organized by the International Society for Rehabilitation of the Disabled met in the United States and decided to "establish a training and research center in Africa in which students from all over African countries shall be trained in the treatment and rehabilitation of leprosy patients" (Terecha 2005: 109).[4] The international center was to be called ALERT, the All Africa Leprosy Rehabilitation and Training Center. The Princess Zennabawarq Leprosarium, located just a short distance from the headquarters of a new symbol of African unity and independence, was chosen as the site for ALERT through an agreement between the Ethiopian imperial government and international patrons. In 1966, the Norwegian and Swedish Save the Children funds agreed to cover the full costs of constructing and equipping the new ALERT center. The following year, European stewards assumed responsibility for running the entire facility and subsequently undertook substantial transformation and expansion projects (Terecha 2005).[5]

The transformation of the Princess Zennabawarq Leprosarium into ALERT meant better facilities and an influx of Ethiopian and European medical practitioners who were willing to take up leprosy work there (Terecha 2005: 175). This, in turn, improved the medical status of people living with Hansen's Disease and the socioeconomic image of Gebre Kristos and the neighborhoods next to ALERT. Further improvements came in the 1970s. The Gebre Kristos village was more fully integrated with the city after the fall of Haile Selassie in 1974. In 1976, the village came under the administrative structure of the municipality, which soon stopped dumping the city's liquid garbage in the area (the solid waste dump is still nearby). Yet despite becoming better integrated with the city and better served by Ethiopian and European health workers, the village of Gebre Kristos continued its evolution into a densely populated slum. Unfortunately, the quality of life experienced by most of its residents would be further eroded in the 1970s and '80s by politically motivated violence.

At That Time, There Was a Revolution

In 1974, the centuries-old Ethiopian monarchy fell to a military junta known as the Derg, which evolved into one of several Afro-Marxisms that emerged on the continent during this period of the Cold War. Marxist-Leninist inspired reforms followed. Notably, the military government attempted to extend primary health care and reform land tenure across the country. Primary health-care reforms had little impact, however, as the government became engulfed in a costly civil war and conflict with neighboring Somalia. These conflicts were fueled by wider geopolitics, as in several other African countries that had gained independence from their European colonizers in the 1950s, '60s, and '70s (Donham 1999). Due to these conflicts, little domestic or international funding was devoted to health care, and hundreds of rural health facilities were damaged or destroyed. Health-services coverage declined to 1960s levels, and modern health-care resources remained concentrated in Addis Ababa (Kloos 1998).

Gebre Kristos village was indirectly impacted by these conflicts. At the end of the 1970s, the village saw the establishment of a nearby military camp for Ethiopian army members wounded in the Ethio-Somali War (also known as the Ogaden War).[6] Later, wounded army members and their families began to construct residences in the area, after receiving land from the municipality. This raised the social status of the area to some degree, yet also attracted beer (*talla*), mead (*tej*), and liquor (*areqe*) houses and a rise in commercial sex work (Terecha 2005).

During this time, young Eskinder and his family lived in a single-room shack, got their water from a shared well, and struggled to get enough to eat by collecting and selling leaves and fuel wood from the forests. He was in and out of school starting at grade six and finally discontinued schooling at grade nine.

School was not the only source of knowledge. Eskinder recounted how he once read about Che Guevara in a book translated into Amharic.

> At that time there was a revolution [in Ethiopia], and so you could only find books related to revolution. It was about Che Guevara's struggle. I think it was for Nicaragua's freedom that he was fighting . . . and Cuba.

At 40 years of age, Eskinder was stockier than the western stereotype of a thin and lanky Ethiopian. He usually wore a T-shirt, baggy blue jeans, and loosely laced work boots, and let his curly hair grow a bit longer than most men his age in Addis Ababa. As a youth, he said he looked up to Che Guevara. Rather than following Che's path, however, under the Derg, adolescent boys in Addis Ababa were more likely to be chased and rounded up by *kebele* officials and agents of several competing parties, to be questioned about their loyalties and harassed. Kebeles are the lowest government administrative unit in Ethiopia and exist in both rural and urban areas. They were created as "peasant associations" by Ethiopia's Derg regime in 1975 to manage land reform in the countryside and promote development. In Addis, kebeles became roughly synonymous with neighborhood associations. They also became associated with rival political factions that fought the Derg and each other for control over the country in the mid-1970s, including the Ethiopian People's Revolutionary Party (EPRP) and the All-Ethiopia Socialist Movement (MEISON). Kebeles thus took on the role of neighborhood "defense" squads that perpetrated violence against suspected rivals.[7] "There were times that I escaped from them by entering into the ravine here by ALERT," Eskinder said. "I was raised beside the river, so I could swim and I knew the way of the water. Other times they came in the middle of the night, asked my father where I was, and left."

Later, when Eskinder would have been close to 20 years old, he was rounded up to serve in the military, to fight against the multiple liberation fronts seeking the downfall of the Derg. Those who had the wherewithal would escape while being transported to *Tateq*, the Derg's military training center outside Addis Ababa. And Eskinder did escape—twice. Had he not, chances are good that he would not be a protagonist in this story. Eskinder simply described this time in his life as "disturbing."

The Derg was finally defeated in 1991, brought down by the Ethiopian People's Revolutionary Democratic Front (EPRDF), a coalition of political parties that holds power in Ethiopia to this day. It was a new era for Ethiopia, one of renewed and deepening ties to western governments, corporations, and donors, as well as the establishment of a federal political system with parliaments and elected officials. It was the beginning of a new era for Eskinder too. Only a week after the EPRDF took over the capital, his father died. As the eldest of his siblings, Eskinder had to take over many household responsibilities. He began working as a daily laborer carrying ceramic wares for 95 cents per day. But this kind of work was literally too heavy for Eskinder: beyond his "capacity," as he put it. So he stopped and eventually began working as a taxi tout or *weyala*— another low-status and low-income job.

Another Life-Altering Infection

Two years before its downfall in 1989, the Derg regime had allowed the Norwegian Save the Children Fund to begin an urban development program in Gebre Kristos. The program brought new houses, schools, clinics, mills, latrines, drainage, and roads, and continued even after the EPRDF took power. When the program came to an end in 1999, the physical status of the village had undergone considerable improvement (Terecha 2005). Poverty was still rampant, and large numbers of people continued to live in squalor. Yet new opportunities also came to some. Around 1993, 25-year-old Eskinder and his mother and siblings, for instance, moved to a new shack next to ALERT and the Gebre Kristos church. For a time, Eskinder worked at a cement factory outside Addis on the Ambo road. He then worked as a welder, making "good income"—about five dollars per day. "I was supporting myself and my family with that, and saving money. At that time, it was good." He also courted a girlfriend, whom he planned to marry.

It was in this context of very modest socioeconomic progress that Eskinder was infected with HIV.[8] Eskinder said he had not had many sexual partners, and thus he was more than surprised when he learned he was infected. He attributed his infection to his girlfriend. He figured she was unfaithful to him when she left Addis with her family to visit Dire Dawa, Harer, and Jimma. He partly blamed himself for being naïve, saying, "When I started to fall for her, I let her fool me. I never thought she would go to another man. I say it is my carelessness—I become close and trust people." Unfortunately, I do not have his ex-girlfriend's side of the story. It would most likely add some complexity to Eskinder's interpretation. However it happened, Eskinder joined a growing population of Ethiopians infected with HIV.[9]

The Ethiopian government's initial response to HIV/AIDS was immediate but far from comprehensive. In 1985, the government convened a National Task Force, which made limited efforts to disseminate information and education about HIV/AIDS, promote condom use, engage in HIV/AIDS surveillance and screening in laboratories at various health institutions, and provide patient care. The government issued its first HIV/AIDS policy in 1998, and a National AIDS Prevention and Control Council was established in 2000. The Council, which brought together representatives of various federal ministries, regional states, NGOs, religious bodies, civil society organizations, and people living with HIV/AIDS (PLWHAs), became responsible for overseeing implementation of federal and regional plans, approving budgets, and monitoring program impact. Subsequently, an HIV/AIDS Prevention and Control Office (HAPCO) was established to coordinate and facilitate Ethiopia's response to HIV/AIDS.[10]

As these new AIDS-focused bureaucracies took shape, Eskinder continued to live with his mother, keeping his HIV status secret and working as a welder. One day, seemingly out of nowhere, his boss said he could no longer employ him. Eskinder was able to find work at a small lumberyard nearby, but not long thereafter he came to work one day and noticed his new boss and another worker talking and looking at him. His boss then approached him and suggested that he go work with some welders in another part of town. Eskinder asked him, "Are they patients [i.e. people with HIV/AIDS]?" His boss replied, "Yes. They organized their own shop, and you can work with them." Somehow, his HIV status had been revealed.

Soon the more pressing issue of bare survival eclipsed Eskinder's twin problems of unemployment and stigmatization. He fell very ill toward the end of 2004, becoming one of the estimated 277,000 people requiring antiretroviral therapies (ART) in Ethiopia at the time—a number that was expected to (and did) rise over the next five years (FMOH/HAPCO 2006a). At this point, Eskinder's life intersected with the set of political and economic processes that brought free ART to Ethiopia and low-income countries in Africa and globally.

During the 1980s and early '90s, an HIV diagnosis was essentially a guarantee of an early death, regardless of socioeconomic status or geographic location. In the United States, deaths attributable to HIV/AIDS rose steadily in the absence of therapies capable of stopping HIV infection from progressing to what came to be called "full-blown" AIDS. In Washington, DC, and New York City, thousands of infected people and their allies and advocates protested, putting pressure on the federal government to make the semi-effective therapies that existed more widely accessible and to devote greater money and political attention to developing and approving newer, more effective therapies. Aside from medical treatment, protestors also demanded the end of discrimination by employers, insurers, and others, as well as better prevention measures and economic support for people living with HIV/AIDS.

Of course, AIDS was not confined to the United States. It was ravaging families, communities, and populations in poor countries, in sub-Saharan Africa in particular. The discovery of effective, "highly active" ART (or HAART) in 1996 inspired some AIDS activists in the United States and analogous advocacy groups in poor countries to join forces. Yet as HIV infection became less of a biological and socioeconomic death sentence in the United States, too little attention was given to popular demands for treatment in poor countries (Messac and Prabhu 2013).

This was especially unfortunate given that prominent experts in global public health circles were at the time arguing *against* treating AIDS in poor countries. In sub-Saharan Africa, prevention and treatment were treated as mutually exclusive strategies for controlling HIV/AIDS epidemics. Global health experts and foreign aid officials came to the conclusion that, given the scarcity of funding for supplying and delivering basic health-care resources (let alone expensive drugs such as HAART), investing in AIDS treatment in poor countries instead of prevention would waste money and cost lives.[11] Others argued that delivering ART in poor countries with crumbling health systems would be counterproductive and dangerous, basically guaranteeing the development of drug-resistant HIV strains that might then travel to wealthy countries. This argument was premised partly on the fact that ART demands strict, lifelong adherence, since anything less increases the risk that resistant strains will develop, and partly on the unfounded assumption that people in poor countries were inherently incapable of adhering carefully to ART (Messac and Prabhu 2013).

The policy norm of denying access to ART for people in poor countries would prove difficult but not impossible to overturn. It would require an inspiring and instructive series of grassroots and global actions, pilot projects demonstrating that successful treatment and high adherence rates were possible in settings of poverty, high-level negotiations between pharmaceutical producers and purchasers, and a historically unprecedented level of donations.[12] Particularly important was overcoming the very high prices of antiretroviral drugs and the unwillingness of donors to pay for these drugs and the delivery of treatment and care.

In 2007, I was at ALERT Hospital when it hosted Bill Clinton, who came to inaugurate the pediatric ART clinic and ward that his Foundation had helped finance (see Figure 2.3). In the previous couple of years, the Clinton Foundation had begun providing direct support to several ART programs in Africa. Before it got involved in supporting ART programs such as ALERT's, the Foundation had played a more fundamental role in the expansion of ART in Africa by helping negotiate down the international price of antiretroviral pharmaceuticals.[13] In the early 2000s, the Foundation began securing promises from the governments of poor countries to place large orders of generic ARV drugs, and reciprocal agreements from generic drug producers in India and South Africa to produce substantially higher quantities of drugs at lower costs. By capitalizing on Clinton's influence over both public and private sector leaders, the Foundation encouraged the formation of new, large-scale ART markets, widely viewed as a "win-win" situation for private producers and public purchasers. Producers of generic ARV drugs ultimately secured higher profits by sacrificing short-term losses, and needy government purchasers secured drastic price reductions (Biehl 2006). Specifically, the price of the most common HAART regimens in poor countries fell from $10,000 to $15,000 per patient per year in the late 1990s to less than $100 in 2007.

The promise of greatly reduced prices for antiretroviral drugs, however, was not yet a sure "win" for the millions of people in need of ART in poor countries, since there still was nowhere near enough money available to purchase and deliver ART and care at that scale (Messac and Prabhu 2013: 125–6). The Global Fund would help change that. In 2001, Jeffrey Sachs and Amir Attaran published an article in the influential medical journal the *Lancet*, proposing a new global fund dedicated to controlling HIV/AIDS, tuberculosis, and malaria, the world's three greatest infectious killers. UN Secretary-General Kofi Annan put the weight of his office behind Sachs and Attaran's proposal, and at the G8 Summit in 2001, leaders of the world's eight largest economies launched the Global Fund to Fight AIDS, Tuberculosis and Malaria.[14] The "3 by 5" Initiative, launched in 2003 by the WHO and the Joint United Nations Programme on HIV/AIDS (UNAIDS), set an interim goal for the Fund: to extend ART to three million people living with AIDS in low- and middle-income countries by the end of 2005. With the 3 by 5 Initiative, the WHO and UNAIDS also put forth an action plan to help make this goal a reality.

The 3 by 5 goal was not met, however: not until 2007 were three million souls receiving HAART in the poorest countries in the world. But according to

FIGURE 2.3 Bill Clinton visits ALERT Hospital in 2007 to inaugurate the pediatric ART clinic and ward. To Clinton's right is Dr. Ruth Leekassa, medical director of ALERT Hospital at the time; Dr. Tedros Adhanom, former minister of health of Ethiopia; and Dr. Yigeremu Abebe, then director of ALERT's HIV/AIDS treatment program (and soon-to-be Ethiopia country director for the Clinton Foundation).

Photo courtesy of the author.

Messac and Prabhu (2013: 114), the 3 by 5 target helped "galvanize" the global AIDS treatment movement and "coalesce a diverse set of actors—multilateral and bilateral donors, health practitioners, international policymakers, governments of AIDS-afflicted countries, AIDS patients and their advocates around the world—around further ART scale-up initiatives."[15] By the end of 2011, the Global Fund would approve $22.9 *billion* in grants for 151 countries. $12.4 billion (54%) of that overall total was designated for HIV/AIDS, and 55% of disbursements went to countries in sub-Saharan Africa. By the end of 2012, the Global Fund estimated that 4.2 million people worldwide were receiving ART (Global Fund 2012).

Only one institution has come close to matching the level at which the multilateral Global Fund financed the rise in ART access in Africa: PEPFAR (the US President's Emergency Plan for AIDS Relief).[16] PEPFAR was initiated unilaterally by the US government in 2003 to focus squarely on mounting an "emergency" response to HIV/AIDS. Between 2004 and 2006, PEPFAR became the second largest AIDS donor in Ethiopia (after the Global Fund) and allocated more than $231 million to recipients in Ethiopia to help rapidly expand access to antiretroviral drugs (Banteyerga et al. 2006: 11). By September 2013, the US State

Department claimed that PEPFAR supported ART for 6.7 million people in 24 nations worldwide, most of them in sub-Saharan Africa.[17]

Meanwhile, the Ethiopian government did its part to pave the way for expanded access to ART. This included issuing a Policy on Supply and Use of Anti-Retroviral Drugs in 2002, and in 2005, a Strategy and Guidelines for Implementation of Anti-Retroviral Therapy. The federal Ministry of Health also put forward a road map for accelerating access to HIV/AIDS treatment, which set goals of creating hundreds of new public ART delivery sites by the end of 2006 (Banteyerga et al. 2006: 10–11).[18]

As a result of these global political-economic developments, Eskinder became one of the first people to access ART for free in Ethiopia. At one point, he was bedridden and barely able to keep down even watery *shiro*, the spicy bean paste that is a staple of local diets. "From 92 kilos, I became 39. My CD4 [count] was five. I was finished." It is common for patients in Eskinder's condition to use their CD4 white blood cell counts as a measure of immune system strength and overall health—that is, as an indicator of how bad a toll HIV has had on one's health and how much ART has helped reconstitute one's health. A normal CD4 count ranges between 500 and 1000 cells per cubic millimeter of blood. Doctors would consider a count of five highly alarming, and to Eskinder it meant impending death.[19] But with ART, Eskinder said he and his CD4 count experienced a rapid turnaround. "I reached 35 and continued to increase," he recalled in 2008. "Now, thanks to God, I am 255."

From Leprosarium to Antiretroviral Center of Excellence

As one of ALERT's first ART patients, Eskinder made his initial recovery from near death while admitted in an officially *public* hospital ward. That's because in 2002, 44 years and two political regimes after European donors and doctors transformed the Princess Zennabawarq Leprosarium into ALERT, Ethiopia's Ministry of Health resumed control over the hospital.[20] Soon thereafter, toward the end of 2004, the Ministry decided that ALERT would become an ART "center of excellence," and so began another transformation of the 75-year-old medical facility.[21]

The fact that the Ministry took control over ALERT in 2002 is momentous given the facility's origins and history. It is also significant in light of recent critiques regarding the hollowing out of public health-care systems and the rise of NGOs and privatized care in sub-Saharan Africa in the late 20th century. Various sources of evidence demonstrate that structural adjustment, which involved placing caps on public sector wage bills and encouraging the private sector to play a bigger role in health-care delivery, undermined public sector health services for poor people, leading to immiseration and intensified suffering in the 1990s and early 2000s (Pfeiffer and Chapman 2010). Anthropologist James Pfeiffer and others have further argued that while international AIDS money greatly expanded the number of people in sub-Saharan Africa who have access to ARV drugs and HIV/AIDS care, it often did little to alleviate the basic constraints imposed on national health systems by structural adjustment, since much of the money flowed not through public health systems but through NGOs that set up parallel, incomplete, and uncoordinated delivery systems. In multiple contexts in sub-Saharan Africa, the result was

> an ART scale-up with millions of new dollars flowing into the health sector but little support for the building blocks of the health system that make the scale-up possible: most glaringly human resources, but also laboratories, supply chains, data collection systems, transport, and bricks and mortar.
>
> *(Pfeiffer 2013: 174; Pfeiffer and Chapman 2010)*[22]

The Ethiopian government's move to take control of ALERT in 2002 and, more generally, its intention to keep primary health care and ART delivery within the public sector, can be understood as a set of political decisions made in response to a trend of weakening public health systems in Africa during the 1990s and to perceived threats to state sovereignty posed by bilateral and multinational institutions that sought to influence political-economic changes in Africa in the 20th and 21st centuries. When the military regime known as the Derg fell in 1991 to the EPRDF, Ethiopia's leadership transferred to a politburo of Marxist-Leninist inspired guerrilla fighters. Ethiopia's new rulers distanced themselves from the policies of the previous regime by allowing some privatization of health care and other sectors and by giving state- and district-level governments more economic autonomy, thus bringing Ethiopia's economic policies and bureaucracies somewhat in line with Washington prescriptions. As in many other parts of Africa, Ethiopia subsequently saw the proliferation of NGOs in the health sector. By 2010, according to Ethiopia's fourth report on its National Health Accounts, 95 international NGOs and 152 local NGOs were "active players in the Ethiopian health sector" (FMOH 2010). An untold number of these NGOs run programs and projects focused on AIDS prevention, care, and treatment support.

Ethiopia's new rulers did not, however, take a simple turn toward the market fundamentalism promoted by the IMF. Instead, the EPRDF leadership, which continues to rule to this day, pursued a so-called third way: a hybrid approach to development that promotes privatization and markets to some extent while maintaining relatively strong state control over the economy, social organization, and the health-care system (Data Dea Barata 2012; de Waal 2012; Feyissa 2011; Meles Zenawi 2012). This approach—and the set of policies and techniques of government that go with it—is dubbed, developed, and promoted by EPRDF leaders as *abyotawi* (revolutionary) democracy (Bach 2011). For Ethiopia's ruling party, having strong control over the economy and over citizens' beliefs and behaviors is deemed necessary to ensure economic growth, poverty reduction, and an eventual Ethiopian "renaissance" amid highly unfavorable international terms of trade as well as domestic opposition (De Waal 2012; Little 2014; Maes et al. 2015). Ethiopia was not colonized by a European power. Yet at the end of the 20th century, after fighting off Italian colonization and then undergoing a violent revolution and the rise of the EPRDF, the Ethiopian state was one of the poorest in the world. Thus the country was in a similar situation to many states that emerged from decades and centuries of colonialism: severely constrained in creating jobs and wealth for its people, in part because of the dominance of neoliberal economic policies on the global level, structural adjustment in Ethiopia, and decades of unfavorable global terms of trade. Ethiopia's leaders have seen the severe constraints that the global political economy puts on poor countries, even as they have seized economic and political opportunities extended by powers beyond their borders. The ways in which the ruling party has attempted to control the Ethiopian population and shape the economy and health system thus reflect not only their explicit ideology and style of government but also a poorly regulated global capitalist system that is unfair to many actors in the global south, including government leaders and impoverished citizens.

As "revolutionary democrats," EPRDF leaders expressed discomfort with IMF and donor-imposed constraints on, for example, growing public health workforces, as well as with the trend toward channeling donor money through an increasing number of NGOs rather than through the government. EPRDF leaders wanted to avoid competition between government and NGOs over scarce human resources, as well as a relentless struggle to coordinate, monitor, and evaluate the "chaotic donor and NGO pet projects" whose resources largely bypass government control—a struggle shared by government bureaucrats across the African continent (Banteyerga et al. 2006; Pfeiffer 2013: 174).[23] Ethiopia's leadership further connected these problems to the vertical structure of much health and development funding. Dr. Tedros Adhanom, Ethiopia's minister of health during this period, and Meles Zenawi, Ethiopia's prime minister up to 2012, thus lobbied international donors to support their program of channeling unearmarked money from multiple international donors through pooled government accounts (Maes et al. 2015). In the AIDS arena, they also pursued an explicit principle of "the three ones"—one consensus HIV/AIDS action framework, one national AIDS coordinating authority, and one country-level monitoring and evaluation system (FMOH/HAPCO 2006a; HAPCO and World Bank 2008). Ethiopia's Ministry of Health and its National HIV/AIDS Prevention and Control Office also made a key decision to have government health centers and hospitals (rather than NGOs and private clinics) play the lead role in ART provision.[24]

Compromise is the upshot of these competing approaches and political and economic interests. ALERT's ART center of excellence provides a clear illustration: the program was closely overseen by the Ethiopian Ministry of Health, yet it was backed by several international NGOs, universities, and donors, including the Christian Children's Fund of Canada, the Ethiopian North American Health

Professionals Association (an association of Ethiopian health professionals within the diasporas in the United States and Canada), JHPIEGO (a non-profit affiliate of Johns Hopkins University), and the Clinton Foundation.[25] These international donors and NGOs, moreover, paid the salaries of many of ALERT's HIV/AIDS-specific hospital staff, from doctors to data clerks.

Meanwhile, ALERT's ART program also followed the global norm of "outsourcing" a great deal of treatment support and care onto CHWs organized by local NGOs. At the time of my research, five local NGOs were integral parts of ALERT's ART center of excellence, and they all relied on unpaid volunteers.[26] Thus when Eskinder was released from ALERT Hospital, his aging mother brought a couple of staff members from one of these local NGOs to visit and counsel him. They came from the Medhin Social Center, founded by an Ethiopian Catholic nun named Sister Tsinkenesh. In the 1980s, she worked in the "social unit" of ALERT, which was then still focused primarily on leprosy. She would frequently visit the homes of people affected by leprosy, learning about their situations and problems. She then decided, in consultation with ALERT's management, to establish a separate "social center" directly adjacent to ALERT, under the auspices of the Ethiopian Catholic Church. At the time of my research, Medhin continued to provide care and support for people with leprosy but had turned much of its attention to HIV/AIDS as the latter epidemic emerged in the 1990s. When Eskinder visited Medhin after being discharged from the hospital, he saw people he knew. He began to visit more, meanwhile struggling to find work. At Medhin, he received counseling and learned that the NGO deployed and supervised a small cadre of CHWs to bring counseling, care, and support into the homes of ALERT's ART patients.

Had Eskinder not lived so close to Medhin, when he left the hospital he may have been connected with another NGO that specialized in HBC for people with HIV/AIDS. Most likely, that NGO would have been the Hiwot HIV/AIDS Prevention, Care and Support Organization, the NGO introduced at the beginning of this book's introduction. Like Medhin, the Hiwot NGO was headquartered in and focused its efforts on ALERT's catchment area. Like Medhin, it started small: founded in 1999 by an Ethiopian nurse named Sister Tibebe Maco, Hiwot initially attempted to address the needs of just a couple dozen people living with HIV/AIDS. And like Medhin, Hiwot trained and coordinated a workforce of CHWs. But by the time of my research, Hiwot was bigger than any of the other NGOs doing HIV/AIDS work in Addis Ababa. It maintained a hierarchy of office and field staff, including a citywide HBC coordinator, HBC team leaders (including one for ALERT's catchment area), social workers, supervisor nurses, and large numbers of CHWs—at least six hundred. The Hiwot NGO also attracted international interns, including some from leading public health schools in the United States. This was all mainly due to the fact that its director had signed a fairly large contract with Family Health International (FHI) in 2003. Hiwot's director recognized her NGO's contract with FHI—and thus her access to PEPFAR funds—as a turning point. Before the contract, Hiwot served only two of Addis Ababa's ten sub-cities or districts. After the contract, the local NGO rapidly scaled up to cover all ten sub-cities and took a lead role among the other AIDS NGOs operating in Addis Ababa. Medhin, the NGO that served as a source of support for Eskinder, received funding from a mix of international donors, including PEPFAR, but was not an "implementing partner" of a big NGO (with massive funding) like Hiwot was for FHI. It thus remained relatively small and focused on the slums immediately adjacent to ALERT.[27] During my research, Medhin deployed only 20 CHWs to serve the growing number of ART patients at ALERT.

Through regular coordination with government authorities, Medhin, Hiwot, and the other NGOs involved in ALERT's ART program made a concerted effort to avoid the "fragmentation" and competition that plague health systems characterized by multiple NGOs and hollowed-out public infrastructures working (or lurching) in parallel (Pfeiffer and Chapman 2010). Their success depended largely on their CHW supervisors, who worked full-time supervising the CHWs' daily activities, making their own home visits with volunteers to supervise adherence to ARV drug regimens, and facilitating referrals of patients to clinical and social services.[28] Nevertheless, as in urban centers throughout Africa, these NGOs were still forced to compete with each other for international funding, including slices of the PEPFAR pie. They were also compelled to rely on unpaid volunteers.

In 2007, Eskinder was invited by the staff at Medhin to become a volunteer CHW, specializing in home-based care and treatment support for other people with HIV/AIDS—people living in his same neighborhood, receiving treatment at the same (albeit transformed) facility that half a century ago had attracted his mother and grandparents. "From the twenty-one volunteers at Medhin, twenty are female. I am the only man. . . . Why?" Eskinder asked rhetorically.

> Because I saw peoples' bodies prepared for burial beside me. Now I am going around as a volunteer caregiver while carrying my own anti-retroviral medication in my pocket. Patients fear that their neighbors, friends, and family will avoid them. I see these matters deeply because I have HIV inside me.

Conclusion

Eskinder suggested that his personal experiences recovering from near death in the hospital, adjacent to other HIV/AIDS patients who did not recover, explains why he is one of the rare men who decided to become volunteer CHWs in Addis Ababa's AIDS care industry. He also said that becoming a volunteer CHW was partly about reciprocity: neighbors, health professionals, and NGO staff had helped him when he was suffering with AIDS, so "today," he said, "I should make an effort for others." He also claimed that during his youth and early adulthood he had many prior experiences helping others, including people with vision impairment, elders, and victims of road accidents. Kindness, as he put it, had "grown up with him."

Most of the women I encountered among the ranks of CHWs made similar comments about their exposure to empathic and compassionate role models, and their internalization of religious and civic values of humble service in support of the well-being of others. These statements about the social development of personal motivations shed light on processes of deep importance. Yet they offer only a partial explanation of why Eskinder and his peers became volunteer CHWs in the age of ART.

Like Eskinder, most of the CHWs in my survey were unemployed or underemployed at the time they were recruited. They were part of the various and massive unemployed and underemployed populations that exist throughout the world today, particularly in low-income countries. In reality, they are not simply jobless—they are in between jobs, or subsisting on informal, insecure work because of a lack of anything better (Han 2013). Before becoming CHWs, some of the older volunteers had held jobs as teachers or factory workers. Some were in secondary school, while others scraped by as house servants, day laborers, food sellers, or parking attendants. Some benefited from a working spouse or relative. A few used to be relatively wealthy, but experienced a socioeconomic descent in the recent past. Some had traveled and worked abroad as house servants in Saudi Arabia and Kuwait, and suffered in doing so, only to return to Addis Ababa and find that decent jobs were still nowhere to be found. Contemporary global health programs look to these populations for volunteer labor.

Addis Ababa's ART center of excellence and its community health workforce came into existence through intersections of colonization, missionization, and imperialization; the evolution of the Princess Zennabawarq Leprosarium and its adjacent slums; the downfall of a monarchy and violent national regime changes; the solidification of a global economy that puts countries such as Ethiopia in very weak trading positions; structural adjustment and the retrenchment of public employment opportunities; the EPRDF's efforts to maintain control over the country's economy and citizenry, and to ally with the United States in its global war on terror; gradual expansions in access to western biomedical care and basic urban infrastructures, buttressed heavily at times by international aid; and compounding health and social problems, including gender discrimination, stigmatization, and epidemics of infectious and non-infectious illnesses.

We see in these histories that the Princess Zennabawarq Leprosarium and ALERT, like so many other early modern health institutions in Ethiopia, were created and transformed through negotiations—about funding and staffing, as well as the use of the labor of much poorer and less powerful people—between Ethiopia's rulers and a series of foreign missions, doctors, donors, and NGOs in the early to mid-20th century. The establishment and evolution of Ethiopia's modern health system and the expansion of biomedical treatment has long involved the flow of money and other resources between international "partners." As others have noted, "partnership" between various public and private actors and institutions is a key concept in the 21st century field of global health. Unfortunately this key concept obscures the fact that these various institutions engage in serious negotiations, competition, and compromise, and maintain competing interests, including diplomatic, commercial, humanitarian, and cultural ones (Crane 2010; Cueto 2013; Whitfield and Fraser 2010). The case of Ethiopia certainly supports this view (Feyissa 2011). The various partners who have shaped Ethiopia's health system over the last century have maintained varied interests, including religious conversion, expanding an empire, building a state, containing diseases and the people infected with them, and providing humanitarian relief. We see in this chapter how the mixed goals of various "partners" have long been associated with violent and harmful practices, including forced resettlement, isolation, and labor exploitation. In addition, we see that lower classes have been largely excluded from or marginalized within these partnerships, unable to weigh in on political and economic decision making.

The biographies of Eskinder and the other CHWs in this book, examined alongside the histories of the institutions, neighborhoods, and epidemics they encountered, thus show us the historical and social processes that entrap individual people in a state of poverty and powerlessness, and throw them into a labor pool targeted by 21st century CHW recruiters. By examining these histories, we are reminded of the lesson of the previous chapter: CHW problems (funding, recruitment, training, supervision, and governance) are embedded in bigger political and social problems that demand great attention and resources. We also confront their historical roots, which need to be grasped by anyone who intends to create stronger CHW programs in the pursuit of health equity.

Finally, this chapter has begun to demonstrate that CHWs are people with as rich and complex and open-ended lives as we live ourselves. Besides health workers, CHWs are many other things: friends, students, churchgoers, and family members, as well as poets, storytellers, and soccer fans. More importantly, CHWs like Eskinder have managed, through great struggle, to survive, get by, and help others amid a series of intergenerational travails and triumphs. Seen this way, it is hard to deny that CHWs can and deserve to play a bigger role in health policy development and implementation, as well as in other important arenas of social change.

Notes

1. For the founder of the SIM, Rowland Victor Bingham, the "Sudan" represented all of sub-Saharan Africa (Donham 1999: 84).

2. Lambie had been engaged in missionary activities representing the SIM since 1918 and first met Ras Tafari in 1922. When the Ras had asked Lambie in 1922 to build a modern hospital in Addis Ababa (the only other one, built by the Russians, was crumbling), Lambie also agreed, raised the money in the United States, and built what became the George Memorial Hospital.

3. As a temporary colonial force, the Italians actually did much of the early work of gathering people with leprosy from all over the country and bringing them to the Princess Zennabawarq Leprosarium.

4. The committee was convened in 1963 in Carville, Louisiana. Carville was also home to the Gillis W. Long Hansen's Disease Center, the last hospital in the industrialized world for the treatment of Hansen's Disease, better known as leprosy.

5. The Europeans constructed a new hospital with 130 beds and, directly adjacent, the Armauer Hansen Research Institute, named in memory of the Norwegian doctor who discovered *Mycobacterium leprae.*

6. The Ethio-Somali War of 1977–8 is a notable example of Cold War proxy fighting between the Soviet Union and the United States. As conflict developed between the Derg regime and Somalia-supported separatists in the Ogaden, the Soviet Union switched from supplying aid to Somalia to supporting Ethiopia, thinking the Derg was developing into a veritable Marxist state. The United States then began to support Somalia. The United States' support would return to Ethiopia after the fall of the Derg and the rise of the current EPRDF government. The war ended when Ethiopian and Cuban soldiers forced the Somali troops to retreat. Contention over the Ogaden region is further rooted in 19th-century European colonialism in east Africa.

7. When Ethiopia's current ruling party took power in 1991, it retained the kebeles as a means to provide government services (e.g., housing, food) as well as surveillance and policing of the population. Later, HIV/AIDS "desks" (i.e., offices) were introduced in kebeles in Addis Ababa in order to coordinate prevention and treatment efforts.

8. The first cases of HIV in Ethiopia were reported in 1986; analysis of the earliest viruses detected in Ethiopia suggest that HIV had arrived in 1983 (FMOH/HAPCO 2006a; Iliffe 2006). The Ethiopian HIV epidemic shared a pattern common throughout the east African region in which the early and undetected spread of the virus occurred through heterosexual infection, fueled by poverty and stark socioeconomic inequalities between women and men (Smith 2014). Initially, the epidemic was concentrated in a large population of sex workers and their clients in Addis Ababa and other major towns, including Nazreth (Adama), Bahir Dar, Gondar, Mekele, and Dessie (Iliffe 2006: 30).

9. In 2005, when free ART was just beginning to be publicly available in Ethiopia, urban areas registered HIV-prevalence estimates around 10%, with rural prevalence estimated around 2%. That translated into approximately 1.3 million people infected, split nearly down the middle between urban and rural areas (FMOH/HAPCO 2006a; Iliffe 2006). Ethiopia's HIV epidemiological profile over the 1990s and 2000s leads Iliffe (2006) to ask why the epidemic was not more extensive and massive. Compared to Kenya and the southern African region, HIV made a very small impact in Ethiopia's rural areas. The most important factor in the opinion of Iliffe was the weakness of Ethiopia's commercial sector. In other parts of eastern Africa, particularly around Lake Victoria and along the trans-African highway, a relatively extensive network of roads fostering commercial and sexual transactions aided and abetted the HIV epidemic, even in relatively remote rural areas. Ethiopia lacked such networks (Iliffe 2006: 32). Ethiopia's National HIV/AIDS Prevention and Control Office's 2006 report shows that urban HIV prevalence appeared to stabilize around 14% between 1996 and 2000 and then began a slow decline. Rural prevalence peaked around 2000 and then stabilized and began to decline slightly as

well (FMOH/HAPCO 2006a). Ethiopia's relatively low HIV-prevalence rates are, however, somewhat misleading. After Nigeria, Ethiopia is the second most populous country in Africa, and its rural population far exceeds its urban population. With Ethiopia's population rapidly increasing and the number of AIDS-related deaths decreasing after the scale-up of ART access, 2010 prevalence estimates of 7.7% for urban areas and 0.9% for rural areas corresponded to 1.2 million people living with HIV (FMOH 2011). Contrast that with less populous countries in southern Africa: in Botswana, the 2012 HIV prevalence among adults aged 15 to 49 was 21% according to UNAIDS, translating into an estimated 340,000 people infected.

10. HAPCO's strategic framework focused on reducing HIV transmission, associated morbidity and mortality, and burdens on individuals, families, and society at large. HAPCO and Ethiopia's Ministry of Health also embraced a policy of decentralization. Thus beneath the national HAPCO was a hierarchy of regional HAPCOs and kebele-level HIV/AIDS coordinating "desks," each tasked with coordinating prevention, treatment, and monitoring and evaluation within their respective jurisdictions (HAPCO and World Bank 2008).

11. Brazil provides a rare example of a developing country that insisted on combining treatment and prevention rather than deciding between them (Berkman et al. 2005; Biehl 2007).

12. For excellent summaries of these transnational scientific and political developments, see Iliffe (2006) and Messac and Prabhu (2013).

13. As president, Bill Clinton both prevented and promoted expanded access to antiretroviral drugs in low-income countries. His administration initially attempted to support western pharmaceutical companies' attempts to protect their patents on antiretroviral drugs, which made it difficult for generic forms to enter global markets. Then, in December 1999, under pressure from global AIDS activists and members of the Congressional Black Caucus in the United States, Bill Clinton made one of his last policy decisions as a two-term president. He announced that the US government would not put pressure on any sub-Saharan African country to purchase brand-name AIDS drugs or give up its rights to import and produce cheaper generic HAART (Messac and Prabhu 2013: 123).

14. The Global Fund would be innovative and progressive in comparison to other funding streams in global health and development. Specifically, it would require "partnership between governments, civil society, UN agencies, the private sector and affected communities, with an operational model based on country ownership and performance based funding." This was supposed to mean that countries would use funding to "implement programs based on their own needs" and be "responsible for the results and impact achieved" (Global Fund 2012).

15. In 2005, when it was clear that the 3 by 5 target would not be met, the G8 leaders pledged to double aid to Africa via the Global Fund in particular, to ensure "as close as possible to universal access to treatment for AIDS" by 2010 (Messac and Prabhu 2013: 126–9). According to a Global Fund Africa report (2011), the Global Fund financed almost all ART costs in Ethiopia in 2010. That year, Ethiopia's Ministry of Health recorded 247,805 people currently on ART out of an estimated 400,000 then eligible: thus about 62% of people with HIV/AIDS were being treated, which the document notes is above the sub-Saharan African average of 53% (FMOH 2011). The goal of universal access to treatment for AIDS by 2010 was not met—not in Ethiopia or in sub-Saharan Africa as a whole. In fact, this goal still has not been met. Yet, according to the Global Fund's 2012 Annual Report Summary, Ethiopia has witnessed significant declines in HIV incidence and mortality and the country would meet the less ambitious target of delivering ART to 80% of people who need it by 2015. In many other countries around the world, even the less ambitious international target (80% coverage by 2015) would not be met, and some countries have even witnessed backsliding in ART coverage in recent years (Global Fund 2012).

16. In addition to being the source of PEPFAR, the United States is also the largest donor to the Global Fund. See http://www.pepfar.gov/funding/results/index.htm (accessed May 6, 2014).

17. The implementation of PEPFAR funding in Ethiopia has been supported by USAID, the United States' federal agency responsible for administering civilian (i.e., non-military) economic and humanitarian aid to other countries. According to PEPFAR's website, "the Emergency Plan, USAID's foreign service officers, trained physicians, epidemiologists, and public health advisors work with governments, NGOs, and the private sector in order to provide training, technical assistance, and commodities (including pharmaceuticals) to prevent and reduce the transmission of HIV/AIDS and to provide treatment and care to people living with HIV/AIDS." See http://www.pepfar.gov/about/agencies/c19395.htm (accessed May 23, 2014).

18. Specifically, the Ministry aimed to create 89 ART delivery sites and 326 additional sites for the delivery of specific ARVs used in the prevention of mother-to-child transmission (PMTCT) in order to serve 100,000 AIDS patients and 10,500 pregnant women and infants, respectively (Banteyerga et al. 2006).

19. Given that ART is still limited in supply in sub-Saharan Africa and other "resource-poor settings," there is debate over the CD4 count cutoff that optimizes (i.e., balances) the goals of saving lives, avoiding the unwanted side effects of ART while rationing the scarce medicines. There is general consensus that ART is recommended for individuals with CD4 counts under 350 (http://www.who.int/hiv/pub/guidelines/arv2013/art/statartadolescents_rationale/en/ [accessed May 6, 2014]).

20. While European and North American doctors and researchers continued to play a role in TB and leprosy treatment, training, and research, the entire medical staff was largely "Ethiopianized" in 2002 (Terecha 2005).

21. There are about ten public hospitals in Addis Ababa. One likely reason that ALERT was chosen as a center of ARV excellence is that it had been recognized nationally and internationally as a center of excellence for leprosy and, later, tuberculosis treatment. Though ALERT offered hospital services for people experiencing various health problems, its focus on AIDS in the 21st century parallels its focus on single diseases (leprosy and TB) in the 20th century.

22. A look at PEPFAR's website suggests that the organization heard these criticisms and perhaps even incorporated them into PEPFAR's mission, goals, and operations, which now maintain a stated focus on strengthening national health systems. The extent to which PEPFAR has changed its actions and not just its rhetoric remains to be seen. Note also that PEPFAR has grown into a program seeking to help national health systems in poor countries tackle not only HIV/AIDS but also other health problems, including malaria and tuberculosis. On July 30, 2008, President Obama signed into law US House Resolution 5501, which authorized up to $48 billion over five years to combat global HIV/AIDS, tuberculosis, and malaria (see http://www.pepfar.gov/about/ and http://www.pepfar.gov/about/138360.htm).

23. EPRDF leaders have sought to curtail the role of NGOs also as a general strategy to solidify their party's status in the minds of citizens as the deliverer of development and to ensure that NGOs do not become conduits for political opposition (Feyissa 2011).

24. While multiple other bilateral donors agreed to contribute to the pooled health system funds that Ethiopia's leaders created and promoted in the first decade of the 21st century, the United States resisted and insisted on targeting non-government projects and partners for support (Global Health Workforce Alliance 2010a). Ethiopian leaders further adapted to this stance by requiring the United States to work with the government in order to minimize difficulties in health sector planning and evaluation. Ethiopia's Ministry of Health sought and achieved a specific Memorandum of Understanding (MOU) with the United States in 2005, requiring the latter to "harmonize" its mainly NGO-channeled funding activities with government priorities and other funding streams, particularly the Global Fund (Banteyerga et al. 2006). Per

the MOU, the Global Fund would provide the majority of ARV drugs to Ethiopia through the Ministry of Health in the form of first-line adult regimens. PEPFAR would provide second-line regimens for adults, as well as first- and second-line regimens for children, directly to programs such as ALERT (Banteyerga et al. 2006: 11).

25. In 2005, officials at ALERT and the Ministry of Health began seeking and obtaining funding and technical assistance from USAID/CDC and others. In an informal presentation to representatives of the Christian Children's Fund of Canada at ALERT in 2006, Dr. Yigeremu claimed that he had approached nearly 40 local and international NGOs to request their help in providing social support to ART patients. The Clinton Foundation later funded the construction of a pediatric HIV ward at ALERT and the salaries of some medical staff.

26. In addition to the Hiwot and Medhin NGOs, which are discussed in this book, the other three NGOs were Tesfa Limat, Mary Joy, and Dawn of Hope. I spoke with officials at the latter two. Due to time and other logistical constraints, I focused my ethnographic work on Medhin and Hiwot.

27. See http://ethiopia.usembassy.gov/pr-2011/u.s.-embassy-provides-five-million-birr-to-support-community-projects (accessed December 11, 2014).

28. The supervisors also helped organize community meetings to promote open dialogue and reduce HIV-related stigma and discrimination, and prepared regular reports on their teams' activities, which they then submitted to higher-level NGO staff and to local government health authorities. In return for their work, supervisor nurses were paid a salary of about 200 USD per month. Some were able to supplement their incomes from time to time by contracting out to various NGOs to run training workshops on, for example, the performance of home-based care. Some also had occasional opportunities to travel to Nairobi and other locations to participate in international workshops, for which they received per diems.

3

SOME ASSEMBLY REQUIRED

Community Health Worker Recruitment and Basic Training

In 2005, Hiwot and FHI rented out a large western-style hall belonging to the Addis Ababa municipality and put on a joint ceremony for two cohorts of CHW initiates and graduates.[1] Within the great hall, Hiwot's graduating and incoming volunteers came together with several higher-status guests and officials from Hiwot, FHI, and the city administration's HIV/AIDS Prevention and Control Office. The CHWs sat toward the back of the hall, behind the officials who were seated directly in front of the high stage. A banner hung across the stage named the event, in Amharic, as the "Home-Based Support- and Care-Givers Blessing Ceremony." The same phrase was printed on the white T-shirts produced for the occasion and worn by all the CHWs present.

Blessing the initiates and graduates, however, was not the only purpose of the ceremony. In a central, symbolic act, the initiates also promised to serve as committed volunteers. After the event got started with a series of ethnic Gurage, Amhara, Tigray, and Oromo dances, performed by a troupe of talented male and female dancers, the CHWs performed a communal song, written by Hiwot's HBC coordinator. The lyrics of the song, which had been passed around to the initiates and the graduates, contained a promise: to carefully look after patients and orphans, to treat them like family, and to fight HIV/AIDS. After the CHWs finished their solemn, collective song, one of the Hiwot NGO's CHW supervisor nurses then took to the stage and instructed the volunteer initiates to hold up the candles that had been given to each of them.

Matches were passed around to light the candles, and then the nurse led the volunteers in performing another promise: a chant entitled (in Amharic) the "Volunteer Home-Based Caregivers' Oath."[2] The term oath, or *qal kidan*, literally translates as "oral covenant" and has obvious Orthodox Christian connotations. Standing in unison, holding candles in their left hands, and placing their right hands over their hearts, the volunteers recited their oath: "With God and the people present as our witness," to give proper care to patients and "feed patients before ourselves," to keep secret the HIV status of patients, until they decide to disclose their status, and to help prevent the spread of HIV.

Several officials then gave speeches. First, Sr. Tibebe, Hiwot's director, took the stage. She expressed her deep gratitude to FHI, the Ethiopian North American Health Professionals Association, and the government representative from HAPCO who was attending the ceremony. She boasted that Hiwot's HBC program had been able to serve over 1,500 beneficiaries in the past year. "Though the volunteer caregivers have worked very hard," Sr. Tibebe said toward the end of her speech, "today they renew their promise."

Dr. Yigeremu, ALERT's ART program director, gave the next speech, boasting that ALERT ran a pioneering ART program—one that depended on the volunteers. He also lamented that many people, including physicians, did not realize the profound importance of the volunteer CHWs and did not show them enough respect (a common challenge across many health-care settings; see Lehmann and Sanders (2007); WHO (1989)). Dr. Yigeremu wanted to bear witness to the incredible job that the volunteers were doing. "They are an example for their friends. They sacrifice so much." He bestowed his appreciation on the volunteers' nurse supervisors, as well.

Subsequently, Hiwot's HBC program coordinator took to the stage and called the volunteer graduates by name. Carrying open umbrellas and backpacks emblazoned with Hiwot's logo,[3] each approached the stage and received a certificate of recognition for completing their service, handed out by the head of Addis Ababa's HAPCO, one of the officials who spoke in the FHI documentary video discussed previously. His message in the video was that, because the burden of care for family members falls disproportionately on the shoulders of women, and because so many women are also infected with HIV, women are the prime beneficiaries of ART. He also said that while strengthening health systems through investments in human resources and other dimensions of the system should be the long-term goal, in the short term, it is necessary to get volunteer caregivers out there to fill the gaps—because people are dying for lack of food, HBC, follow-up, and drugs. At the initiation ceremony, his comments to the assembled crowd were geared more toward sustaining, and less toward justifying, a reliance on unpaid health-care labor. He promised the incoming volunteers that they would become satisfied when they saw their patients' health improve and vowed that he and his fellow officials were there to help and encourage them. He then reminded the volunteer initiates to keep *their* promise.

This chapter examines recruitment, initiation, and training processes as reflections of the specific concerns that officials and supervisors have with volunteer CHWs' motivations, expectations, orientations, and skills, showing how those concerns shape the forms of participation in which CHWs engage and how CHWs understand and experience their role. The initiation ceremony described here—which brought recruits together to listen to NGO and government officials, encourage them to sacrifice for the good of people with AIDS and the country, and to expect emotional and spiritual rewards in return—provides an initial glimpse at how institutions turn recruits into volunteer CHWs. Recruitment interviews, initiation ceremonies, and training sessions in Addis Ababa gave officials and supervisors opportunities to try to shape and reinforce a certain set of skills as well as expectations and motivations, by circulating and reinforcing specific moral sentiments of sacrifice and satisfaction, and by including and excluding particular kinds of knowledge and practice within training sessions. CHWs in Addis Ababa were being oriented toward cold data collection and drug adherence functions as well as compassionate, empathic care, and they were not being turned into agents of structural changes aimed at health equity and social justice. They were being encouraged to sacrifice and seek not material but spiritual and mental rewards. By paying attention to these various inclusions and exclusions, a nuanced picture of CHW participation begins to emerge—one that involves CHWs' interactions not only with patients but also with the NGO staff, government officials, and doctors who seek to recruit, train, and rely on them. By understanding these dynamics, we are better prepared to debate and come to negotiated decisions about how to reform and redesign CHW recruitment and training programs.

Recruiting CHWs

The turn of the Ethiopian millennium saw the Hiwot NGO seeking to recruit 60 new volunteer CHWs from the two city districts served by ALERT. Elsa, Hiwot's HBC program coordinator, told me that "many, many, many" people were coming forward to volunteer based on their own interest. Training Hiwot's new recruits was even delayed, she claimed, because such a large number of people had come forward to volunteer, and the NGO supervisors needed more time to select the best. Thus the NGOs felt that they were in a position to employ some criteria to choose a subset of applicants.

As they sought to assemble the volunteer workforce, NGO recruiters took into account a number of sociodemographic and behavioral characteristics, including HIV status and gender. Supervisors and coordinators at both Hiwot and Medhin told me that they sought people who, like Eskinder, had recovered from AIDS. They had experiential knowledge of ARV drug adherence and other challenges, and were thought to be more compassionate and willing to "stand the smell" of sores, feces, and vomit—as Sister Nebyat, Medhin's HBC coordinator put it. Women were also encouraged to volunteer by NGO officials, and nine out of ten of the volunteer CHWs we surveyed were women, consistent with a trend extending across sub-Saharan Africa and globally. In Ethiopia, as in many parts of the world, this imbalance is the result of several interacting factors: women's disadvantages in labor markets, the prevalent social norm that deems unpaid caregiving and community health work women's work, and the widespread idea that women are better caregivers than men (Akintola 2008; Maes and Kalofonos 2013). Illustrating the latter stereotype, Sister Selamawit, one of the Hiwot NGO's supervisor nurses, said that men were "more focused on their own benefit," and "don't like to do 'women's work.'" They were more likely to "disappear" after being confronted with the real challenges of the service, such as dealing with bedridden patients.[4]

Age was another characteristic that recruiters and others had in mind when it came to conceptions of an ideal workforce. A third of the volunteers we surveyed were between the ages of 18 and 25 and many of them were unmarried, consistent with sociodemographic and economic conditions in Addis Ababa (Amare 2010; Gurmu and Mace 2008). Only 10% were over 40. For some officials, unemployed youth represented a large demographic pool that simply had to be targeted for recruiting. At the same time, several people expressed concern that younger volunteers were less reliable and effective caregivers. Meselech, one of ALERT's HIV/AIDS data clerks, once told me that younger caregivers were less willing to treat patients "properly." They often seemed to be in a hurry, whereas older caregivers were more patient and attentive to their patients, at least when accompanying them to the clinic.

The volunteer CHW role was not, however, reserved exclusively for women, people living with HIV/AIDS, or older people. Negative HIV status, after all, was reported by 73% of the volunteers we randomly surveyed. Men were far outnumbered by women, but they still played important roles that were recognized by supervisors. Sister Selamawit, for instance, admitted that there were men who were dedicated and very helpful volunteers. NGO recruiters welcomed—and attempted to attract—men who were relatively compassionate, humble, and respectful towards women. Likewise, many admitted that there were plenty of young volunteers who were caring, patient, and warm. Alemayehu, a 33-year-old male volunteer whose story is examined more closely in the next chapter, told me he thought that youth these days were more selfish and disrespectful, not like the youth of earlier generations. Yet he was referring to youth who were *not* becoming CHWs. He thought that the ones who became CHWs—his colleagues—were generally humble, respectful, and compassionate.

The only hard and fast rule used to judge a recruit was his or her "moral acceptability"—which basically meant having a reputation free of things such as theft, stinginess, laziness, and abuse of alcohol, cigarettes, and drugs, as well as, preferably, a reputation for helpfulness, humility, and energy. To recruit morally acceptable volunteers, Hiwot and Medhin relied on existing and current volunteer CHWs, who would sometimes persuade a friend or relative to seek the position. They also relied on the help of local community organizations known as *iddirs*. Strictly speaking, *iddirs* are neighborhood-based social insurance associations, common throughout Addis Ababa, which function primarily to help members meet the costs of funerals and burials. Thus they are referred to in English as a form of "burial society."[5] *Iddirs* were formalized in Addis Ababa in the 20th century with the establishment of organizing committees and meeting spaces (Pankhurst and Haile-Mariam 2000). With the rise of AIDS-related mortality in the late 20th century, and then AIDS treatment programs in the early 21st century, *iddirs* in Addis Ababa evolved to fulfill functions related to community health and well-being. CHW recruitment became one of these functions. Thus a handful of relatively respected men and women on the organizing committee of cooperating *iddirs* would assist with volunteer CHW recruitment, putting out calls for recruits, registering those who came forward, and then making preliminary selections.

The cases of Alemnesh and Birtukan, two women recruited as CHWs by the Hiwot and Medhin NGOs, respectively, further reveal how CHW recruitment can involve not only identifying acceptable recruits but also attempting to *shape* CHW motivations.

What If She Is Planning to Fly Abroad?

Alemnesh ended up in the batch of volunteers recruited by Hiwot at the end of 2007. She was 26 years old, unmarried, unemployed, and living with her parents, who according to Alemnesh had raised her and her two brothers "properly," advising them not to make mistakes. She described her mother, the family's homemaker, as "our foundation" (*meseret*). As children, she and her siblings feared her temper, but in hindsight recognized that she wanted her children to reach a "good level." Her mother was also the kind of person who maintained close relationships with others. Whenever her mother heard about a sick neighbor, for instance, she would go and "help with all her capacity." "I got that from her," Alemnesh said. "I have many friends and I can be close with anyone."

Alemnesh described her father, a pensionless ex-soldier who served under the Derg, as meek (*yewah*), someone who "doesn't know how to be disgusted by others." "He always has a good perception of others," she added. Her brothers, who held professional jobs in Addis Ababa (which helped raise the economic status of her family), took after their father: "Once they become close to you," Alemnesh said, "they can do anything to help you. In general, my family has a good spirit (*tiru menfes*)."

Alemnesh perceived that volunteer caregiving and community health work was made necessary by the commonplace abandonment of people living with HIV/AIDS by their family members and friends: "Nowadays, even close kin abandon each other." She recognized that such abandonment was connected to poverty and that her own family was "living in a good condition" and thus positioned to "take responsibility" for the welfare of others, even unrelated people. Her initial interest in becoming a volunteer CHW, she claimed, was ignited by a spark of what she called "spiritual envy" (*menfesawi qinat*). She explained that when she was preparing to retake the twelfth grade "school-leaving" examination (she was unhappy with her first result), she heard on the state television and radio about volunteer caregivers. "When you hear about people who do good deeds, you may have spiritual envy. I thought, 'What if I do something like them?'"

After deciding to become a volunteer CHW, Alemnesh received sincere support from her parents and siblings.

> They know that it is good work (*tiru sera*). They encourage me by saying, 'you are helping your fellow people with what you have.' My mom worries a lot when I go out, but she is astounded by the problems that people face, and so she supports it.

One of Alemnesh's brothers, whom she described as a close follower of the Orthodox church, told her that "'By volunteering and lowering oneself"—that is, by humbling oneself—"you get something from God (*amlak*), even if you do not get anything from humans."

Alemnesh's comments about her family, and her own initial interest in volunteering, might make her seem like the perfect recruit. She and her family not only had untarnished reputations but also were accustomed to humbly helping others. Yet Alemnesh was not treated as an ideal recruit during her interview. The reason, it seems, is that although Alemnesh was unemployed at the time of her recruitment, she had worked as a domestic servant in an "Arab country," as the Gulf States are typically called in Ethiopia. In fact, she had worked in two: Saudi Arabia and Kuwait.[6]

Alemnesh had long dreamed of leaving Ethiopia. She and one of her close childhood friends had promised each other long ago that whoever got the chance to go out of Ethiopia first would take the other with her. "We loved each other very much," Alemnesh explained. Her friend ended up going first, to Jeddah, and helped Alemnesh come up with the 13,000 birr it cost to make the trip. "It was very difficult. But she had been working there for over two years, and she helped me cover the cost."

Alemnesh worked in Jeddah for two years. After spending one year back in Addis Ababa, she registered with an agency and paid 1,500 birr to work in Kuwait, where she spent two additional years. She admitted that on her first trip to Saudi Arabia, she spent a lot of money on herself. "I was young—I was not very mature. At that time, I did not understand things well." But looking back, she also said that she went abroad for her family. Especially by working in Kuwait, she had supported her parents and helped put her two siblings through college. For Alemnesh, working abroad and supporting her family in this way was a major achievement.[7]

For the nurse supervisor who interviewed her, however, Alemnesh's international work experience was apparently a red flag. A leader of her family's *iddir* had presented Alemnesh with the opportunity to volunteer. He informed her that Hiwot was recruiting volunteers tasked with "helping our poor people, spreading awareness, and ridding the disease from our country." According to protocol, the *iddir* leader then brought Alemnesh to Sister Meheret, one of Hiwot's supervisor nurses, for an interview. At the beginning of her recruitment interview, Alemnesh recounted, Sister Meheret was told by the *iddir* leader that Alemnesh "came from abroad"—in other words, from working in an "Arab country." This piece of information apparently pushed Sister Meheret to judge her as an unfit recruit. "'Never! What if she is planning to fly abroad now?'" Alemnesh asserted that she was not and that she was ready to "do this work for a year and six months," the length of service expected of everyone. The *iddir* leader reassured Sister Meheret, saying he had spoken with Alemnesh and that she had no plans to leave Ethiopia.

Don't Think That You Will Get Something

But according to Alemnesh, Sister Meheret still grilled her on her willingness to work without any pay. Meheret knew that she had no other income and, like other educated Ethiopian youth, was expected to not only materially support her family but also to achieve some socioeconomic progress for herself and move out of her parents' house and into her own, ideally with a good husband. "Sister Meheret asked me repeatedly, 'How can you serve without being compensated?'" Alemnesh raised her voice as she related a sense of indignation.

> They were frustrating me. I was so angry. If you come to serve with good will, then they should give you a kind face (*melkam fit*). But they said, "There is no money, there is nothing. The work is heavy and you will get tired." I told Sister Meheret, "I came with good will (*bebego feqadeñanet*), and I knew that we were not going to get anything. I simply wanted to help my people with all my capacity."

Alemnesh thus asserted that the NGO supervisors failed to provide willing recruits with what they deserved: a "kind face," or, in other words, admiration and respect. Alemnesh's recruitment experience was not unique. Tsehay, another young woman who had also migrated to work in Saudi Arabia and Kuwait, told a similar story. In her recruitment interview, Sister Meheret openly doubted Tsehay's willingness and ability to volunteer, in part because of her history of working abroad and in part because of her nicer clothing. "At first, they thought we wouldn't work. They made this judgment after only seeing us." Tsehay added that the indignation (in Amharic, *illih*) she experienced during her recruitment interview only motivated her to work harder. "I thought, 'I have to do this thing and show them.' This kind of thing—*illih*—will be inside you, so you will work even more."

Alemnesh and Tsehay received special scrutiny perhaps because of their work histories, youth, and outward appearances. Yet other recruits who had considerably more difficult backgrounds—including hard childhoods, living with AIDS, and working in low-level positions in Addis Ababa just to scrape by—were also warned to work hard and to eschew expectation of material reward. For example, Asayech was a 32-year-old married woman who also began volunteering with Hiwot in early 2008. She had worked in a low-level factory job before she became sick with TB, found out she had HIV/AIDS, and lost her job. One of the first patients in Ethiopia to receive free ART, she recovered from TB and AIDS. Afterwards, she "simply sat" jobless for a couple of years, partly out of fear of getting sick on the job again and partly because it was difficult to find good work anyway. Her husband struggled to support her and their one child by working at an industrial firm located just outside Addis Ababa. His position was insecure and not well remunerated, yet it was still highly desirable considering the high levels of unemployment in the capital.

During her recruitment interview, Asayech's willingness to work for free was not taken for granted. Nurse Tirusew,[8] the young man who would serve as supervisor nurse to Asayech and about 20 of her fellow volunteers, did not just check to make sure that Asayech knew that she was being asked to donate her labor. He told her specifically not to expect any material rewards for her service as a volunteer. " 'There is no salary and nothing material that you will get. Don't think that you will get something.' "

. . . Except Mental Satisfaction

During recruitment, volunteers were not just discouraged from seeking material rewards for their service. They were also encouraged to expect that volunteering would provide nonmaterial mental and spiritual satisfaction and to accept the idea that such benefits are the appropriate reward for volunteers. This is uniquely illustrated by the case of Birtukan, one of Medhin's volunteers.

Medhin's HBC program coordinator, Sister Nebyat, told me she "handpicked" Birtukan to become a volunteer. On Saturdays, Medhin would play videos for kids from the surrounding slum, serving as "a kind of a moral or ethics center" for the community. One Saturday, an eight-year-old boy was watching videos when he had a seizure and fainted. He eventually woke up and seemed fine, but Sister Nebyat noticed that his cheek was swollen. With a quick inspection, she observed that two of his teeth were seriously decayed. Sister Nebyat then went with the boy to his mother and father. They told her they knew nothing about the boy having seizures, and they could not take him to the dentist for lack of money.

Birtukan, the boy's mother, explained to Sister Nebyat that she was unable to find work. She and her husband used to be relatively well off, thanks to profits from their small shop selling leather products next to Addis Ababa's national stadium.

After the regime change in 1991, though, they lost their business. Now, Birtukan's husband worked for a Protestant church as a guard—a low-status and low-paying job in Addis. They owned a modest house, which meant they did not have to pay rent and that they had income from renting out one or two rooms.[9] Yet these resources came up short in supporting Birtukan's basic needs during the height of the 2008 food crisis, when she reported moderate food insecurity. Losing the business and the status she and her husband once enjoyed took a psychological toll on Birtukan. Her situation once came up in a conversation I had with Eskinder, her fellow volunteer. He explained that Birtukan had some kind of "mental problem" (*aymero chigger*). "It is from having something and losing it. She used to work and have a shop and cars. But now she just works with us as a volunteer."

When Sister Nebyat saw how "messy" Birtukan's house was, in addition to the lack of care her son was receiving, she concluded that Birtukan was depressed. "She didn't say that she had depression, but she explained the symptoms. They have a good house, but she didn't clean, and she didn't care—for the house or the boy." Sister Nebyat could have judged Birtukan morally unacceptable for not taking care of her home and children. Instead, she perceived that Birtukan was suffering. So Sister Nebyat and Sister Tsinkenesh (Medhin's director) decided to help by taking the child to the dentist and paying the bill of 700 birr (~70 USD).

Sister Nebyat then asked Birtukan, "Why don't you join the home-based caregivers? Instead of spending your days depressed and crying, come give service and take care of your children." Sister Nebyat apparently thought that volunteering and "giving service" would be a sort of therapy for Birtukan and, indirectly, her son. Birtukan was reluctant. Volunteering as a CHW was probably not the form of economic and social therapy she had in mind. Nevertheless, according to Sister Nebyat, she finally agreed to volunteer.

Sister Nebyat thus recruited a woman who was not necessarily interested or prepared to volunteer her time and energy, but whom she deemed in need of the emotional benefits that supposedly result from volunteering. Birtukan's case may be unique given her socioeconomic descent and struggle with a high level of mental distress. Yet there is no easy distinction between Birtukan, Asayech, and many of the other CHWs in terms of psychosocial well-being. So many of them had similar histories of unemployment and insecure, unstable employment, and many likely experienced intermittent and variable levels of psychological distress related to their experiences of poverty, unemployment, and food insecurity, which I explore further in the following chapter.

Health officials and supervisors, meanwhile, often claimed that volunteer CHWs would experience psychological and spiritual benefits. We have seen evidence of that in the context of initiation and recognition ceremonies. Recruitment interviews also provided key opportunities for Hiwot's supervisor nurses to reinforce recruits' expectations of psychological benefits. When Tirusew interviewed Asayech, for example, and told her that she should not expect any payment, he also added, " 'You will only get mental satisfaction (*yehilina irkata*).' "

The Moral Economy of CHWs

In anthropological terms, what begins to emerge in these descriptions of recruitment is the ground-level *moral economy* of a CHW program. Material economies involve the circulation and exchange of different material resources, including money. Political economies involve the distribution of political power and its relationship to the production, distribution, and utilization of material resources. *Moral* economies involve other kinds of currencies: sentiments, emotions, and values, felt and experienced internally by individuals and expressed verbally in a social milieu. A broad conceptualization of moral economy involves different people producing, distributing, circulating, using, and experiencing particular moral sentiments, emotions, values, norms, and obligations in relation to specific social issues in particular historical contexts (Daston 1995; Fassin 2005; 2013; Scott 1976; Thompson 1971).

Anthropologist Didier Fassin (2013) has marshaled a great deal of historical and ethnographic evidence to argue persuasively that moral economies generally eclipse political economies. For example, people often openly express and seek to act on empathy and concern for certain categories of people—for instance, people suffering with HIV/AIDS (and particularly women and children within that category)—while avoiding "the necessary analysis of the structural determinants of their exposure to health risks and social hazards" in the first place (p. 129). When certain moral sentiments, emotions, and values become normative—that is, when they become common and move actors to a common mode of humanitarian action—Fassin suggests that wider structural determinants of suffering can become ignored and even unspeakable (p. 111). In the CHW arena, Closser (2015) uses the concept of moral economy to examine how the moral sentiments of those in positions of power in the Global Polio Eradication Initiative (GPEI) overshadow and drown out the moral sentiments and desires of unhappy CHWs involved in polio eradication and primary health care in Pakistan. Nading (2013) uses the concept to draw attention to how CHWs in Nicaragua are involved in two moral economies, one of obligations to patients and one of obligations to (government) employers. Swartz (2013) also uses the moral economy concept to examine how CHWs in South Africa experience and understand legitimacy vis-à-vis *other CHWs* who are perceived to have alternative values, commitments, and goals.

The concept of moral economy is thus invoked by a number of anthropologists who have recently studied the multiple and context-specific relationships, expectations, and exchanges involved in CHW programs. The concept is popular among researchers because it helps in the development of answers to the same kinds of compelling questions raised in the introduction to this book regarding the negotiations and exchanges that take place between CHWs and higher-status, health-system actors as well as the relationships and forms of care that exist between CHWs and their care recipients.[10] In the next few chapters, I use the moral economy concept to help understand the emotions, morals, and values involved in day-to-day care work with vulnerable and stigmatized patients amid widespread poverty and unemployment, and to help make sense of CHWs' attempts to take greater control over their lives through seeking better jobs and job conditions, and negotiating with supervisors and directors about mutual obligations and expectations. What we have seen so far in this chapter is how unpaid CHWs entered into a moral economy involving powerful ideas about saving lives, sacrificing, and experiencing emotional and spiritual satisfaction, circulated by officials and supervisors as a way to socialize the CHWs—that is, to try to get CHWs to internalize and express the same moral sentiments of sacrifice and satisfaction, and thereby keep labor cheap and hopefully effective in Addis Ababa's ART center of excellence. Recruitment interactions gave supervisors more than a chance to weed out people who, despite their reputation of moral acceptability in the community, seemed overly self-interested. Interviews also served supervisors' and officials' interests in shaping a moral economy involving certain expectations, moral sentiments, emotions, and motivations, in hopes of producing a workforce of women and men willing to donate their emotional and physical labor to an ART program, and expect little more than mental and spiritual satisfaction in return.

Ideas of sacrificing as a CHW and reaping the spiritual rewards may be convenient and potentially effective for CHW employers because they resonate with many local and global religious belief systems in the 21st century.[11] Orthodox Christianity, the religion with which most government officials and volunteer CHWs (85%) in Addis Ababa identified, has a lot to say about sacrifice, spirituality, and the rejection of material self-interest. For example P. Yohannes, a scholar of the Orthodox Church, writes that a devotee sacrifices possessions or parts of her or his self to God "out of love in order to express thankful dependence on . . . the creator and sustainer of life." This, furthermore, is the highest form of worship, "by which humanity affirms its faith" (Yohannes 1988: 171). Not all of the volunteers were religious in the sense of always attending church or adhering to every doctrine. And not all were Orthodox Christians. About 15% were Protestant, and a few were Muslim. The vast majority, nonetheless, valued spirituality and things sacred, and maintained some connection to religious institutions, teachings, and models. Eskinder, for instance, did not closely follow the church like his father, and he even espoused some unorthodox beliefs about the non-existence of an afterlife. Yet it was clear that Eskinder remained a spiritual person and never cut himself off from the Orthodox religion and its values of humility, service, and respect. Likewise, Alemnesh was not religiously devout, yet volunteering as a CHW still struck her as a virtuous activity; hearing about others doing it sparked a "spiritual envy" and a desire to do the same.[12] Other CHWs spoke of how volunteering to help others with AIDS involved a willingness to "lower" or humble oneself—to forget about climbing the worldly socioeconomic ladder in order to help others, please God, and reap spiritual rewards. Further, it was not only supervisors and officials who reinforced these ideas; close family members and friends did, too. Thus the moral economies of CHW programs can be intertwined with religious traditions and interpretations of key religious teachings.

The fact that ideas of sacrifice and mental satisfaction resonate with the spiritual traditions of CHWs and their families, friends, and supervisors, demands that we pay not less but more attention to the political-economic context surrounding supervisors' and officials' attempts to shape their motivations. On the one hand, it is important to take seriously the religious and moral sentiments of supervisors, CHWs, and others with regard to improving the lives and deaths of suffering people. Such beliefs can be important resources in CHW programs that are empowering and effective.[13] From another perspective articulated long ago by Karl Marx, connecting volunteering to popular religious and moral values and expectations is a way for supervisors and officials to produce a workforce of underemployed, economically insecure people nonetheless willing to donate their labor. Supervisors and health officials in Addis Ababa probably genuinely believed that volunteers enjoyed spiritual and mental benefits through sacrificing and "lowering themselves" to help others.[14] Yet officials also used these popular and salient religious values, beliefs, and associated emotions. By reinforcing volunteers' intuition that humbly serving others generates mental and spiritual satisfaction, officials attempted to maintain volunteers' willingness to donate their labor.

During recruitment and deployment, the CHWs were not given opportunities and resources to understand why, in so many contexts of poverty and unemployment across Africa, CHWs are not remunerated for their work, or why so many places across Africa were stricken with such severe poverty and unemployment in the first place. As we will see later in this chapter, some public health experts and longtime allies of CHWs argue that such knowledge should be a key part of CHW orientation and training in order to empower CHWs as agents of change within structures that perpetuate inequality and suffering. Such knowledge was not deemed important to CHW recruiters, trainers, and supervisors in Addis Ababa. The focus instead was on a goal of saving and improving the lives of people living with HIV/AIDS, a set of technical and interpersonal skills deemed necessary for the CHWs to achieve this goal, and a set of moral sentiments and emotions constructed to rationalize volunteerism. This is an example of how humanitarian sentiments that circulate globally and on the ground go hand-in-hand with failures to understand and grapple with the political economies that shape the global health industry and that make so many people vulnerable to poverty, unemployment, violence, and poor health (Fassin 2013).

In examining how NGO and government officials shape the moral economies of community health workers, the goal is not to criticize them for exploiting people or manipulating their emotions and religious beliefs. The supervisor nurses and staff I encountered at Hiwot and Medhin were kind, intelligent, energetic, and respected by the volunteers who served under them. Pretty much everyone who knew Sister Meheret, for example, was quickly charmed by her warmth and humor. Alemnesh and Tsehay, too, ended up sharing very positive relationships with her. How great it would be if CHW supervisors everywhere were as compassionate, dedicated, and humble as these supervisors were. The ways they attempted to shape the expectations of recruits, with promises of mental satisfaction and discouragement of material self-interest, were encouraged by the circulation of certain morals and policies at the global level, in particular the humanitarian moral imperative to save lives through ART, and the so-called global sustainability doctrine, which was called into question in the context of rural primary health care in Ethiopia, while maintained in the urban AIDS treatment sector. There is a reason why Swidler and Watkins (2009) refer to a sustainability *doctrine*—to emphasize that a reliance on volunteerism, a policy encouraged by powerful donors, is virtually unquestionable for people in positions of little power. From supervisors' and other officials' perspectives, there was little to be gained by openly recognizing that a reliance on volunteerism was problematic. Conversely, there was much to be gained—the "sustainability" of their organizations and programs in the eyes of key donors—by defending a policy of relying on volunteers and reinforcing a vision of the ideal volunteer. The sustainability doctrine forced CHW supervisors around Africa to encourage volunteerism in settings of deep poverty, where would-be volunteers are unemployed and interested in climbing the socioeconomic ladder. Thus by examining the moral economy in which volunteers, supervisors, and officials all participate, we see important links that exist between decisions at the global level and local forms of CHW participation.

There is another set of processes by which officials attempted to produce their ideal workforce: basic training. After making it through their recruitment interviews, new CHWs-to-be entered into fairly extensive training programs. These contexts provided officials and supervisors with further opportunities to shape recruits' understandings and orientations, and to impart specific skills deemed important to their day-to-day work.

Training Rituals

On the first day of basic training for Hiwot's newly recruited CHWs, a middle-aged man named Tesfaye, one of the NGO's two HBC team leaders tasked primarily with overseeing and supporting the supervisor nurses, delivered a speech.[15] Standing at the front of a local government hall, in front of rows of seated CHW trainees, Tesfaye began by reminding the trainees that they were expected to work for 18 months. He warned that missing even one day of the training was grounds for dismissal. He then gave a brief history of the NGO, starting with its founding by Sister Tibebe, and identified the contract with FHI and access to PEPFAR funds as a turning point in the growth of the organization.

After the first morning's opening speech, the supervisor nurses went over some ground rules for the training. With magic markers, they wrote the rules on a white sheet of paper that was then taped to the wall:

> Do not be late or absent
> No coming and going during the lesson
> Respect each other's ideas
> Turn off cell phones
> No chewing gum
> No talking to your neighbor
> Pay attention to the lessons
> Love each other
> No sleeping
> Be thankful and polite to each other
> Obey commands
> Listen to each other
> Participate actively
> No laughing without good reason
> Maintain secrecy and trust

On another big sheet of white paper, one of the trainers, a young man named Million who also served as a salaried social worker for the Hiwot NGO, drew three cartoon faces.[16] Next to each cartoon face, he wrote a short phrase: "I'm feeling happy," for the top face, "I'm feeling so-so," for the middle face, and "I'm feeling unhappy" for the bottom face. Next to the faces were columns for Monday through Friday, forming a simple matrix. Million instructed the trainees to write a check mark somewhere in the matrix at the end of each day to provide a gauge of their mood as the training progressed.

Later in the day, the trainees were led outside the big hall for an exercise. Under the bright sun and over the sounds of chirping birds and trucks shifting their gears on the ring road below, Sister Selamawit (a supervisor nurse mentioned in a previous chapter) instructed the trainees to link hands and form a big human circle. As Selamawit choreographed, the human chain folded in on itself. Some trainees were instructed to pass under the linked arms of another part of the chain until everyone was standing closely together, tangled up with hands still clasped. Two trainees, one man and one woman, had been told to wait inside the training hall during the process of entanglement. When Selamawit called for them to come out, she announced to all that they would play the role of "authority figures" tasked with solving the community's "problem," symbolized by the bodily morass. Each was given two minutes to unfold the trainees into the original circle *without* breaking the chain. Both gave it their best shot. Both failed, to the amusement of the group.

Then came Sister Selamawit's lesson: "Why couldn't these authority figures solve the community's problem without rupturing its existing links?" she shouted. Because only community members know how local health problems and people's relationships intertwine, and only community members can solve local problems in ways that minimize such rupturing. The volunteer CHWs are "one with" the poor and sick in the community. They and their patients know the problems they face and are in a position to solve them.

Thus began four weeks of basic CHW training. A typical day ran from 9:00 a.m. to 4:30 p.m., with lectures and activities filling both morning and afternoon sessions. Each day, the trainees received a hearty lunch replete with several kinds of *wat* (stew), *injera*, rice, and Coca-Cola and Pepsi. Every day there were also mid-morning and mid-afternoon breaks, during which the trainees enjoyed refreshments including milk, tea, coffee, and fresh plain donuts.[17] On top of the daily lunches and refreshments, trainees received 20 birr per day, for a total of 400 birr (about 40 US) over the course of the training. Four hundred birr was on par with the monthly salaries of some low-level jobs in Addis. For many trainees, 20 birr per day was not enough to pay for a private taxi between their neighborhoods and the training facility, but it was enough to cover the cost of collective transport and still pocket several birr.

In Africa's AIDS industry, training is one of the most pervasive and standardized industrial practices. Based on their extensive observations in rural Malawi of trainings of volunteer youth peer educators, Watkins and Swidler (2013) argue that trainings comprise a highly ritualized set of practices, typically composed of "scripted minutiae": PowerPoint presentations, dramas and skits, group work, songs, rules, energizers, introductions, and so on, all emanating from a cultural model of "training." "Just as a Catholic Mass would not be a Mass without wine and wafers," they write, "a training is not a 'training' without allowances [i.e., per diems] for attending the training, flip charts and magic markers, a 'bun' [small loaf of bread] and a 'Fanta' at mid-morning and mid-afternoon breaks, and an ample lunch" (Watkins and Swidler 2013: 208).

The resemblance between their observations and mine may seem uncanny. The similarity is understandable, however, when we see that it is determined by a cultural model—a series of stereotypes widely shared throughout the AIDS industry—of how a training should unfold. As a social form determined by a coherent cultural model, trainings are highly standardized and circulated to countless locales across the continent and globe.[18]

Take, for example, the fact that trainees in Addis Ababa were paid relatively generous per diems and provided meals for each day of training—which were generally very pleasing to the trainees. Why provide the trainees with such material benefits after telling them during recruitment interviews not to expect any material benefits? Perhaps NGO officials figured that the per diems and meals were necessary incentives in a context of rapidly rising food prices, bus fares, and rents. The CHWs' deployment, however, also involved using public transport and being away from home during meal times, and it occurred in the same context of rapid inflation. Why, then, were these material benefits provided only during training? An important part of the answer is that it was simply a globally common practice. Donors and international NGOs such as FHI rarely aim to create salaried jobs for CHWs and typically rely on "volunteers." Nevertheless, they habitually fund per diems and lunches for trainings and workshops (Smith 2003; Swidler and Watkins 2009; Watkins and Swidler 2013).

CHW Orientation and Training in Three Dimensions

The training of CHWs in Addis Ababa did more than adhere to a script or ritual formula, however. We also must understand that NGO and government officials who designed basic CHW training in Addis Ababa, included certain kinds of knowledge and competencies and left out others, and thus prepared trainees for a specific mission and conveyed a certain understanding of the CHW role.

Below I describe more of what was included, prioritized, and excluded in this particular CHW training program, guided by a review of the public health and social science literature on CHWs, which suggests that the competencies targeted by CHW trainers can be categorized into three areas: (1) empathic care, (2) technical care, and (3) the pursuit of social justice. A distinction between the first two dimensions—empathic and technical care—is commonly raised in critical discussions of the conduct of biomedicine and public health. Empathic care is typically associated with forms of care involving intimacy, listening, respect, and thoughtful, personalized attention, including help with meeting basic domestic needs. Technical care, in contrast, is typically associated with impersonal, bureaucratic, and "cold" forms of care that treat people as patients who must comply with doctors' notions of treatment adherence, or as just another data point in a handwritten or electronic spreadsheet (Fassin 2008). Many medical anthropologists argue that empathic caregiving has been problematically marginalized to make room for the hegemony of technical forms of care and knowledge within modern-day western medicine. "[I]n the broader system of healthcare," Arthur Kleinman and Bridget Hanna write, "[medical] students can all-too-readily discern that medicine largely leaves caregiving to others. Those others include nurses, whose professional science has made caregiving a central element of knowledge production and training" (Kleinman and Hanna 2008: 291–2; see also Kleinman 2008: 2009).

In addition to nurses, CHWs represent a major category of health-care worker taking on the "nitty-gritty of caregiving" (Kleinman and Hanna 2008: 291) left behind by most physicians. Yet critical medical anthropologists and other scholars are concerned that even this cadre is becoming distanced from empathic caregiving by a relentless drive to confine medical care to narrow technical procedures. The displacement of empathic care within CHW programs is particularly troubling when one considers that empathic caregiving in many ways depends on a set of skills that CHWs, as human beings, already have, even without specialized training. Training CHWs narrowly in technical forms of care can mean disempowering them by failing to acknowledge and encourage what they already know, while reinforcing an inequality between professional trainers who have technical knowledge and trainees who do not.

Anthropologist Alex Nading (2013) has taken up the distinction between empathic and technical care, arguing that CHWs end up in a sense caught between the desires of health institutions for cold, technical labor fixated on adherence to biomedical prescriptions and quantitative data reporting, on the one hand, and the desire of intended beneficiaries for compassionate, respectful, quality care on the other hand. The Nicaraguan government generally seeks to use dengue-focused CHWs as delivery mechanisms for public health technologies and as the eyes and ears of the state, concerned first with observing, reporting, and altering the behaviors of people. Many CHWs, however, continue to treat intended beneficiaries in empathic, neighborly ways. Nading thus constructs an image of CHWs as "Janus-faced," go-betweens connecting a citizenry that desires to be treated humanely to a state bureaucracy that functions primarily to monitor and produce a disciplined citizenry. CHWs combine empathic and technical forms of care because beneficiaries demand the former, while the state demands the latter.

A clear ethnographic account of the marginalization of empathic care within a CHW training program is provided by anthropologist Ippolytos Kalofonos, who has worked for several years alongside CHWs providing HBC amid a massive scale-up of ART access in urban Mozambique. According to Kalofonos (2014), during the 1990s when HIV/AIDS was wreaking havoc in a population devoid of ART, "volunteers focused on palliative and comfort-oriented care, education and improving basic health and social relationships through a diverse set of techniques and approaches, including bodily care, prayer, food, help with domestic chores, compassion and counseling" (Kalofonos 2014: 8). In the context of ART scale-up in urban Mozambique, which was roughly concurrent with ART scale-up in urban Ethiopia, a committee convened by the Mozambique Ministry of Health drew up a national model for HIV/AIDS care and treatment support programs. The committee's model sought to establish "minimum quality standards" for care, focusing on adherence to medications, tuberculosis screening, and management of opportunistic infection prophylaxis. Existing volunteer CHWs were deemed unprepared to meet the new technical standards. The committee members were concerned that CHWs were "just praying"—that is, only engaging in empathic, intimate, and spiritual forms of care—and incompetent when it came to technical forms of care. Following Akintola (2008) and Kleinman and Hanna (2008), Kalofonos argues that this perception was anchored by taken-for-granted views of intimate care as a "natural woman's activity." Ministry of Health officials saw the dedication of the CHWs as a strength, yet also believed that they were in need of reorientation from the spiritual, empathic, and intimate aspects of care to the clinical priorities identified by the committee. Thus as a consequence of donor-funded ART scale-up and the efforts of a clinically oriented committee to devise quality standards, the training of CHWs in Mozambique was remodeled into a "more technically comprehensive" form that re-defined care "as clinically oriented work that unfortunately bracketed out much of the more intimate, spiritual, and empathic forms of care in which volunteers typically engaged (Kalofonos 2014: 2).

The third dimension listed earlier—the pursuit of social justice (i.e., an equitable distribution of power, resources, and well-being)—was important to former WHO director General Halfdan Mahler and many of his colleagues in the field of international health in the 1970s, yet seems to be largely neglected or marginalized in today's CHW programs (Pérez and Martinez 2008). In some places, CHWs do engage in the pursuit of social justice through community organizing, advocacy, and other activities. The 2010 US National Community Health Workers Advocacy Study (NCHWAS) found that CHWs were significantly more likely to engage in political and civic advocacy, seeking goals of social justice, if they received advocacy training (Sabo et al. 2013).[19]

How exactly does one go about training CHWs to engage in political advocacy and pursue structural changes in the distribution of basic resources? That is, what forms of training would a CHW program need to provide in order for someone to conclude that CHWs are being prepared for a mission that involves the pursuit of social justice and not just the mechanistic delivery of health care? One answer is a type of critical pedagogy known as *popular education*, translated from the Spanish *educación popular*, or the Portuguese *educação popular*. Closely associated with the literacy instruction methods of the Brazilian educator, philosopher, and activist Paulo Freire, popular education has been adapted for use in many fields, including health education and the training of CHWs. Oregon's Community Capacitation Center which maintains strong ties with the Oregon Community Health Worker Association, is one example of an institution that incorporates principles of popular education into CHW training, with a goal of empowering CHWs to pursue social justice. According to Noelle Wiggins (2012), who has decades of experience working with CHWs in Latin America and who currently heads the Community Capacitation Center, the ultimate goal of popular education is "the redistribution of power from privileged groups to oppressed groups" and "the creation of just and equitable social, economic and political relationships at every level of society and along every axis of diversity" (Wallerstein 2002; Wiggins 2012).

Popular education comprises multiple principles designed to increase the chances of attaining the ultimate goal (Wiggins 2012). Some of these principles are overtly political, for instance, "The current distribution of the world's resources is unjust and change is possible; The purpose of developing critical consciousness is to be able to take organized action to change the world. Critical thinking alone is not enough." There are also several principles of popular education that are less overtly political. These include the following: (1) In each situation in which we try to teach or organize, the conditions should reflect the conditions of the society we are trying to construct. This means equality between "teacher" and "student" and democratic decision making. (2) Educators and organizers should share the life experience of those they want to teach or organize. (3) It is important to create an atmosphere of trust so that people can share their ideas and experiences. (4) We all know a great deal. As educators and organizers, we should always start with what people already know and do. (5) Education should cycle between action, reflection, and action. (6) The knowledge we gain through life experience is as important as the knowledge we gain through formal education. (7) People should be active participants, rather than passive recipients, in their own learning process. (8) Popular education is an inclusive movement that combines influences from many sources. (9) We learn with our heads, our hearts, and our bodies. (10) The arts (music, drama, visual arts, etc.) are important tools for teaching and organizing.

For Wiggins and many others, popular education for CHWs is an ideal toward which we must strive, for this form of training is a necessary if not sufficient ingredient to uphold the notion of participation put forward in the Declaration of Alma Ata. The United States, of course, is very different from Ethiopia. But the basic idea is that CHWs, regardless of context, can pursue structural changes through engaging in some manner with political policy makers in public and private sectors. With popular education adhering to the principles listed above and tailored to specific settings, CHWs can develop a critical consciousness of the global and local political-economic structure of which they are a part and begin to collectively organize and advocate to alter that structure through engaging with legislators, bureaucrats, and other power holders. Without popular education, CHWs are more likely to participate as mere health-care delivery mechanisms deployed by experts. One envisions that in CHW settings that emphasize popular education and the involvement of CHWs in changing social and political determinants of health, recruitment interviews and initial training sessions are the beginning of ongoing, frank discussions of local and global health policy, arenas in which CHWs form opinions on certain health policies and ideas for improvement. In these settings, laypeople with relatively limited understanding of political structures and their own potential power within those structures evolve into well-informed, critical, and constructive shapers and controllers of health policy and implementation.[20]

To what extent did the training of volunteer CHWs in Addis Ababa include or exclude these three dimensions? Considering the third dimension of pursuing social justice, it was evident that some of the less overtly political principles of popular education were upheld, including the maxim that education should cycle between action, reflection, and action. The truisms that people learn with their heads, hearts, and bodies and should be active participants in the learning process were also to some extent endorsed. But what about the other principles, including equality between "teacher" and "student," democratic decision making, and recognition of the value of people's life experiences as a source of important knowledge? Several observations from the training show that these principles were not on the minds of trainers. The happy face matrix that the trainers constructed, for instance, was intended to provide the trainees with a way to communicate their feelings. However, it did not lead to any sort of democratic decision making. It was instead a rather infantilizing means of communication, which perhaps functioned more to reinforce the normative expectation that volunteers should be happy and derive positive emotions from their work.

The rules that the trainees ostensibly agreed to at the start of the training program further suggest that a stark inequality existed between teacher and student. Some of the rules sent a message that love and respect were highly valued, particularly among the trainees. Rules about respecting and loving other trainees, and refraining from gossip, take on significance in light of the diversity of the workforce. They also contribute to fostering an atmosphere of trust among the trainees—one of the principles of popular education. Yet other rules, particularly the ones about being absent or tardy and obeying commands, emphasize the subordinate status of the trainees. Indeed, some of the trainers were late on the first day of training; it was generally acceptable for the trainers to make trainees wait, but not vice versa. Then there were the classroom-like setup and didactic nature of many training sessions, which emphasized the inequality between expert trainers and novice trainees (Figure 3.1). During lunch and tea

FIGURE 3.1   CHW trainees listening to a lecture, February 2008.

Photo courtesy of the author.

breaks, too, volunteers would typically sit together and socialize among themselves, while NGO officials and invited guests would sit together, apart from the trainees. All of this suggests that the trainees—a mix of young and middle-aged adults who had survived difficult circumstances and acquired valuable life skills—had a status more or less equivalent to that of children-students who were not to openly question their supervisors or other health officials. This is clearly at odds with the ideal relationship between teachers and students within popular education. It is nevertheless entirely consistent with local traditions (Poluha 2004) and an international norm: "The structure of a training" in the global AIDS industry, argue Watkins and Swidler (2013), "which donors might imagine as an equalizing activity, in fact mirrors local understandings of the social hierarchy. The more educated enlighten the less educated, who defer to their expertise" (p. 210).

What about the overtly political principles of popular education that state that the current distribution of the world's resources is unjust, that change is possible, and that people should be prepared through education to take action to change the world? Selamawit's human chain exercise emphasized the problems faced by the sick and poor in CHWs' own communities, and made an important distinction between CHWs, who live and know intimately the problems their patients face and thus represent key ingredients in local solutions to those problems, and outside "authority figures," who, despite their recognized authority, are not experts in understanding and solving local problems. The distinction suggests a social critique: that local people living in poverty are knowledgeable and important resources for solving community problems but are too often treated as ignorant by outside authority figures. These authority figures descend upon their communities to tell them how to solve their problems, leading to negative rather than positive social outcomes. However, the activity never attempted to teach the CHWs about the distribution of power and resources in their lives, or about how to seek a more just distribution of power and resources. During her human chain activity, Sister Selamawit proposed that the CHWs were more knowledgeable and capable problem-solvers than bureaucrats and authority figures. Yet she and the other trainers refrained from relating poverty or human rights abuses to the failures of government or to the labor norms that reigned within globalized industries in the 21st century.[21] Expressions about human rights did emerge in the training and orientation of the CHWs, but they were mainly oriented toward the stigmatization and discrimination of people living with HIV/AIDS. I never once witnessed supervisors and CHWs engaged in serious discussion of politics and human civil, economic, or social rights and justice. Though this may be partly because they did not want to engage in such talk in front of me, it would still suggest that such discussions were seen as taboo, and definitely not the primary concern of CHWs and others in the program.

The post-training reflections that I collected from several of the trainees further suggest that after a month of basic training, recruits conceived of themselves primarily as people who were supposed to provide quality, one-on-one care to patients: "I now understand how to take care of a patient and help him get out of bed and get well again." "The training has helped me to know the steps to take care of patients." None of the post-training reflections were about how the training imparted a better understanding of the distribution of basic resources in the world or the steps that CHWs and other citizens can take to change the norms, laws, and structures responsible for keeping such a large number of Ethiopia's and Africa's people poor, sick, fed up with and fearful of their governments, and unable to find work. The trainees did not say that they now had a critical understanding of why the global health industry so often relies on the "volunteer" labor of poorer people, even as it has moved so many resources and well-paid elites around the globe.

Thus, the overall training, a reflection of the CHW job description and mission envisioned by ART programmers, sidelined ideas of social justice and the work of political activism. During training, NGOs did not encourage volunteers to become political forces intent on raising awareness about injustices or advocating for the rights of the poor to share in the benefits that elites enjoy. The ART program and the local, national, and transnational bureaucracies that governed the program were not rendered as phenomena or structures for the CHWs to control and alter, to fit their own visions of justice and quality care. They were rendered as structures for the trainees to understand just enough in order to perform their CHW role according to supervisors' expectations.

To what extent did basic training in Addis Ababa balance the dimensions of empathic and technical care? The situation in Addis Ababa was likely on a trajectory similar to the one in Mozambique described by Kalofonos (2014). The displacement of quality, empathic care, and service to make room for technical specifications and practices brought in by transnationally trained biomedical and health systems experts, is indeed a global phenomenon. Yet it appeared to me that empathic forms of care still received emphasis during the CHWs' basic training in the early years of ART scale-up in Addis Ababa.[22]

To be sure, drug adherence and compliance with "doctor's orders" were clearly emphasized during the training. Collecting and generating data for monitoring and evaluation—other forms of cold, technical performance—were also emphasized. For instance, during the first week of training, Dr. Mengistu, an authoritative older physician from ALERT, delivered an invited lecture on TB, STDs, and HIV-related opportunistic infections. "People who get sick with HIV have less immunity. These opportunistic and related diseases can be the cause of death." As Dr. Mengistu described the handful of common opportunistic infections observed in ALERT's patients, Sr. Meheret leaned over to whisper in my ear that "the volunteers have to know how to treat each of these opportunistic infections." Zewdu, a 50-year-old male nurse from ALERT, later lectured about ART. Dressed in a suit, Zewdu explained that ART defies HIV replication and allows the body to rebuild its immune system so that it can fight infections, and that ART reduces the chance that a mother will pass HIV to her baby during birth or breastfeeding. He explained that the WHO and CDC maintained different guidelines for when to start ART in settings of resource scarcity, noting that Ethiopia followed the WHO's guidelines, and went over the various first-line ARV regimens in use in Ethiopia. He further emphasized that ART is not a cure and cannot completely eliminate HIV; that if treatment is stopped, the virus will come back; that poor adherence leads to the development of resistant strains of HIV; and that strict adherence to ART is thus hugely important. He also pointed out that while ARVs have side effects, so do common painkillers and antibiotics. Patients, he continued, must therefore carefully follow doctor's orders, especially by taking their medicines at the appropriate times, and they must see their doctors on their scheduled dates. This would "help the doctors confirm how the medicine and the patients are adapting to each other." He noted that the CHWs bore important responsibilities to help identify and promptly notify health professionals about apparent side effects and drug interactions, so that such problems could be appropriately managed.

During the third week of the training, Tirusew instructed the trainees on how to collect and report data—specifically data describing their CHW activities, which were to be used for monitoring and evaluation (Figure 3.2). Tirusew defined monitoring and evaluation, noting that the former enables the latter.

FIGURE 3.2 A group of CHW trainees study their data collection forms, 2008.

Photo courtesy of the author.

He expounded on the importance of data quality and "good record keeping," starting at the volunteer CHW level. "Well organized records will show whether your work is improving and which areas need improvement or change." During his lecture, Tirusew showed the trainees an organogram depicting the hierarchical relationship between patients, volunteers, supervisors, team leaders, coordinators, directors, and finally, FHI. In the organogram, data and evaluation reports moved up and down this hierarchy, and each level in the hierarchy had its associated forms to fill and weekly, monthly, or quarterly "review meetings," comprising a "monitoring system." Tirusew summarized this set of relationships by emphasizing that "it is very necessary for volunteers to be familiar with their forms, because this will help the supervisors present their reports to their coordinator."

After introducing the forms and their use in lecture, Tirusew and the other supervisors led the trainees outside the hall and divided them into groups of seven or eight individuals. They received and studied copies of the forms that the they would use in data collection and weekly reporting: a volunteer CHW's Weekly Activity Planning form, a Weekly Activity Reporting form, and a Self-Reflection Form, all adorned by FHI's logo. Given hypothetical narrative descriptions of a patient and a volunteer's visit to that patient's home, including the name and age of the patient, whether or not she was a new patient, some clinical and demographic data, the time of the visit, and what kinds of services were performed during the visit (cleaning, medicine assistance, sick care, etc.), the trainee groups practiced filling out both the weekly reporting form and the planning form for the next week. Finally, the groups discussed how well each had filled out their planning form, identifying and building consensus on errors and inconsistencies.

CHWs were thus expected to work with multiple kinds of technical, biomedical, and bureaucratic knowledge and practices: HIV subtypes, opportunistic infections, and ART regimens; wards, labs, pharmacies, HIV/AIDS desks, and data card rooms; data collection for monitoring and evaluation, and so on (Figure 3.3). The tendency to refer to patients with bureaucratic terms like "client" or "beneficiary," and the white coats that the trainees wore while at the hospital and in a group photo-op on the last day of training, can be read as signs that CHWs were seen and saw themselves as extensions of biomedicine and of bureaucratic institutions.

Yet if mediating technical forms of biomedicine and collecting data were important parts of their job, from the looks of the training, so was being a force of anti-stigmatization, solidarity, support, hope, and improved quality of life for patients and families. Even as NGO and government health officials in charge of scaling-up ART access in Addis Ababa emphasized technical aspects of the volunteer CHW job description, they continued to encourage and train volunteers to engage in intimate and empathic care.[23] They used multiple media and formats, furthermore, including not just lectures but also dramatic performances

FIGURE 3.3 CHW trainees visit ALERT Hospital's ART pharmacy, 2008.

Photo courtesy of the author.

and community discussions to encourage the CHWs to become forces of anti-stigmatization and care at the interpersonal, familial, and community levels, as well as mediators of social services that provided access to basic resources like food, housing, and school supplies.

For instance, during the first week of the training, Sister Haimanot and Sister Meheret led the CHWs in discussions of intimate care focused on treating the mind and soul of patients. The CHWs were encouraged and guided to simply "spend time and listen" to their patients, to "communicate love and acceptance," and to encourage their patients and families to engage in and deepen their religious or spiritual practices. During one exercise, Sister Haimanot asked the trainees to contemplate the desires that a patient might maintain, including "things related to their bodies, their health, their home, their job, their children, their spouse, or their community." She instructed them to be as specific as possible and gave them a few examples to get things started: "I want to feel well enough to sing in the choir, I want my children to finish school, I want to feel loved by my family." The trainees were told that they could explore these desires with their patients, and help them choose a few that they could expect to achieve. Together with the patient, the CHWs could then make "action plans" for achieving these goals. Sr. Haimanot also introduced several simple exercises that CHWs could teach to patients who felt a need to get their emotions out but feared disclosing their feelings to anyone, including writing a letter or having an imagined conversation with the virus living inside their body.

During the second week of training, groups of trainees performed short social dramas dealing with issues of stigma, abandonment, and acceptance of people with HIV (Figure 3.4). In one, the father of a household, played very well by a CHW named Fikirte, angrily reveals to his family that he has tested positive for HIV. The mother of the household reacts frenziedly, and their two children are unable to calm her. An elderly neighbor enters the house and, through a process of counseling the mother and father, succeeds in reconciling them. The following week, Fikirte and a group of trainees performed another, longer social drama, also featuring themes of stigma, family conflict, and reconciliation. These dramas were performed with great seriousness and skill on the part of the trainees. Fikirte later told me she believed deeply in the power of dramatic performances to shape cultural understandings and values. "In our society it is known that dramas are very good—better than simply talking—at getting people to understand. Dramas make them see the disadvantages of stigmatization and conflict."

Toward the end of the month-long training, the trainees also spent multiple consecutive days in the hospital wards at ALERT practicing intimacy with bedridden AIDS patients. I watched Tsehay, for instance, sit for minutes simply staring at the face of a very thin and weak male patient, with her elbows on the mattress and her head resting in her hands. A couple of trainees brought a pot

FIGURE 3.4 A group of CHW trainees perform a social drama about stigmatization and reconciliation, 2008.

Photo courtesy of the author.

of water to the bedside of another male patient to carefully wash him without disturbing his IV drip. Eden, another trainee, told me that earlier she had put Vaseline on his noticeably dry skin. At ALERT, the trainees also confronted the task of preparing dead bodies. Some practiced post-mortem care on a mannequin. Another group practiced on a fellow volunteer, Eden, who enthusiastically volunteered. Her peers took turns wrapping her in a white cloth and carefully placing her in a coffin. A brochure produced by Hiwot in 2005 indicated that, "After preparing a dead body for funeral, volunteers and nurses complete their care for the patient." Sister Meheret also emphasized to the trainees that post-mortem care was an important task for a volunteer, since even family members were often afraid to handle the dead bodies of their deceased relatives.

These are just some of the ways in which the dimension of empathic care was targeted by trainers and trainees. Kleinman argues that medical training must help doctors

> to master the art of acknowledging and affirming the patient as a suffering human being; imagining alternative contexts and practices for responding to calamity; and conversing with and supporting patients in desperate situations where the emphasis is on what really matters to the patient and his or her intimates.
>
> *(Kleinman 2008: 23)*

Trainers made real attempts to help trainees practice these arts and to think of beneficiaries as human beings with multiple needs, desires, emotions, and relationships.

In sum, changing social structures through advocacy and organizing was not part of the CHW role envisioned by program staff in Addis Ababa, but both empathic and technical care were. The role CHWs played—in the minds of the CHWs and their superiors and in many cases in reality—was not just about dispensing medicines and reminding patients when to take the pills. Their role was also one of the empathic caregiver who established intimate relationships with stigmatized patients; reconciled conflicts within their families and social networks; openly confronted difficult existential questions, questions of abandonment and support, and questions of quality of life and death; and helped maintain hope in a better future and faith in God.

Popular education was not the modus operandi of the CHW training program because, simply put, it was politically problematic. Popular education is not a politically neutral form of education. It has a progressive, system-changing, revolutionary quality that does not sit well with many in power. Like Lehmann and Sanders (2007), who have pointed out that CHWs are much more likely to be oriented to social justice when embedded in larger popular movements, Wiggins (2012) points out that popular education is likely to be unsuccessful when embedded in an antagonistic, unsupportive political context.[24] Ethiopia's ruling party did not want its poor to become activists and human rights defenders speaking out about injustices and seeking to change laws and policies. Popular education was also unwanted by donors and international NGOs. Such actors typically do not want CHWs who understand norms such as the "sustainability doctrine" and who are prepared to question and alter such doctrines, even as they provide care to their fellow community members. Certainly, they were not encouraging local "implementing partners" such as Hiwot to use popular education to turn their CHWs into critical thinkers prepared to question and alter the economic and power inequalities within the global health industry.

Why was empathic care so strongly emphasized? There are at least two reasons. On the one hand, empathic forms of care remained within the training and orientation of CHWs in Addis Ababa because supervisors and officials genuinely valued CHWs who were willing and able to engage in empathic and intimate care for people living amid widespread unemployment, insecure access to food and housing, and social abandonment. Supervisors, officials, and CHWs all consistently expressed concern for patients as people who lived very difficult material and social lives, and I believe that their concern was genuine. On the other hand, from the perspectives of supervisors and directors, emphasizing these forms of care was expedient, given a policy that CHWs engage in unpaid "volunteer" service. Empathic forms of care (as opposed to technical forms) are more readily linked to sentiments of sacrifice and mental satisfaction. Thus during training, the CHWs were told that by serving as empathic caregivers and by seeing patients get healthy—not filling out standardized report forms—they would derive profound mental and spiritual satisfaction. In the next chapter, we will also see that, once deployed, the CHWs would connect the intimate and empathic aspects of their care work to their experience of emotional and spiritual satisfaction. It is worth noting the non-mutual-exclusivity of these two explanations for why empathic caregiving was maintained in Addis Ababa's ARV center of excellence. Supervisors and directors can genuinely see value in empathic forms of care and support for patients and simultaneously find it helpful to connect these forms of care to sentiments of sacrifice and satisfaction to get people to do community health work for less material remuneration. Thus the production of CHW workforces involves interactions between the pre-existing moral sentiments of local actors and policies handed down from above.

Conclusion

Like the Ethiopian Volunteers Day event, the initiation ceremony, recruitment interviews, and training sessions described in this chapter were opportunities that supervisors and officials created for themselves, aimed at imparting a specific set of skills and at socializing their emotions, expectations, and motivations through discourses of sacrifice and mental satisfaction. Recruits participated in these interviews, ceremonies, and activities in obviously limited ways. During the initiation ceremony, when it was the volunteers' turn to talk, they collectively promised their willingness to take up the task as described, responding to cues and using words that had been prepared by supervisors and coordinators. Narratives of recruitment interviews suggest that recruits participated in them mainly by defending themselves as pro-socially and unselfishly motivated, making it clear that their moral sentiments were consistent with the expectations of the recruiters, or, in Birtukan's case, by reluctantly accepting an offer to provide unpaid but mentally and spiritually gratifying work. While many CHWs were likely happy with their interview and initiation experiences, being provoked to defend their motivations caused some, including Alemnesh and Tsehay, to experience a sense of indignation and to begin forming opinions on the fairness of the ways in which they were treated. Yet from the stage at the CHW initiation ceremony to the global stage, such emotions and opinions were not parts of the story, because they were inconsistent with the public emotions and moral sentiments of higher-status actors. What these actors wanted was exactly the kinds of statements the CHWs wrote down at the end of their month-long basic training, that they were now prepared to care for vulnerable and suffering patients, help them regain some measure of health and well-being, and experience the mental and spiritual rewards.

Recruitment and basic training are of obvious interest to CHW supervisors, directors, and policy makers who often aim to produce CHW workforces with certain sets of capabilities and motivations. The recruitment and training of CHWs are also clearly important to the patients, who will receive the care and support that CHWs are prepared to give, and to CHWs, who may be interested in having greater influence over how they are recruited and trained. This chapter provides an understanding of how recruiters, trainers, supervisors, and officials went about trying to produce their ideal workforce. In so doing, it also shows how recruitment and basic training are entry points for CHWs into a moral economy involving negotiations among various actors with different and overlapping interests, values, and power. The ground-level moral economy in which CHWs in Addis Ababa participated was in turn shaped by global norms and local politics between the state, NGOs, and citizens, which influenced the ways that officials and staff went about recruiting CHWs and deciding what to include within and exclude from their basic training. Thus we see how CHW recruitment and basic training occur at the intersection of global policies and local moral, economic, and social dynamics.

Notes

1. Hiwot's HBC coordinator lent me a VHS recording of the event in September 2007. Elsa and others at Hiwot told me that a similar ceremony would happen in late 2007 or early 2008, but it never did. I was told by Hiwot staff that the reason why the ceremony kept getting delayed, and eventually was never held in 2007 or 2008, had to do with uncertainty over the continuation of Hiwot's contract with FHI.

2. *Qal kidan* also connotes the traditional form of Orthodox education (mainly for boys) consisting largely of learning and reciting prayers and hymns.

3. Umbrellas for protection from Addis Ababa's highland sunlight and rainy season downpours, and backpacks for carrying various supplies, were "incentives" provided to the volunteers. These items also identified the volunteers as NGO-based CHWs as they moved about public spaces. In practice, the CHWs often left these items behind when they visited the homes of patients in order to avoid attention and HIV-related stigma. But they also sometimes used them in public, in part out of a collective goal to destigmatize HIV/AIDS by confidently and openly providing care and support.

4. After getting to know Selamawit over the course of a couple months, I learned that she was a 32-year-old mother of two sons and had recently finalized a divorce. Her husband, according to her, was not providing any financial child support.

5. Historical evidence suggests that *iddirs* came to Addis Ababa during the early 20th century with ethnic Gurage migrants and spread throughout the capital in the aftermath of the Italian occupation (1936–41). Many *iddirs* in Addis Ababa are based on locality, with membership open to anyone in the neighborhood who can pay the monthly dues, regardless of status or other social divisions. According to Pankhurst and Haile-Mariam (2000: 49), membership of *iddirs* in Addis Ababa ranges from 15 to 800 people, with a mean of about 250 people. The size of the membership and monthly contributions at *iddirs* vary, with dues at the time of my research ranging from 1 to 10 birr per month (~1 USD). With dues so low, even very poor people maintain membership in an *iddir*, though extreme poverty does force some in Addis Ababa to let their membership lapse.

6. It is difficult to obtain reliable data on the number of Ethiopian women migrating to work in the Gulf States, yet it clearly became a common goal and experience for large numbers of Ethiopian women in the early 21st century (Endeshaw et al. 2010). One reason is that many travel on tourist visas. In addition, due to the Ethiopian government's recent attempts to regulate more closely this form of labor migration, some Ethiopian women have begun migrating first to neighboring countries in East Africa and then making the journey to the Middle East (Endeshaw et al. 2010). While reliable data are hard to come by, long queues of young women processing their visas at Ethiopia's central immigration offices were visible to anyone who happened to be downtown on a weekday. And those who departed Ethiopia from Bole International Airport with an economy class ticket typically waited in the same line as several dozen young women waiting to board their flights.

7. The fact that Alemnesh had gone to and returned from two countries in the Middle East—and had made money and stayed healthy—means that she avoided some of the horrible fates that other Ethiopian women have faced while working as domestic servants abroad, including suicide, murder, sexual abuse, beatings, burnings, revoked passports, and unpaid wages (Anbesse et al. 2009). Unfortunately, with severely limited work opportunities within urban Ethiopia, many women are willing to brave these forms of violence in order to gain income as domestic servants.

8. Female nurses are typically referred to with the title of "Sister," while male nurses are called "Nurse."

9. Technically, they did not own their house because only the Ethiopian state owns land; citizens are only given long-term leases for land, and the government can take it away at any time.

10. Studying moral and political economies in the arena of global health and development is one way to answer anthropologist James Ferguson's (2010) call for studies of the mix of "funds, energies and affects" involved in global health and development action.

11. It is important to point out that the claim that volunteering as a CHW in Ethiopia or other low-income countries offers a psychosocial "bonus" is not based on any careful

epidemiological study. There is a considerable body of research in social psychology and epidemiology that tests the link between volunteering and mental well-being (e.g., Borgonovi 2008; Piliavin and Siegl 2007), but most of this research has been conducted in North America, with relatively well-off volunteers (and not specifically CHWs). In settings of poverty and unemployment, where people are uniquely in need of both "mental satisfaction" and economic security, the link between volunteering and well-being seems to operate less as a hypothesis to be rigorously tested and more as a belief that is convenient for those who seek cheap labor.

12. I came to interpret her use of the term *qinat* not as envy, exactly, but as a form of what cultural psychologist Jonathan Haidt calls elevation, a positive feeling of exaltation or proximity to the divine, and a reflection of a "third dimension of morality," a common interest across cultural groups to seek right behavior in regards to one's peers, one's superiors, and the divine (Haidt 2003; Shweder et al. 2003; 2008). For Haidt, the emotion of elevation is the opposite of disgust and can be triggered by behaving or witnessing other people behaving in a virtuous way (Haidt 2003; 2007).

13. By having volunteers don the same T-shirts and hats and swear the same oath, and by reinforcing the shared goals, roles, orientations, and desires of the volunteers present, officials perhaps also attempted and succeeded in fostering solidarity among new CHWs.

14. When CHWs, supervisors, and others express these moral sentiments, we are presented with a problem of interpretation due to the limitations of interviews and even participant observation: it is admittedly difficult to know the extent to which CHWs genuinely believe versus just pay lip service to the moral sentiments of their supervisors and superiors.

15. Once deployed, the volunteers would only occasionally interact with team leaders like Tesfaye, or with the team leaders' immediate superior, Elsa, the coordinator of the NGO's HBC program.

16. Aside from office cleaners, social workers such as Million were the lowest-rank salaried workers in Hiwot's hierarchy of staff; many of the NGO's social workers used to volunteer as CHWs.

17. Another daily occurrence was the afternoon "energizer," a brief group exercise used to fend off the torpor that quickly set in during the first lecture after lunch. Trainees were assigned the responsibility of leading energizers on specific days. Sometimes, energizer leaders told jokes. A young man and trainee named Abebe impressed his peers and supervisors with a few short lines of poetry he had composed. Others led the group in a lightly physical, rhythmic group exercise. The trainees might stand up together, stretch freestyle, and then repeat a little chant like "ba da dam" while snapping their fingers and slapping their butts to the beat. They would laugh and then sit, and the lecture would resume as a new one would begin.

18. Donors, international NGO reps, and local NGO and government officials, according to Watkins and Swidler, are all convinced that "whatever the problem, training is the solution" (2013: 208; cf. Smith 2003).

19. Sabo et al. (2013) caution that the National Community Health Workers Advocacy Study is based on a non-random sample that includes "a disproportional number of Hispanic and female respondents and may not be representative to the CHW profession in the United States. CHW respondents may also be different from those CHWs not affiliated with a CHW professional organization" (p. e72).

20. I say "one envisions" because at present there are few ethnographic studies of how people experience and evolve as a result of CHW trainings including popular education.

21. She also told the soon-to-be CHWs that the activity reflected the importance of a grassroots community "movement," using the Amharic term *neqnaqe*. *Neqnaqe* is the "N" in MEISON, the All-Ethiopia Socialist Movement, the Marxist-Leninist

political party that, along with the Ethiopian People's Revolutionary Party (EPRP), vied for control of Ethiopia in the mid-1970s, after the fall of Haile Selassie and before the consolidation of power by the Derg. The term *neqnaqe* is thus associated with overtly political movements seeking a redistribution of power and resources and even connotes a revolutionary goal or motive. Not surprisingly, Selamawit did not make these connotations explicit.

22. Without longitudinal data, however, it is impossible for me to characterize change or stasis in the training and orientation of CHWs in my field site.

23. The bureaucratic collection of data for monitoring and evaluation was also framed during the training as important not just for preventing the rise of drug resistance or for meeting donors' demands but also for meeting the changing needs of patients and their families. These changing needs, Tirusew explained, were generated partly through ART and its restoration of the immune system, which challenges programs to keep up by tailoring services to individuals in various situations, in order to continue to "ensure the quality of life" of those patients.

24. According to Wiggins (2012: 13), "When the pre-existing level of sense of community is very low, or the structural barriers are very great, it may be unreasonable to expect that a popular education intervention can lead to improvements in community-level empowerment, at least in the short or medium term." Though it is difficult to measure, there surely existed some sense of community among CHWs and many others living in Addis Ababa's various neighborhoods. But the structural barriers to community empowerment, involving a government increasingly seen as repressive and violent toward opposing parties and critics, seemed massive.

4

TO CARE AND TO SUFFER

Community Health Work Amid Unemployment and Food Insecurity

The PEPFAR-funded documentary that FHI produced to highlight ALERT's ART program features scenes of volunteer CHWs going about their daily work: walking along a dirt path and entering a mud house; helping a man step out of his house, onto a stretcher, and into a doctor's office; spoon-feeding and fixing an IV to the arm of a bedridden woman in her home. Two profiles of volunteer CHWs and their now-healthy patients are also featured in the film. In the first, Abebech, a volunteer, enters a home constructed of corrugated tin walls and eucalyptus poles to find Fikirte, her patient, knitting. Abebech fans a small indoor cook fire, as Fikirte's children look on and talk with Abebech. Speaking to the camera, Abebech gives a brief overview of her relationship to Fikirte.

> Fikirte is the first of my patients to start treatment. At first, I was keeping Fikirte's pills with me at my house and giving her only her daily pills. She had many complications. I was giving her simple medications, according to my training: painkillers and oral rehydration salts for diarrhea. If there is no improvement, I take her to Dr. Yigeremu. If she is strong enough to walk, I support her. Sometimes I ask for transport from the home-based care program.

Fikirte, the patient, then testifies to the profound significance of Abebech's care. She also identifies food support as a crucial aspect of her care.

> They assigned Abebech to follow me closely. She is coming to me hour after hour and reminding me to take the pills . . . She gave me a watch and taught me to tell time. . . . If Abebech had not been with me, there would be no life. I say this in all respects. She helps me when I have nothing at

home, until I get food items like sugar and wheat from the home-based care program. You can't take the pills without food since it burns the stomach and gives you a hard time. Sometimes I wake up in the middle of the night feeling hungry. At these times she goes to the neighbors and says, "There is this woman with three children who is very sick and has nothing to eat," and she brings me food to eat. She is my life. Without her I would not have been alive.

Later in the documentary, another patient, Almaz, backs up this testimony with her own reflections on the importance of food and emotional support, in addition to drug adherence support, all provided by her volunteer CHW.

I'm here because of them. If they had not given me emotional support and visited me time and again, what would have happened to me? What would I have given my children to eat? What would I have eaten to take the drugs? It would have been impossible to feel better.

Success stories and testimonies of happy patients are exactly what PEPFAR administrators and other donors want to see and circulate to the public. In composing such stories, the documentary champions the social and emotional work and efficacy of the volunteer CHWs in ALERT Hospital's ART program. Yet these testimonies tell us little about how Abebech and patients like Fikirte actually became close and built trust in challenging circumstances, or about how CHWs dealt with the more difficult parts of their work, such as caring for patients who were abandoned, hungry, and, in some cases, dying. This chapter examines several of the key capacities for intimate care that were commonly exercised by these CHWs, exploring how they maintained empathy for patients, gained the trust of their patients, reconciled disputes within patients' families, and gave patients who died on them a better death. The capacities of CHWs for intimate and empathic care can be understood through careful, in-depth work that attends to the actual formation and maintenance of intimate relationships in a particular social and economic world, and to the values and skills that go into these processes. These practices demand this kind of close attention, for they are important both to patients and to a vision of care within community health work that is empathic and empowering, not just technical and disciplining (Nading 2013). Understanding these practices should contribute to efforts to amplify and multiply them.

The exercise of intimate care, furthermore, greatly impacts the emotional lives of CHWs. Contrary to a simple portrait of volunteer CHWs deriving mental satisfaction through caring for others, this chapter will show that community health work involved both profoundly positive and negative effects and experiences. After all, some patients did not survive, some kids were orphaned, some patients were not simply happy and doing fine, and many CHWs had to deal emotionally with these people too. CHWs' emotions and well-being were also shaped by factors outside of community health work, involving their own experiences of food insecurity, unemployment, and difficulties with loved ones. Unemployment generated substantial distress for many CHWs and their families, and was a major factor behind their willingness to become volunteer CHWs and to subsequently experience both the mental satisfaction and deep distress that came with this unpaid work.

By examining both the exercise of empathic care and the complex production of psychological distress and satisfaction among CHWs, this chapter further advances an understanding of the moral economies in which CHWs, patients, and supervisors participated. The quantitative data and narratives discussed in this chapter also clarify the multidimensional social, emotional, and health gains that can come from investments in CHWs. Many important publications about CHWs and the issue of payment assert that the creation of well-paid CHW jobs can function as an economic stimulus and empowerment, especially for women, since CHWs around the world so often are women. The data presented here can be used not only to scrutinize claims that CHWs are adequately compensated for their work by feelings of mental and spiritual satisfaction but also to show more precisely the kinds of meaningful social, economic, and emotional benefits that generous payment and good job conditions can bring.

Getting Close

A capacity to develop intimate relationships with marginalized people forms the foundation for the multiple ways in which CHWs support, heal, and otherwise serve their intended beneficiaries. In Addis, among CHWs serving highly stigmatized people, this capacity was partly dependent on an explicit desire to include the poor and suffering within a category of fellow human beings deemed deserving of intimate care. CHWs and others in their networks often used the Amharic term *wegen* (literally, one's clan, faction, or party) to refer to this category of care-deserving people. For Eskinder, who had recovered from AIDS after beginning ART in 2004, treating people with HIV/AIDS as *wegen*—regardless of their religious, ethnic, or social background—was partly about reciprocity: he had been helped by unrelated neighbors and health professionals, so "Today," he said, "I should make an effort for my *wegen*." Other CHWs suggested that churches played a big role in promoting the *wegen* idiom. Rahel, one of Medhin's volunteers whose situation we will examine later in this chapter, affirmed, "We are caregivers because we want to help our *wegen*." Rahel also reiterated the anti-discrimination messages that, according to her, were voiced in every local religious organization: "People with HIV, the poor, and the hungry are *wegen*. Do not discriminate or distance yourself from them. Help them and treat them like *wegen*, and pray to God." Likewise, Alemnesh offered that "living in harmony" with others, regardless of social status, was a core message of the "spiritual teachings" she had internalized.

In addition to churches, families reinforced the *wegen* idiom. Alemnesh said that her family members praised her for becoming a CHW and "helping your *wegen* with what you have." Fasika, a 36-year-old married woman who worked as a CHW for the Hiwot NGO, narrated how several years back, in her hometown in northern Ethiopia, her mother had taken in an HIV-positive man who had been thrown out of a neighbor's house. "My mother said, 'Bring him—he can lie down in my home. My house belongs to *Medhane Alem* [literally Savior of the World (i.e., Christ)].'" While caring for him, Fasika's mother contracted HIV, developed AIDS, and died. When Fasika first became a volunteer CHW, a young woman near death was assigned as her patient. She was told the woman had a history as a sex worker in Djibouti before falling ill and returning to Addis Ababa. When Fasika visited the woman, she found her lying naked in a back room of her brother's house: "Her brother and his wife were there, but nobody was putting clothes on her. She was alone. Everybody else had retreated." Fasika said she envisioned the patient dying alone and asked herself, "Who is going to prepare this woman's body? My mother died because she was taking care of what my people threw away. How can I do nothing when I see the disease attacking so many people?" In this particular situation, and in the daily experiences of Fasika and her fellow CHWs, the alternative to doing nothing was to provide intimate care to people with HIV/AIDS.

A desire and commitment to treating people no matter their background as *wegen* may have encouraged CHWs to care for and become close with care recipients.[1] Yet the *wegen* idiom reflects only an abstract value of inclusiveness and reveals little about how CHWs and care recipients forged relationships, involving mutual expectations and obligations, with patients who were not necessarily willing to trust a stranger, even one who seemed nice and offered some helpful resources (Bornstein 2012). In explaining how they actually established close, trusting relationships with their patients, CHWs often stressed the importance of adopting a deliberate approach, one that involved frequent contact, patience, humility, and the construction of hope—a fundamental challenge shared by broad segments of urban Ethiopian populations (Mains 2012).[2]

"The important thing is your approach," Asayech explained. "If you go too fast, thinking that you are knowledgeable, they may be uncomfortable. If you are careful, and simply visit them frequently and talk with them, you become close." Fasika said that "if you approach them nicely, show them love, and visit them morning and night, they will be yours." Eskinder told of a patient named Silennat, whom he visited on a regular basis. "She was crying one day, and she told me something that touched me inside. She told me that there is nobody like me, who is close with her and who follows her. 'You know about my inside life, and you speak to me closely,' she said. So I went back on Saturday to visit her again."

The importance of constructing hope was emphasized by Markos, a young man who, in addition to serving as a CHW, had gotten his parents' permission to invite a woman with HIV/AIDS to live rent-free in their family's modest home. When Markos met her, she was alone, having trouble renting a house, and distraught. Care recipients such as this woman, Markos said, need to be carefully told by their CHW, "I am here for you. You will not stay sick. You will get better and work again." If convinced, "they will have hope for the future and be stronger."

Keeping secrets (*mistir tebbeqe*) emerged as another important part of CHWs' capacity to establish and maintain close relationships. "Care recipients will become close to you," Markos said, "if you do not tell their secrets." The woman who came to live with his family did so, for instance, only after she had told him "all of her secrets." "She told me everything openly, and I kept those secrets. Then I asked my parents and invited her to live here." In his classic ethnography of Amhara ethnic tradition and change, Donald Levine (1965) discusses the importance of keeping secrets with close friends in both rural and urban settings. The male students he surveyed in Addis Ababa, who were experiencing the novel situation of mingling with peers from various backgrounds, described their close friends "as confidants, as individuals with whom they can disclose 'secrets' and discuss personal problems" (Levine 1965: 117). The HIV/AIDS care and treatment support program is another novel situation in which relative strangers build solid relationships, in part by keeping secrets. "I am my patients' confidant (*mistireñña*)," declared Fikirte, suggesting that being a CHW and keeping secrets was an important part of her identity and confirming comments, made by several CHWs, that care recipients often entrust their secrets to nobody but their CHW.

CHWs act not only as guardians of personal information but also as advocates who divulge their knowledge when it appears to be in a care recipient's interest. Tsehay, for example, spoke about a father of three young children who had been excluded from the government's food support rosters. She distinguished between the man's outer clothing, which he acquired while employed and signaled a better economic status to the bureaucrats, and his "inside" lifestyle and history, with which she had become familiar:

> I was so angry. Because even though he has a good physical appearance, his house and his life were not good. That is because he used to have a good job, and he used to have assets, but he was fired from his job when he got sick. Eventually I got him and his children to enter the wheat support program by arguing [with the bureaucrats]: "Why do you exclude him? Because he wears a leather jacket? Does that mean he has wealth? You can come and see his inside lifestyle."

Reconciliation

Reconciling conflicts among loved ones, involving difficult questions of stigma and the provision of care and support, was another important activity of CHWs in Addis Ababa. The CHWs' involvement as mediators within care recipients' biosocial problems was an important mechanism by which the program for which they worked improved the social and emotional lives of care recipients and their families. Sitting across a basic wooden coffee table in the front room of his two-room shack, Eskinder told me about the time he reconciled a hospitalized 17-year-old girl and her aggressive father, who wanted to withhold ART from the girl, saying, "She should die."

> I said to her father, "Calm down. We don't know from where this child got HIV. She could have come in contact with somebody's blood." He couldn't believe me. His daughter stayed in hospital for more than a month. I was visiting them all that time, consoling the father, and I finally got him to agree with his daughter. Now, he has given her a room in his house, and she is living properly.

"When you reconcile others," Eskinder reflected, "you will give them happiness, and you will also be satisfied. You will be blessed." He recounted that when he recently met the hospitalized girl, she told him, " 'Now I agree with my father and I love him. He gave me a room where I can live and eat, and he gives me money.' " "For me," Eskinder asserted, "that is big happiness." In addition to mending relationships between children and their parents, several respondents told stories about reconciling spouses, some of whom repeatedly fought verbally and physically in front of their children.

As conflict mediators and reconcilers, CHWs were supported by a widely recognized cultural model, known as *shimgilinna*. For instance, in 2007 a high-profile political drama involving shïmgïlïnna took place as part of the unfolding of Ethiopia's 2005 election-related protests and the state's violent response. After the election and protests, the government had imprisoned opposition party leaders and supporters to the dismay of many Ethiopians and international observers. In the months leading up to the Ethiopian millennium celebrations in September 2007, as reported and read widely in the local press, a group of respected elders mediated a sort of reconciliation between the ruling party and its prisoners, leading to the latter's release (Halpern 2007).[3] In more mundane agrarian contexts, *shimgilinna*—conflict mediation and reconciliation—is a key role performed by elders, as reflected in the Amharic term often used for elder: *shimagille*. Markos explained, however, that "Today, one does not have to be old to be a *shimagille*."

Eskinder and his peers further connected reconciliation to values of peace and the emotional and spiritual benefits experienced not only by the reconciled parties but also by the reconciler, friends, and family. "If it is within your capacity," Rahel affirmed, "you must try to reconcile people when you see them separated." Reconciling others was so desirable, Tsehay explained, because it meant pleasing God and preventing Satan (*seytan*)—the embodiment of hateful feelings—from separating people: "God says, 'Above all, reconcile others and give love.' Why? To cool the *seytan* between people." Tsehay said she found happiness in the fact that relatives and neighbors frequently sought her father's skillful arbitration. "He is not highly educated," she pointed out, "but he simply has a nature of convincing others." CHWs thus exercised an important capacity to effectively reconcile conflicts within their care recipients' social networks, which did not require elderly status or formal schooling, but rather a desire to generate and experience the emotional benefits of reconciling others, sensitivity to the desires and concerns of the conflicting parties, and patience.

In sum, CHWs built and maintained close relationships with care recipients with a deliberate approach and a desire to see others as deserving of intimate care, regardless of background. Of note, CHWs' intimate knowledge of their care recipients' situations was not limited to HIV status, but included various other kinds of personal information, emotions, and experiences. This suggests the relevance of secret keeping and divulging to the establishment of close, supportive relationships in CHW contexts in Ethiopia beyond HIV/AIDS care. The close relationships that CHWs developed with patients were important for many aspects of the latter's care and quality of life, including the reconciliation of conflicts between spouses and close family members. Conversely, the close relationships that all CHWs experienced with at least some of their patients were important for the mental and spiritual satisfaction of the former.

Confronting Death

CHWs by definition struggle to improve people's health. Yet an important aspect of community health work—particularly in settings of elevated mortality—involves struggling to confront the mortality of care recipients. The capacities of CHWs to confront death deserve greater appreciation and understanding in terms of the forms in which they are enacted and the life experiences and values that encourage and support them. In Addis Ababa's ARV center of excellence, CHWs helped some patients (and their families) experience "better" deaths. The capacity to help stigmatized patients have "better" deaths was partly illustrated by CHWs' comments about *adera*: the entrustment of something or someone to another's care at the time of death. While a close relative typically handles a person's *adera*, Rahel affirmed that patients often chose CHWs to take on their *adera* because of the key role they played in their care: "They say, 'You were there for me while my relatives were not.'" She also described *adera* as a potential burden: "Here, you are not afraid of death, but you are afraid of the *adera*. It is very heavy, and it is not good for your mind." Rahel and Eskinder each spoke of accepting the *adera* of care recipients, by securing care for their children or selling a possession to settle a debt, out of a sense of obligation and a desire to ease their worries.

Many CHWs also spoke about providing patients with better deaths by carefully preparing their corpses for burial, a salient experience for CHWs because of the emotional and physical difficulties involved. Several CHWs spoke about

adapting to these difficulties, narrating how they became fearlessly able to prepare the bodies of patients who had died, through either repetition or specific
experiences. Eskinder said that when he first became a volunteer CHW, he used
to have "the fear," but over time, "I got used to it, because I see dead people every
day." Rahel said she got over her fear thanks to her first experience with a dead
patient, which occurred in a hospital ward: "It is better if I learn than this woman's body gets spoiled," she told herself. With another volunteer and the nurses,
she prepared the woman's body. "After that, I was no longer afraid." Tsehay
recounted a specific experience in which she was called to attend to the death of
a woman in her neighborhood. After several difficult hours of the woman's soul
"leaving her and coming back again," she finally died. "We prepared her body
and put her into the coffin. After this, I stopped fearing death. An experience
like that makes you brave."

Yet other CHWs suggested that at least some encounters with death were
experiences that they could not simply "get over." Asayech narrated a specific
experience in which she was called to attend to the death of a patient who lived
in her neighborhood:

> The woman's bed was soiled. Her mouth was open, and her body had
> sores. I saw all of that when we were washing her body. And though men
> usually put the body in a coffin, I did that. Let alone the things that you
> touch, the smell will hurt you deep inside. If you see the work deeply, it is
> difficult. It is not simple.

Tsehay described how her first encounter with a dead patient led to a great deal
of embodied stress: "My body was shaking the whole day. For several weeks, I
was waking up in the middle of the night and couldn't sleep. I lost weight." After
11 months of experience as a CHW, she admitted that she was still in the process
of adapting to the emotional challenges presented by caregiving.

Underlying this capacity to confront the challenges posed by death, and in
some cases to provide patients with better deaths, were ideas about God's non-
discriminatory love, a belief that God gives life and death to all humans equally,
and desires to please God. Eskinder connected the *wegen* idiom to his willingness
to attend to the deaths of patients: "When people are convulsing, gasping, and
falling from bed," he said, "we [CHWs] correct it. We pick them up and prepare
them. We wash them and we bury them. Why? They are *wegen*."

Providing Good Care and Seeking
Socioeconomic Progress

While confronting death may have been one of the more dramatic features of
CHWs' work, relationships with living patients were also a source of stress. This
was because many patients and their families were struggling to find employment

and secure access to food and other basic necessities. The CHWs could not help but closely witness their patients' frustrating experiences of chronic unemployment and food insecurity.

In 2008, the World Food Programme began to require that people living with HIV/AIDS have a body mass index below 18.5 (kg/m^2) to be eligible for food aid, exacerbating the problems experienced by patients. Alemayehu visited a dozen patients, which was roughly average among his volunteer peers. He told me, "When I wake up in the middle of the night, I think about my patients. I think about what they tell me in the day about their problems. . . . Yesterday there was one woman who was lying on the ground. She had nothing to eat. The [antiretroviral] medication was there in her room, unused. Now they get food aid only when their body mass index is less than 18.5 $[kg/m^2]$. And I can see these things . . . So these things worry me."

The witnessing and distress Alemayehu describes were mentioned by many volunteers, including Markos, who said, "Now I am beginning to feel awful. Almost half of [the patients who were previously receiving food aid] have been dropped from the food aid program. They are just angry. Now you will go to a care recipient's home and all you see is crying. And they start to cry when they see you." The emotion that these volunteers described was not just a feeling of pity or disappointment with the apparent capriciousness of donor aid but also a shameful feeling of not being able to provide patients with the material support they needed. They could listen and offer their patients advice, mediate their family conflicts, remind them when to take their pills, explain to them urban gardening and micro-enterprise entrepreneurship, and link them with erratic NGO and government sources of material support. But they were powerless to give them what they truly wanted: some kind of formal, secure employment with a decent wage. CHWs often gave patients some of their own food; on a few occasions, they even gave money to patients. But such transfers were on a very small scale, for the majority of CHWs also came from food-insecure households.

It was further emotionally distressing when volunteers became the target of patients' frustrations. This could come in the form of challenging questions posed by patients. For example, Alemayehu said that some care recipients would ask him, "With what can I take the medication? My insides are burning with medication only" (cf. Kalofonos 2010). Asayech explained,

> It seems that some patients don't want you as a volunteer caregiver because there is no benefit they receive from you. . . . When they meet us on the road, they think there is food or something in the backpacks we carry. But the backpack contains our first aid materials. "What do you carry in this bag?" they ask. "Why do you have it if it is empty?"

Beyond challenging questions like these, volunteers faced insults and even physical abuse. As Fikirte explained, "There are many patients, and sometimes they will insult you. Forget the insults, but they might [physically harm] you." Serving as a volunteer CHW was indeed "a sacrifice," Fikirte said. She also identified it as "a risk—when the patients' stomachs are empty."

Unemployment and food insecurity often generate psychological distress by introducing uncertainty and shame into peoples' lives and eroding meaningful forms of reciprocity (Amare 2010; Hadley et al. 2012). The experiences of the volunteers and patients I encountered in Addis Ababa provide unique support for this broad understanding of how unemployment and food insecurity put strain on relationships and cause distress. Much of the time, CHWs and patients enjoyed solid, positive relationships of mutual respect and intimacy. But it was also common for CHWs and the people they were meant to serve to interact and talk about each other in more antagonistic ways. Strife—instead of solidarity—between CHWs and patients in the context of ART was clearly driven largely by unemployment and food insecurity. These key features of the local ecology, furthermore, reflect a broad pattern across various global health interventions that make sophisticated drugs and medical technologies more accessible than basics like food and jobs (Biehl 2007; Han 2013; Kalofonos 2010).

The three waves of surveys that my research assistants and I conducted with a random sample of 110 volunteer CHWs, which included a checklist of psychological distress symptoms, provided one way to both describe and quantify their distress. The term "common mental disorder" or CMD denotes a non-specific category of mental or psychological distress that can include somatic and psychological symptoms of depression and/or anxiety. The surveys we conducted showed that 37% of the sample reported experiencing eight or more CMD symptoms in the 30 days prior to the first wave of data collection, eight or more symptoms being an optimal cutoff for a probable diagnosis of a common mental disorder among urban Amharic speakers (Zilber et al. 2004).[4] The most commonly reported symptoms over the three rounds of data collection were frequent headaches, trouble sleeping, feeling tense or worried, poor appetite, poor digestion, feeling unhappy, losing interest in things, having uncomfortable feelings in one's stomach, being easily tired, experiencing interference or trouble thinking, and easily getting angry at others.

The common experience of these symptoms and others may have been related to the feeling of not being able to help patients who were unemployed and food insecure. In addition, a great deal of the distress experienced by CHWs in Addis Ababa was because of their own experiences of unemployment and food insecurity. A growing body of qualitative and quantitative research shows that mental disorders that are commonly experienced by people living in poverty, such as depression and anxiety, are tightly linked to uncertainty, shame, and strain on relationships due to being unemployed, insecurely employed, and food insecure (Cole and Tembo 2011; Hadley and Crooks 2012; Hadley and Patil 2006; Han 2013; Lund et al. 2010; Nanama and Frongillo 2012; Patel et al. 1999; on common mental disorders or CMD and their relationship to poverty and food insecurity in Ethiopia, see Hadley et al. 2012; Hadley et al. 2008; Hanlon et al. 2009; 2010; Maes et al. 2010a). Over half of the CHWs we randomly surveyed in Addis Ababa experienced moderate to severe food insecurity, which was closely associated with very low household per capita income levels (well under 1 USD per day). The survey data further confirmed a strong, dose-dependent relationship between food insecurity and psychological distress: the more severe the level of household food insecurity reported by the CHW, the more distress symptoms she or he reported experiencing in the previous four weeks (p < 0.0001).[5]

Survey data only tell us so much, however. In-depth interviews and observations of daily life offer an opportunity to develop a richer understanding of CHWs' experiences of food insecurity, unemployment, and psychological distress.

There Is No Happiness with Me

At 33 years of age, Alemayehu had not yet married and still lived with his mother, an aging homemaker, and his father, a retired soldier. Tall like his son but not as lanky, Alemayehu's father began a career in the military during the latter years of Haile Selassie's reign and continued as a soldier through the regime change that put the Derg into power. "I was a soldier, and who toppled Haile-Selassie?" asked Alemayehu's father rhetorically. "It was the soldiers." Multiple battles lay in store for the Derg regime, battles that took Alemayehu's father far from Addis, his wife, and their young children. Eventually, Alemayehu's father was shot and wounded in his hand and neck, and he finally returned to Addis Ababa. He retired from the military with the fall of the Derg in 1991 and became a house guard in a middle-class neighborhood. This kind of low-paid work was about all that was available to a man with his set of skills and injuries. Now in his 70s, Alemayehu's father no longer worked.

Two years after his father retired from the military, Alemayehu dropped out of secondary school. He was not bored with the classroom. Rather, he recognized the economic hardships now facing his parents, and he wanted to contribute to the family income. His parents found it difficult to dissuade him from doing so. So Alemayehu began working. First, he worked in a cotton-processing factory. He also tried out day labor in Addis' construction industry. The pay was low, however, and to Alemayehu, these jobs seemed menial and—perhaps more importantly—meaningless. Unfortunately, there were not many good job options that would both support his family and provide for a more meaningful existence.

It was around 2004 when Alemayehu decided to become a volunteer CHW. At that time, the vast majority of people in need of ART still did not have access. "I was watching many people dying from this disease (HIV/AIDS), and I also saw when they were insulted and discriminated." Initially, his parents had reservations. They said to him, " 'With this work, you will spend your time without getting any *santeem* (i.e., money) and come home with something else: disease.' " Alemayehu convinced them to be supportive by "counseling them slowly." "I told them my interest was not *santeem*. I said, for example, 'what if your daughter was caught by HIV, and there was nobody to help her? What would you feel?' "

He volunteered with the Medhin NGO for 18 months, completing his term of service in 2006. During the time he was there, his parents grew supportive of his volunteer efforts, even though it was unsalaried work. When he subsequently joined up to volunteer *again*, this time with the Hiwot NGO, his parents even joked, asking, " 'Did you get addicted to this?' " When I interviewed Alemayehu's father, he unequivocally supported his son's efforts as a volunteer, explaining that he recognized HIV/AIDS as a major problem that demanded such efforts.

> HIV/AIDS is attacking and killing, and people have been dying. When HIV entered this country, it was presented like a beast or a wildfire. Yet if you go out in the night, you see most young people just messing around, disregarding this disease. Finally, some of them are volunteering to help, saying, "This is just a disease, and we don't have to be disgusted by it."

Alemayehu's parents' house had a nice garden full of flowers and vegetables. The living room had enough space for a dining table and couches, in addition to a TV and DVD player. When I visited, Alemayehu's mother served a big breakfast of fresh injera, shiro, scrambled eggs, Coca-Cola, and tea. She was laying on the hospitality. The comfortable home and generous meal, however, disguised a more complex situation: a generous family more fortunate than many others, but stretched thin by skyrocketing food prices, illness, and the difficulties of international labor migration.

The house in which Alemayehu and his parents lived was bought several years back by Alemayehu's older sister and her husband. They now lived in another neighborhood about 15 minutes away, in a government-owned kebele house that used to belong to Alemayehu's parents. When Alemayehu's sister was about to give birth to her second child, her husband had become bedridden with hypertension and paralysis in his leg. It was not possible for her to work and care for her husband and children at the same time, so the family decided that the kids would stay with their grandparents and Alemayehu. The small kebele house, however, could not hold all of them. So Alemayehu's sister and her husband moved into the kebele house, and Alemayehu, his parents, and his sister's two children took up residence in the bigger, newer house.

In Addis Ababa, poor people can become eligible to rent houses from the kebele (the local government administration) for a very low monthly rate. The rent his sister paid for the kebele house was less than two birr per month. Yet Alemayehu's sister had many other expenses besides rent. With her job, she was just barely able to provide food and other basic necessities for her parents, her husband and kids, and Alemayehu. Alemayehu's father pitched in about 15 USD per month, the meager monthly pension he received in return for his service in the military. In addition, Alemayehu's two younger sisters had recently migrated to work as domestic servants in the Middle East. They would send about 1000 birr (~100 USD) to their parents every few months, particularly on holidays, so that the family could enjoy a good meal.

While Alemayehu's sisters had married, moved out, and begun to support their parents and their own families in various ways, Alemayehu remained unmarried and dependent on his parents and sisters. As a volunteer for Medhin in 2005 and 2006, Alemayehu had received a monthly allotment of wheat and cooking oil. "I would bring the wheat home and give it to my family one month," Alemayehu explained, "and sell it the next month and keep the money for myself." He never sold the oil, however, because it made more sense to give it to his mother to use at home. He affirmed that the food aid was considered *demoz*, which is Amharic for a salary, but also translates into "blood and sweat." " 'This is your *demoz*,' " his supervisors at Medhin would tell the volunteers. Eskinder, who also volunteered for Medhin, confirmed that the supervisors and volunteers considered the food aid package a kind of salary. Now that Alemayehu was volunteering for Hiwot, he did not receive food as remuneration, partly because international food aid supplies had dwindled as a result of the 2007–2008 food crisis. He only received five USD per month to offset transportation and telecommunication costs.

When we met for another of our interviews, the white T-shirt Alemayehu had received at the 2008 Ethiopian Volunteers Day event was visible beneath his collared shirt. He joked that it was a bit rushed because of the late-arriving invited guests. But once things got started, he said, "The mood of the celebration was beautiful. It made me so happy that everyone gathered together and the volunteers were recognized." Alemayehu insisted that he did not get anything material, but affirmed that volunteering made him happy. "I also get spiritual satisfaction," he continued, "thinking that I might get something good from God." He saw volunteering "as an obligation, as citizenship." It was also clear that his parents continued to support and encourage his volunteer efforts. Even though he was not materially supporting the family, they believed he was meeting an important need of their country, and it resonated with their civic and religious values.

Nevertheless, Alemayehu reported 17 CMD symptoms at both the first and second survey waves. During one of our later interviews in 2008, Alemayehu explained in his own words what was behind the high level of psychological distress he reported. He said that he had lately been experiencing a "sleeping problem." "Now at least three times in a week, I wake up in the middle of the night." As we saw earlier, Alemayehu would think about his struggling patients when he awoke in the night. During our interview, he added that he often thought about his family, specifically "about supporting them with a good job." Whenever he had these bouts of insomnia, he explained, he would feel tired and dejected all day. "There is no happiness with me. When I can't sleep, I will feel depressed all day."

Markos, the 19-year-old male volunteer whose family had taken in a young woman living with HIV/AIDS, served alongside Alemayehu and lived in the same neighborhood. He provided his own perspective on Alemayehu's situation. "At his age, Alemayehu should build a house and support his mother. Instead of supporting her, she is supporting him, because he doesn't have any income. He just works with us as a volunteer." When I asked Alemayehu how people can avoid anxiety and sadness, he replied,

> I think that if you work, then the pressure of life can decrease and you will not be worried by anything. And if you do good things for human beings, then you will not worry. You will get mental rest (*aymero ereft*).

Alemayehu was far from alone in his socioeconomic experiences and expectations. Eskinder reported a high level of CMD symptoms in survey waves two and three (11 and 10 symptoms, respectively). He also had no substantial source of income and depended on the Medhin NGO, neighbors, and extended family for food. During the time we spoke, he received some support from his brothers and sisters and their spouses. His sister would sometimes come and wash clothes. His brother-in-law would sometimes take him out to eat with his friends. His sister-in-law would send him soap. Having little to give in return, Eskinder would sometimes sit for their children. He contrasted his present situation from his previous experiences, after his father died and before he himself became sick, when he was able to *work*, and thus furnish a small shack house and live in mutual support with his mother and siblings. During one of our interviews, Eskinder further explained his stress:

> This chair is not edible. The television and these cupboards are not edible . . . I got all these things previously when I was healthy—when I was working . . . I am stressed because I am not working, not because the virus is inside me. I also worry about how long I will rely on the support of others. I have to work and I have to change myself . . . What shall I do working at something [i.e., volunteering as a CHW] that has no prospects for improvement . . . How can a woman accept me as a husband?

Like half of the survey sample, Alemayehu and Eskinder reported moderate to severe food insecurity. For many CHWs in the sample—HIV-positive and negative—food insecurity pointed to their underlying unemployment. Even if they were not interested in getting *santeem* when they began volunteering as CHWs, after a couple years of relentless inflation and chronic unemployment, they felt the stress of not being able to provide for themselves, their parents, and their families and friends.

I Brought Them into a Life They Don't Want

Rahel, divorced, was the mother of grade school-aged twins. She reported in the survey that she was 28 years old, but she looked significantly older. In addition to her prominent cheekbones and broad smile, one could not help but notice her tattooed gums, a sign of her origins in rural northern Ethiopia. In fact, Rahel's mother raised her and her siblings outside the northern city of Gondar. Thus Rahel is one example of the important demographic phenomenon of migration within Ethiopia, from the countryside or smaller towns to the big city. Rahel talked about her childhood with enthusiastic detail. She had loved music and idolized Yirga Dubale, a famous poet and musician who hailed from Gondar. Yet her early life was not easy. Her father died when she was too young to know him, and she described her family as very poor. "We were five with my mother, and we took turns sleeping on the *medeb* (a bed made of mud)."

Rahel discontinued school at grade four. She began working as a house servant to support her mother, who struggled to provide food for the family by working a small plot of land and selling small amounts of produce in the local market. After their mother died, Rahel and her sister Hannah decided to migrate together to Addis Ababa. At first, Rahel worked as a house servant. At times, she sold vegetables on the streets of the slum where she lived. By the time of my research, she was unemployed and living with her twin children, a brother and sister named Robel and Samrawit, in the Gebre Kristos neighborhood next to ALERT.

Several years back, Rahel had also begun to provide independent, voluntary care for sick people in her neighborhood. She explained,

> In all my life, what makes me happiest is to see patients being human—being able to work and feed themselves. When I see others doing good things, I say, "I wish to be like this person. Why doesn't God make me the same? This is work that God likes."

Thus Rahel expressed a sort of spiritual envy, much like Alemnesh had, in order to explain her interest in becoming a CHW. She also suggested that she might need the same kind of help and support someday, affirming the locally common anti-stigmatization message that "HIV/AIDS will knock at each of our doors." Rahel had internalized at a young age the conviction that it was good to serve others. Her mother told her, "'You will be blessed if you help your neighbors. Being good is good. When I die and can no longer support you, you will encounter good things in return.'" Rahel tried to live according to this bit of wisdom. Helping others was thus a way to survive amid poverty, illness, and other poverty-related troubles. She said she aimed to pass this on to her children, recognizing that she could "die tomorrow or the day after tomorrow." She hoped that her good deeds would continue to bear fruit for her children in the event of her death.

Eventually, Rahel claimed, Medhin learned of her helpful reputation and invited her to volunteer for the NGO. "They said [about me], 'She will be qualified.'" Volunteering as a CHW with Medhin soon led to another opportunity:

foster parenting. At the time of my research, in addition to Robel and Samrawit, Rahel was raising a young boy named Daniel, an AIDS orphan. Sister Nebyat, Medhin's HBC coordinator, had asked Rahel to adopt the boy. "They offered me Daniel, saying, 'We trust that she will raise him properly.'" Rahel agreed to take him in, despite her lack of a partner and her poverty, saying,

> Nobody accepts another child with this cost of living. It is difficult even to hold your own children. But I do it out of kindness. I treat Daniel like my child. I don't have anything, but if I did, I would give it to them equally.

She may also have been convinced to take in Daniel by the fact that, in return, she would receive modest food support from the World Food Programme, via Medhin. With the donated wheat, cooking oil, and beans, she might be able to feed Daniel and perhaps also nourish Robel and Samrawit.

According to Rahel, however, the food support was not enough to cover her family's needs. With the high and rapidly increasing cost of living in Addis Ababa in 2007 and 2008, she was always in need of money and basic necessities. Her benevolent landlord kept her rent low, and her neighbors provided her with occasional handouts, partly because they appreciated her work as a volunteer caregiver in the neighborhood. But she constantly worried about feeding her children. She could not afford even the few birr each month it would take to join a small *iddir*, and she barely managed to wash the children's clothes once a week with a one-birr bar of soap. In our surveys, Rahel also reported severe food insecurity.

Rahel dutifully attempted to keep all of her children clean, disciplined, fed, and in school. "I brought them into a life they don't want. As long as I brought them here, I should face it all and raise them properly. It's my responsibility." She was also thankful that her landlord and neighbors were helpful, that Medhin provided the monthly food aid, and that God had given her children who were "not like children that bother a [poor] family." Most children, Rahel explained, come home from school and ask their parents for supper (*mekses*). "But my children put down their bags and study. If I don't have anything for them to eat, they simply go to sleep." Thus she managed through great hardship to continue serving as a volunteer CHW and raising her children, focusing on her blessings. But the future was uncertain, and Rahel was very much troubled by her chronic dependency on others and inability to feed her children. In addition to severe food insecurity, Rahel reported several symptoms of psychological distress, and during the first survey wave, she reported that she even sometimes thought of taking her own life. In a subsequent interview, she reassured me that she was not repeatedly or seriously thinking about killing herself, but had contemplated suicide a few weeks before the first survey wave, on a day like any other when she had no food to feed her children.[6]

My Sadness Comes When I Have a Fight with My Husband

We briefly met Asayech in the previous chapter: she used to work in a factory before she became sick with TB and AIDS; now at 32 years old, she was raising a young child with her husband, who supported the family with a low-level position at an industrial firm located just outside Addis Ababa. By the time she began volunteering for Hiwot in early 2008, Asayech had been unemployed and following her ARV regimen for about three years.

Asayech narrated her childhood and adolescent years with a mix of tears, regret, gratitude, and acceptance. Her father died when she was a child. And her mother "didn't have good love" for Asayech. "Her friends would tell her, 'An only child is like a jewel,'" Asayech recalled. "But she didn't see me like an only child. I think she simply had to live her own life."

In grade eight, Asayech found herself doing housework every morning before school and returning to housework as soon as she got home. This may sound like a fairly normal life to some Ethiopian girls, but according to Asayech, her mother was an extremely strict, unloving, and "powerful" (*haylegna*) tyrant. When her friends would come to the house, her mother would insult them and send them away. Asayech recalled that when she was in high school, there were times that she would leave for school crying. And when she returned to her neighborhood and saw her house from a distance, she said her "face would change" as she would contemplate what awaited her at home. "I finally gave up hope, and I left our house." The parents of one of her close friends took Asayech in and treated her like one of their own. "They said, 'She can live here with us, eating what we eat.' Thanks to God, people loved me." She lived with them until she completed secondary school.

At that point, Asayech's narrative turned from sadness at not having been cared for by her own mom and gratitude toward the family who took her in, to regrets about not taking her education seriously and not making a greater effort to find good work. "I could have taken night classes and worked during the day. But I didn't think like that. I didn't do good things for myself." Looking back, she imagined that she could have built a "foundation" for a better life if she had done "good things" and followed her education. "Instead, I was just playing and relaxing. I was crazy and spoiled." She did work a little, washing dishes and cleaning cafes and hotels. But according to her, she wasted her time and money hanging out with friends, drinking tea in cafes, and relaxing. "We treated those times as one good part of our life. But I wasted my time." Asayech said she now considered herself an example for other young women of what *not* to do. "I tell others that if you do not get educated, you will not reach a good level. You will stay in your house, chopping onions and tomatoes."

Asayech thought of herself as a good mother, which was especially important to her given her relationship with her own mother. "Sometimes when life makes you bitter (*mirir*), you blame your child. I do not." Like Rahel, Asayech said,

"I am the one who brought him into this world—with God's power. My child should not suffer like me. And if I can, I will be happy to help him have a better life." But Asayech was unemployed. For Asayech, being unemployed meant sitting idle and "thinking too much" about her illness, being overly dependent on her husband, and being unable to give her son a better life. Asayech was either unable to find work or hesitant to work in a setting in which her HIV status might invite discrimination. She said that after she lost her factory job, she was not able to do any job out of fear that she would get sick at work.

Volunteering as a CHW was thus partly beneficial to Asayech, because it allowed her to be active. Asayech also had her friends and neighbors to thank for her ability to volunteer. They would look after her child when she left to visit patients and attend meetings. Now that she was volunteering, she said she often forgot that she even had HIV and felt peaceful on the inside.

> If you have your own work, you never think that you have a disease. [But] if you are getting aid [from an organization], you always think of your pain . . . [and] if you are just sitting in the house, waiting for what the [aid] organization is doing for you, it is very difficult . . . This [volunteer caregiving] gets me to go out, rather than sit idle at home. It gives me hope.

Asayech's sense of well-being was also connected to her hope for a better future and her faith in the divine intervention of God. She expressed her hope and expectation that in the future, "God will help me in some way."

In surveys, Asayech never reported more than three psychological distress symptoms. When we asked if she had ever felt a long sadness, a depression, during our in-depth interviews, however, Asayech responded by narrating how her occasional periods of sadness resulted from being unemployed and HIV-positive, which interacted and generated marital strife with her HIV-negative husband.

> My sadness comes when I have a fight with my husband at home . . . When I am thinking about my sickness, I am not comfortable to have sexual contact. I will be happy if he doesn't even touch my clothes. Sometimes he plans to have sexual contact, and I may not be ready, and we simply fight because of that. We even say bad things to each other. That disturbs me for some time.

It was not just sex that generated strife in their relationship. Recently, their tension was related to the fact that Asayech was working but not getting paid.

> Sometimes my husband says, "I can give you what I have, but you should also work." At first, he was supportive of my volunteering. But now, he says, "Volunteering does not pay anything, and it is tiresome . . . Why don't you find another job?" . . . I am ready to do any job that God

gives me . . . If I get a chance to be employed in an organization [i.e., an NGO, government office, or private company], I can do that. I want to live, working. If I had my own job with good income, I would have freedom.

Asayech, like many of her peers, was thus caught in an unpaid position that relieved some of the distress of sitting idle while failing to deliver a living wage. A living wage was important to her because it would help provide for her child, repay her helpful neighbors and friends for all they had done, and perhaps grant her greater freedom within her marriage.

I Didn't Do Anything for Myself

Alemnesh, recall, was 26 years old, unmarried, and living with her parents after working in Saudi Arabia and Kuwait. Unlike the majority of volunteers in the survey sample, she did not report household food insecurity. This was apparently because her father, an ex-soldier who served during the military Marxist regime (the *Derg*), currently worked, while her two siblings held professional jobs in Addis Ababa.

Nevertheless, Alemnesh reported a high level of psychological distress symptoms in the first and second survey waves (11 symptoms and 7 symptoms, respectively). The satisfaction Alemnesh experienced through volunteering was evident. But so was her frustration with the lack of modestly paid jobs in Addis Ababa. "Let alone 150 [US] dollars, there is no job in Addis Ababa that will pay you 50 dollars per month!" She had worked abroad as a lowly house servant and had suffered untold hardships for years to raise her brothers and family to a higher level. Now back in Addis Ababa, she had not yet attained the life she envisioned for herself. Alemnesh described her understanding of a "good life" as one that combines "money with love and peace." A good job for Alemnesh would translate into a good life that involved being "a respected person," fulfilling her family's needs, and "feeding and clothing the poor." "If God gives me wealth, I will be happy if I can do such things. My dream is like that."

The Social, Economic, and Emotional Impacts of Unpaid Community Health Work

Developing trust and intimacy with stigmatized, non-kin care recipients, reconciling social conflicts, and providing care recipients with "better" deaths: each of these capacities draws on a constellation of moral values, desires, abilities, and positive emotions encouraged by CHWs' families and religious teachings. These capacities are important yet poorly understood parts of the social and emotional resilience and dignity that exist within contexts of intense poverty, competition, and violence (Hussen et al. 2014; Klaits 2010). Supervisors and officials in Addis Ababa valued these empathic and intimate forms of care, as well as the drug adherence support and data collection in which CHWs engaged, and connected their work as empathic caregivers to sentiments of sacrifice and satisfaction.

We have seen that CHWs in Addis Ababa often concurred that their unpaid work pleased God, others, and themselves. Alemnesh once told me about a patient for whom she had cared. "When she was told that she had HIV, she was crying on the road. But now she accepts it, and she is peaceful. She is changed a lot now. When you see that, you will become happy. That is *aymero irkata* (mental satisfaction)." Serving as a CHW was particularly psychosocially therapeutic for HIV-positive volunteers such as Eskinder and Asayech, because it allowed them to be socially active and efficacious in a space where their positive HIV serostatus did not pose a problem. Eskinder also reflected that by reconciling people, he and his fellow CHWs created happiness and peace for the conflicting parties, pleased God, and generated emotional and spiritual benefits for themselves.

CHWs' statements about deriving happiness and spiritual satisfaction, however, should not necessarily reinforce the idea that these are sufficient rewards for doing what they do. Clearly, the difficult work of being an unpaid CHW in Addis took its toll. Seeing patients suffer without any clear path to economic security, bearing the brunt of patients' frustrations, and confronting death and loss were inevitable parts of the job. In addition, CHWs struggled with their own experiences of chronic and at times severe food insecurity, which were closely correlated to their levels of psychological distress, and driven by their lack of income and in turn, employment.

For these CHWs, being unemployed meant more than food insecurity and psychological distress. Anthropologist Daniel Mains argues that work is valued by young men in urban Ethiopia not only for the money it pays. What a job does to one's relationships and social position is just as important, if not more. Working in different occupations, as well remaining unemployed, places men in particular relationships to others, and these relationships have an important impact on psychological distress and well-being. Unemployment and many forms of low-level work are stressful because they translate into an inability to become adults, get married, and gain the respect that comes with reciprocating material support with family members and others (Mains 2012). Thus young urban men are not satisfied with achieving food security through food aid or work that is not respected by their families and peers—they want good, respectable jobs in order to achieve food security and much more. The narratives we have seen in this chapter suggest that this applies to men and women serving as CHWs in urban Ethiopia. Like Alemayehu and Eskinder, the women I encountered among the ranks of CHWs also wanted to be able to financially support their families and other community members in need, but were confronted with a frustrating lack of work options in Addis Ababa. Being a volunteer CHW in

Addis Ababa allowed women and men to form solid relationships with others, particularly patients with a stigmatized illness, and in some instances pleased their parents and family members, which had positive and negative impacts on their mental health. But the CHW role did not position these women and men within their ideal social networks, partly due to the fact that it was unpaid. From their perspectives, good jobs would bring positive socioeconomic change, a repositioning from dependence on others to supporting others. For instance, Eskinder used the Amharic term *lewt* ("change") to describe both the process of furnishing his house in the past and improving his life in the future.[7] Similarly, others said employment would help them reach a "good level" or experience greater freedom.

As anthropologist Clara Han (2013) and others have shown, massive numbers of global subjects have little choice but to toil through trajectories of unemployment and unstable, insecure employment. It is precarious, uncertain living: sometimes individuals and families get by, sometimes they slip behind. Sometimes they maintain hope for a better future, often they fear what may come next. It is no surprise that many in these situations experience high levels of depression and anxiety symptoms. CHWs are no exception, despite their abilities to engage in intimate work that is sometimes emotionally rewarding. The various experiences of distress voiced by CHWs are clearly important aspects of their lives and of their participation in the moral and political economies of today's global health systems. These experiences demand greater attention, lest they be obscured by normative sentiments of sacrifice and satisfaction.

Recent documents have addressed how paying CHWs a living wage can be an economic stimulus for their families and communities, and contribute to "broader development" (CHW Investment Case [Dahn et al.] 2015; WHO 2008). This chapter drives home that CHWs have severe economic troubles that could be greatly eased with a living wage and shows how well-paid work can have a multidimensional psychosocial impact, involving the quality of intimate relationships, forms of care that build and mend bridges between close kin and between strangers from diverse backgrounds, experiences of social prestige, and individual and collective experiences of hope. Receiving generous and predictable remuneration for the work they do may thus constitute a powerful mix of emotional, social, and economic therapy—not only for individual CHWs but also for families and communities. While many global health leaders say they recognize this and call for CHW job creation and the improvement of pay levels and benefits, there is still much to be done to answer this call. At the same time, there is and will remain a great need for research that documents the context-specific social, economic, and emotional impacts of CHW job creation and job conditions.

Still, pay levels and job conditions are not the only problems facing CHWs. As many have noted, the underlying problem is that CHWs have too little *control* over their job conditions and other social policies. The following chapter examines this issue more deeply, focusing on how CHWs attempt to take greater control over their economic lives and job conditions, in part through negotiations with their supervisors and directors.

Notes

1. The *wegen* idiom may also help explain our survey finding that close care relationships created links across ethnicity and religion 57% and 29% of the time, respectively. In the first wave of the survey, in February 2008, we asked each respondent to think of their two closest patients and then to answer questions about those patients (e.g., age, gender, ethnicity, and religion). In 8% and 2% of cases, CHWs were unsure of their close patients' ethnic and religious affiliations, respectively.

2. The Amharic term used for approach (noun: *meqqareb*) is related to the adjective close (*qirb*). Since we posed the question in general terms, responses did not always refer to the close relationships that respondents identified during surveys.

3. This narrative was presented in an article in the *Christian Science Monitor* (Halpern 2007), and reprinted on August 12, 2007 in one of Addis Ababa's English-language weekly newspapers (*Fortune*, Volume 8, Number 30).

4. The CMD symptom checklist I used, a locally tailored version of the WHO's Self-Reporting Questionnaire (SRQ), had previously been validated as a tool to screen CMD cases among urban, Amharic-speaking Ethiopians (Zilber et al. 2004). To provide some context for the figure of 37% of CHWs reporting eight or more CMD symptoms, a 20-year-old study using a 20-item version of the SRQ estimated the prevalence of CMD in Addis Ababa at 12% (Kebede et al. 1999). In that study, female gender, older age, less educational attainment, and unemployment were associated with greater risk of CMD. A 2002 study that focused on patients with leprosy who received treatment at ALERT Hospital in Addis Ababa estimated the prevalence of CMD at 52% using the SRQ, suggesting the importance of stigmatization in generating mental distress in this context (Leekassa et al. 2004). A more recent study focusing on postnatal women attending vaccination clinics in Addis Ababa, which employed local psychiatrists' diagnoses, identified CMD in 19% of the subjects (Tesfaye et al. 2010). Unfortunately, it is problematic to compare prevalence estimates across studies, in large part because different analyses use slightly or markedly different ways of identifying probable cases of CMD.

5. Using the severe food insecurity group as the reference, a generalized estimating equation that accounted for the non-independence of data contributed by the same participants at multiple survey rounds demonstrated that moderate food insecurity was associated with fewer distress symptoms (beta = 0.86, $p < 0.01$), mild food insecurity was associated with even fewer symptoms (beta = 1.93, $p < 0.0001$), and food *security* was associated with the fewest symptoms (beta = 4.31, $p < 0.0001$). The data revealed another interesting pattern in which newcomers reported less food insecurity and psychological distress in the face of a worsening ecology of food access. I cautiously interpret this as having to do with response shifts related to new CHWs' changing tendencies to compare their own situations to those of patients who are perceived to be doing worse (Maes et al. 2010a). This underscores the social complexity of experiences of poverty and its associated distresses, and again reflects the capacities that people have for empathizing with those who are worse off and humbling themselves. Yet it shouldn't detract from the other finding that food insecurity and distress were very common and tightly linked over all.

6. After I learned that Rahel had reported suicidal thoughts in the survey, I spoke with my advisor in the Department of Community Health at Addis Ababa University. He said that such thoughts were common among the city's poor and that there was

little that Ethiopia's health system could currently do for people expressing suicidal thoughts and high levels of psychological distress in response to grinding poverty. He suggested that the appropriate thing for me to do was to speak with a high-level staff person at Rahel's organization, about the presence of psychological distress among the organization's CHWs, while maintaining the privacy of each of my research participants and the confidentiality of the data. I then met with Sr. Nebyat, the HBC coordinator at Medhin, and told her that two of her organization's volunteer CHWs had reported suicidal thoughts and that a good percentage of them had reported a high number of psychological distress symptoms. Sr. Nebyat was surprised and concerned about the levels of psychological distress, but she did not take the suicidal thoughts too seriously. She confirmed, as did other people with whom I spoke about suicidal thoughts among the very poor of Addis Ababa, that such thoughts were unfortunately all too common, a response to chronic and at times acute poverty and suffering.

7. This is the same term that young men in Jimma used to talk about their frustrations and hopes for social and economic progress in their lives (Mains 2012).

5

WHERE THERE IS NO LABOR MOVEMENT

At the turn of Addis Ababa's new millennium, tens of thousands of NGO- and government-deployed CHWs were actively serving in communities across Ethiopia. A large proportion of these CHWs faced difficult job conditions and poverty. But there was no CHW association that Eskinder, Alemnesh, Asayech, or any of their peers could have joined to coordinate and advance their various interests. They were certainly not part of any labor movement. Meanwhile, Ethiopian workers in general were and are in weak positions. According to the International Trade Union Confederation (ITUC), Ethiopia has registered numerous trade union rights violations in recent years. The country's Labor Proclamation does not proclaim a right to freedom of association and collective bargaining, and the government can dissolve trade unions that carry out a strike in an essential service (ITUC 2013). Further, after Ethiopia's contested and violent 2005 elections, when the ruling party demonstrated its willingness to kill and imprison political opponents and protestors, citizens have grown fearful of popular protest, and the EPRDF-led government has tightened its grip on journalists and bloggers as well as civil society organizations and trade unions (ITUC 2013). In 2009, the party-controlled legislature passed a law that requires all civil society organizations in the country that receive more than 10% of their budgets from abroad to desist from any work in the arena of civil or human rights advocacy or monitoring, and that provides government authorities open access to their records and their meetings at any time, without warning (Feyissa 2011). NGOs involved in health, education, and other development sectors, including Hiwot and Medhin, have had to adjust to these controversial new rules. Some civil society organizations— for instance, the Ethiopian Women Lawyer's Association (EWLA), one of the most prominent organizations in Ethiopia—have even seen their funds confiscated by the government and have had to shut down or close many offices and branches (Burgess 2013).[1]

Thus in Ethiopia in the early 21st century, major labor associations are beholden to the ruling party. But at least some trades have associations. Even if their existence requires cooperating with the ruling party, they can still serve some of their members' collective interests in social policies and exchanges. For instance, currently the Ethiopian Medical Association (EMA) and the Ethiopian Public Health Association (EPHA) are active, the latter established in 1991 with the rise of the EPRDF.[2] These organizations function to advance some of the interests of their members and to influence health and social policies in Ethiopia. CHWs in Ethiopia do not even have coopted state-level associations of their own or formal representation in the EPHA.[3]

And yet, even if CHWs in Addis Ababa at the turn of Ethiopia's millennium did not have a way to collectively bargain with their NGO supervisors and directors, propose legislation, or hold their own rallies and demonstrations as a labor union or CHW association might, this chapter will show that they still made attempts to communicate their frustrations to their supervisors and take greater control over their own lives. Thus even where there is no CHW labor movement or association—as is likely true in many parts of the world—there are still labor relations. In such contexts, what do CHW interactions with management regarding their job conditions look like and what further insights can we draw from them?

From ceremonies like Ethiopian Volunteers Day to the more mundane processes of recruitment, basic training, and caring for others, this book has examined a series of relationships, interactions, and discourses comprising a moral economy linking CHWs, patients, supervisors, and Ethiopian and international health officials. This final chapter examines another kind of interaction in which CHWs express their desires and frustrations regarding their employment or lack thereof to their supervisors and directors, driving home that CHWs everywhere are political and moral actors who interact with, and often oppose, a hierarchy of managers, bureaucrats, and donors, sometimes in efforts to improve their own job conditions and livelihoods. While labor relations and movements have many context-specific features, there are some commonalities that emerge from a comparative analysis of CHWs in different parts of the world. Both the unique and common features deserve much greater attention from those who seek to plan CHW programs and constructively deal with individual CHWs and CHW collectives. Thus this chapter will examine the experiences of CHWs in Addis Ababa alongside the actions of CHW associations and labor movements in Massachusetts and Pakistan, where CHWs have organized, demonstrated, protested, lobbied, and/or pursued legislation to advance their own collective interests. This analysis offers further insight into the challenges that low-level laborers in the global health industry face and the particular kinds of efforts that CHWs have made to wrestle greater control over their lives amid more powerful actors and structural forces.[4]

How Can I Tell Sister Meheret?

Recall that at the end of 2007, Alemnesh had passed her recruitment interview, in which Sister Meheret repeatedly asked her, "How can you work without compensation?" At the beginning of 2008, she had participated in all of the scripted and practical exercises that took place during her month-long basic training program. A few months into her deployment, Alemnesh also participated in the Ethiopian Volunteers Day event described at the beginning of this book. She stood in that crowded traffic circle, wearing the T-shirt and visor given to her and listening as multiple officials testified to the necessity of volunteerism in combating Ethiopia's poverty and HIV/AIDS epidemic in particular. She heard Sister Tibebe, the Hiwot NGO's director, compare the volunteer CHWs to candles, sacrificing themselves and melting away to give light to others. Meanwhile, she got to work building close ties with her fellow volunteers, with her supervisor, Sister Meheret, and with her patients. Then, in November 2008, Alemnesh learned that her cousin had arranged an entry-level job for her with a company in Dubai. Ten months prior to completing the eighteen-month commitment expected of her, Alemnesh dropped out of the volunteer CHW program.

A few days before her scheduled departure to Dubai from Bole International Airport, Alemnesh and I sat down for our sixth and final interview. She was anxious because she had not yet told Sister Meheret, and she seemed to welcome the chance to rationalize her decision to drop out. She put it like this:

> I joined this [volunteer] work. But if it is God's will that I get some other opportunity, I will not hold myself back. I served eight months, and I am very, very close with the patients, [especially] with the children. And it is difficult [to leave . . .]—but it is life. You have to do something for yourself, too.

Privately, I also asked one of Alemnesh's fellow volunteers, Shewaye, for her impressions of Alemnesh's decision to go abroad. Before Alemnesh told Sister Meheret, she had talked it over with Shewaye, Tsehay, and her fellow volunteer CHWs.

> Alemnesh told us, "I don't want to go." But we encouraged her not to reject the opportunity. Alemnesh's mother raised her with much effort. It is good if she changes [i.e., improves the life of] her mother, as her mother worked hard to raise her. It is good if she changes herself and changes her family, too.

Alemnesh waited until the day before her departure for Dubai to tell Sister Meheret that she was dropping out of the program and leaving Ethiopia. Alemnesh called Sister Meheret on the phone to deliver the news. According to Alemnesh, Sister Meheret replied, " 'What!? You shocked me! I depended on you!' " Alemnesh told Sister Meheret, " 'I can't do anything—this opportunity to go abroad happened without my expectation.'" Sister Meheret then kindly told Alemnesh, "'May God make you successful. May we meet peacefully.'"

Everybody Complained

In late 2008, Eskinder and his fellow volunteers at the Medhin NGO were about to finish their 18 months of service—or "graduate," as the NGO staff termed it. Eskinder was among the few CHWs asked to continue for another term of service. Sister Tsinkenesh, the NGO's director, explained to me that she and her staff wanted to further retain those volunteer CHWs who went "out of their way" to help others. She complained that most of the CHWs did not fully grasp that they were volunteers—they thought of their service like a job or a potential job. Her ideal volunteers would clearly understand their role: to temporarily devote themselves to the goal of saving and improving the lives of others, without any desire to receive material benefits in return, and then move on to find a job on their own. Sister Tsinkenesh called the disconnect between the NGO's expectations and those of the CHWs an "information gap" and said she had been trying to close it through dialogue. She was clearly frustrated by the apparent refusal of the CHWs to see things her way.

In this regard, Eskinder is an interesting case. Asked to stay on for another term of service, he apparently better approximated the ideal volunteer from Sister Tsinkenesh's perspective than most CHWs. Indeed, Eskinder was compassionate and admired by his peers, supervisors, and neighbors for going out of his way to help others. Yet he clearly saw his volunteer service as a potential job, too. Eskinder claimed that if he had income from another job, he would be happy serving on the side as a CHW for free, because "when you go to the hospital and visit patients; when you help them; when you give them food; when they get up and thank you; and when you see them stand up and walk—it makes you happy." But this was not actually an option, given the difficulties in finding decent work. Thus he thought that the NGO had an obligation to provide better remuneration. During one of our interviews, he lamented the monthly cash stipend of 100 birr (about 10 USD) that the NGO now gave its CHWs, after the food aid from the WFP (worth abut 300 birr at the time) was cut off.

> We depended on [the food aid package]. We entered in the first place depending on that. Most of us volunteers were managing our household needs with that food stipend . . . We considered that as a salary (*demoz*). What can I do with 100 birr? How can a woman accept me as a husband? [. . .] The [NGO] supervisors know how much a sack of wheat costs. If they don't increase our stipend, how can we live with this life condition? This is troubling my mind . . . It is not only me, but many of us . . . Many of my sisters [i.e., fellow volunteers] are stressed about it. They say, "What are we going to do?" We don't have any other thing—no salary. When the

stipend was changed, everybody complained. We said, "We will not volunteer if it is like that. Can a person work without eating?" We respected our word [to volunteer for 18 months], and the [NGO] supervisors should respect theirs [i.e., to support the volunteers] . . . They are reducing things; but we are not reducing our love [for the patients].

Unhappy with their economic prospects and with their graduation on the horizon, Eskinder and his sisters asked the Medhin staff to help them obtain low-level, salaried positions at ALERT Hospital—as cleaners, gardeners, or office assistants—upon departing from their volunteer roles. For Eskinder, such work would be physically less demanding than other kinds of work, and at a hospital housing an ARV center of excellence, he could be relatively open about his HIV status without fear of discrimination. Eskinder felt that, at the very least, he and his fellow volunteer CHWs deserved to get recommendations from the NGO director so that they could get a leg up on the competition.

We were saying to the staff, "You can write letters of recommendation to the hospital. We live around the hospital; we were raised around here— why don't we get hired in the hospital and work? We were even giving good service [to patients] in the hospital. We were getting familiar with the doctors, the nurses, the health assistants, and the guards. We know all of them. If you write us letters of recommendation, the people responsible for hiring at ALERT can give us priority."

Sister Tsinkenesh was reluctant to write letters of recommendation, figuring that helping the volunteers get jobs would send the wrong message. From her perspective, constrained as it was by norms in the industry, the correct message was that volunteers should be happy with what they had.

Articulating a "We"

Alemnesh and Eskinder were not willing to sacrifice, experience mental satisfaction, and wait for some better future; they wanted paid jobs and socioeconomic change now. As their narratives demonstrate, these CHWs were not acting alone in seeking the change they wanted. Instead, they articulated a "we"—a collectivity—in addressing and opposing their superiors. For instance, Alemnesh mustered up the confidence to inform her supervisor of her decision to drop out from the program by convening with her co-workers. Her co-workers, in turn, asserted that Alemnesh should have no qualms about pursuing an opportunity for better work that could help her improve her family's socioeconomic status. Eskinder provides an even clearer case of CHWs articulating a "we" within Addis Ababa's ART center of excellence. He repeatedly spoke in the first person plural, narrating how he and his sisters discussed their collective grievances vis-à-vis their NGO supervisors, making known to each other their common desires that the NGO reciprocate the commitments made by the CHWs and maintain a higher level of material support.

Not individually but together with their co-workers, Alemnesh and Eskinder responded to and resisted the discourses and policies of their respective NGOs. Thus in contexts in which formal CHW associations do not exist, CHWs still develop collective opinions on the fairness of their job conditions and become collective forces within a hierarchy of program staff and, ultimately, payers and donors. In a metaphorical sense, these CHWs began to spin their own webs with other co-workers, not only to tie up life-threatening diseases but also to catch the elusive issue of their own unemployment and lack of pay within a globally funded health program. Here we see faint reflections of negotiation and collective bargaining between NGOs and CHWs who lacked any formal, autonomous organization. Articulating a "we" in these ways did not necessarily help them gain much power or leverage—after all, they had a very limited understanding of the transnational hierarchies, norms, and relationships that governed their unpaid positions. These are nevertheless important examples of the kinds of early steps that CHWs make toward organizing their own ranks and forging relationships with allies, and thus convening people with common interests and diverse skills, resources, and connections.

When CHWs in other contexts have sought structural changes and better job conditions, they, too, have started by articulating small collectives, which then led to the formation of official associations and the assembling of allies in diverse positions of power, including professionals in government health agencies and associations, state legislative bodies, and other civil society organizations. The United States provides many examples: in several US states, CHWs have formed autonomous associations as well as national networks and a vibrant section within the American Public Health Association. Mason and colleagues (2010) tell the instructive story of Massachusetts, which began in the mid-1990s when a number of ardent CHWs began to discuss their poor working conditions: low wages, lack of appreciation from other health-system actors, limited training opportunities, and high turnover rates, based in part on the insecure and short-term nature of program grants focused on specific diseases or populations. They then went about establishing ties, first formalizing a collaborative relationship with staff at the Massachusetts Department of Public Health (MDPH). This led to the formation of the Massachusetts Association of Community Health Workers (MACHW) in 2000. MACHW's leadership, which consisted of CHWs as a matter of principle, identified the Massachusetts Public Health Association (MPHA) as another key ally and financial sponsor—one that shared a similar vision of CHW leaders effectively advocating for changes in state policy (Mason et al. 2010: 2212). The partnership between MACHW, MDPH, and MPHA gained further traction in 2003, when the Blue Cross Blue Shield of Massachusetts Foundation began to provide significant funding for CHW-led policy initiatives. MACHW also found an ally within the Massachusetts House of Representatives, a lawmaker and CHW "champion" who sponsored the legislation that MACHW pursued.[5]

With all of these partners, MACHW leaders were successful when they introduced a bill in the 2005–2006 session of the Massachusetts state legislature to require the Massachusetts Department of Public Health to conduct a study of CHWs' activities, distribution, relationship to the health system, and effectiveness in reducing health disparities, the results of which would be used to seek even greater recognition, influence over policy change, employment stability, and wages.[6] Subsequently, in 2009, MACHW and their collaborators drafted and proposed legislation to establish a board of certification for CHWs as a way to strengthen the workforce alongside new and improved training, an issue prioritized after convening a series of meetings with CHWs across the state. MACHW was again successful.[7] Ms. Lisa Renee Holderby-Fox, one of the leaders of MACHW's first legislative initiative, noted to me that MACHW leaders had never written a bill before. Their hope was that proposing legislation would be a way to educate legislators about CHWs in Massachusetts and thereby set the stage for future gains. Yet with the support of others well versed in the workings of the state legislature, MACHW leaders found that writing a bill was not only fairly simple but also a viable way to advance some of their interests. More generally, MACHW's recent successes depended on having "big allies" who "understood who we were and wanted to help us help improve public health" (Holderby-Fox, personal communication, April 2015). The future for MACHW is of course uncertain. But these alliances and recent successes have created motivation and momentum. CHWs in Massachusetts continue to receive strong support from the MDPH and are vocal about CHW needs and contributions to public health, with an aim to further strengthen their role.[8]

The future for the thousands of CHWs who work in *kebeles* and districts across Ethiopia is also uncertain. Currently, the extent to which they can self-organize, develop power, and genuinely negotiate and collaborate with government, NGO, and donor actors seems highly limited. But this chapter demonstrates that CHWs in Ethiopia can and should be expected to make some moves toward becoming collective forces—if small ones—in the future. In fact, recent work in rural Ethiopia suggests that Health Extension Workers have begun to carefully form small groups to petition the government health bureaucracy for work transfers and other changes in their work conditions (Maes et al. 2015). It remains to be seen how government, NGO, and donor officials will encourage, seek to control, and otherwise engage with such action in the future.

Legitimizing Self-Interest

CHWs serving Ethiopia's antiretroviral center of excellence clearly had little power over their job conditions. A basic law of labor relations is that the bargaining power of workers and managers is contingent upon the state of the economy.

In theory, when unemployment levels are low and the economy is strong, workers have more bargaining power. They can quit if they are not happy with their job conditions, with the confidence that they can find a new job. When unemployment is high, on the other hand, workers have a weak hand, and managers can work them harder and pay them less—or nothing. Thus CHWs in Addis Ababa didn't have much power partly because of high unemployment rates. The NGOs that deployed them—and by extension, the donors that funded the NGOs and the public health systems that depended on the NGOs—could simply dismiss them and recruit and train others. The CHWs, furthermore, didn't have any laws protecting them. The only protection they had was a norm that volunteers should work no longer than 18 months—which could be broken (and was) and which did not seem to help them very much anyway. Under these circumstances, the CHWs did what they could, such as seek out work in another country and begin to speak up about their own expectations regarding the NGOs' obligations.

Their power in negotiating better job conditions seemed to be further reduced by the humanitarian ethos that dominated the moral economy. When Alemnesh spoke with me about her impending departure from the program, she emphasized her close engagement with care recipients, especially children. Alemnesh was dropping out, but that did not mean she never became close to her patients or no longer cared about her relationships. Eskinder also made a point to defend himself and his sisters as unselfish people, emphasizing not only their socioeconomic deprivations but also the love and intimate care that they continued to give their patients. Thus both Alemnesh and Eskinder seemed compelled not only to seek better job conditions (within or beyond the NGO) but also to defend their dedication to patients. This, I argue, is partly due to the messages these CHWs faced throughout their trajectories as unpaid workers: about saving lives, improving health, and seeking nothing more than spiritual and mental rewards. Through government- and NGO-sponsored ad campaigns, recruitment interviews, trainings, and ceremonies, these CHWs came to know that they were expected to put their patients' well-being before their own and to desire the mental and spiritual satisfaction that could come from the their work. Sentiments of sacrifice and satisfaction, and the primacy of saving people's lives or offering them health care, are not inherently problematic. They can and perhaps should be used to help build solidarity among CHWs and others, and thus to form more effective alliances seeking social change. But in this case, such sentiments can also contribute to the difficulties facing CHWs in asserting their desires for better lives, giving rise to additional concerns about being labeled as selfish, unhumanitarian, and therefore undeserving of better work conditions by more powerful stakeholders including NGO and government officials. Thus the humanitarian goal to save lives, in conjunction with the disparities in power that existed between CHWs and the officials, legislators, and donors who typically set policy and practice standards, made for a uniquely challenging landscape for CHWs who sought to legitimize their demands and desires.

Efforts among CHWs to avoid labels of selfishness can also be better understood through comparative analysis. Medical anthropologist Svea Closser has examined the ground-level functioning and global context of Pakistan's national contingent of CHWs known as Lady Health Workers (LHWs) (Closser 2010).[9] Drawing on the work of James Scott (1985; 1990), she investigated the "arts of resistance" practiced by CHWs—in other words, CHWs' efforts to resist the directives of their superiors. She observed, for instance, LHWs' small-scale refusals to work, falsifications of recorded data used to monitor immunization campaign quality, and direct confrontations and insubordinations vis-à-vis superiors. Closser suggests that these arts of resistance pose a substantial barrier to major public health goals. She also explains what lies behind the resistance of LHWs in Pakistan: basically, lack of pay, benefits, and respect.[10] It is likely that CHWs in Addis Ababa's ARV center of excellence also engaged in some foot dragging and falsification of data. They also directly confronted their superiors, as we have seen in the cases of Alemnesh and Eskinder. The earlier narratives, however, highlight another kind of CHW resistance that may be just as important for CHW programs and labor relations: resistance to being seen as insufficiently dedicated to patients and public health. Their rhetorical efforts to stress their love and dedication for patients can be seen as a tactic aimed at maximizing their legitimacy and thus their ability to achieve change in and greater control over their lives. Mason et al. (2010) point out that there is an inherent tension between promoting heightened professional status (including job security, better pay, and greater respect) for CHWs, and retaining the very characteristics that make CHWs distinctive and effective: their ties and orientation to the communities they serve. Thus expressions of dedication to patients may be common across various CHW settings because of the humanitarian nature of health industries and systems in many parts of the world today.

Beyond asserting their commitments to patients, how else do CHWs in different contexts go about rhetorically defending their legitimacy and advancing their interests? CHWs in Massachusetts made concerted efforts to convince others that their interests in job security and certification were coupled to their abilities to serve underserved people (Mason et al. 2010). Thus, in pursuing their legislative agenda, the CHWs were careful to emphasize that job losses interrupted "vital relationships between CHWs and the people they serve" (2212) and that the problems facing their workforce "influenced their effectiveness in improving access to care and health outcomes in their communities" (2213). Likewise, Shewaye, Tsehay, Alemnesh, and many of the CHWs with whom I spoke emphasized that their goals of climbing the socioeconomic ladder were actually a means to a pro-social, not just a selfish, end: doing so would allow them to fulfill their desire to help disadvantaged people in their communities as well as meet the needs of their own parents and relatives, who had health problems of their own and insecure access to basic resources and quality health care.

In Pakistan, LHWs have in recent years developed a large CHW labor movement, focused primarily on pay and other regular benefits, and involving public

strikes that have closed train stations, blocked roads, and occupied other prominent public spaces.[11] LHWs have emphasized their inability, because of poverty,
to meet the basic needs of their own children. In interviews, Closser (2015)
heard pleas like, "I have small children. My daughter is three months old . . . I'm
away from the house from 8 to 4 pm. And when my older children come home
from school, who will give them food?" These women said the challenges they
faced in balancing work and their children's well-being would be manageable
if they were making more money. Then they could afford to, for example, hire
someone to watch their children or pay for the extra transport costs needed to
make midday trips home to breastfeed. On the one hand, calling attention to
the suffering of one's children is a common feature of labor and other social
justice movements in many different times, places, and industries. On the other
hand, emphasizing the needs of one's own children may be particularly important for CHWs because of the unique challenges they face in legitimizing their
desires for better pay and better jobs to stakeholders fixated on saving lives and
fighting disease. Thus one way that CHWs advance their interests is by asserting that job security and better pay for themselves translates into higher quality
care for vulnerable people within and beyond their kin networks. Now and in
the future, some CHWs may be increasingly inclined to back up this claim with
evidence.

CHWs in different contexts have also attempted to gain traction by pointing
to the unfairness of being paid less or receiving fewer benefits than other workers in the health system. One of the messages LHWs have attempted to get across
is that it was not fair that they did not receive the promotions or benefits, such
as retirement pensions, enjoyed by other employees of the Ministry of Health
(Closser 2010; 2015). Health Extension Workers in rural Ethiopia claim their
low salaries are unfair, since they work much harder than health officials who
only "sit in offices," yet get paid less (Maes et al. 2015). And in Massachusetts,
MACHW members do not only assert that better pay for CHWs translates into
greater well-being for their communities; they also feel strongly that payment
levels are about fairness in a health system that remunerates other health workers
well above the minimum wage (Lisa Renee Holderby-Fox, personal communication, April 2015).

To advance their interests in securing material improvements in their lives,
CHWs in Addis Ababa also articulated alternative rhetorical relationships between
their work conditions and the divine. Recall that the Medhin NGO's director did
not want to write letters of recommendation to help her crew of CHWs obtain
paid jobs after volunteering. Eskinder was understandably upset about this. In
lamenting her decision, he said, "Sister Kidan looks towards God, right? If she
helped each of us get jobs, it would mean she would get great gratitude from
God. She would also get big thanks from us and our families." Eskinder and his
peers had been encouraged by their superiors to seek spiritual satisfaction and
please God by sacrificing themselves to serve vulnerable patients. Now he was

suggesting that the same superiors ought to seek divine reward through providing for the material well-being of their CHWs and not only patients. Alemnesh also pointed to "God's will" to defend her decision to drop out and take up an opportunity to work in Dubai. CHWs may very well gain mental and spiritual satisfaction, and move closer to God, by lowering themselves to work with the sick and the poor. But God, Alemnesh asserted, may also will them to move up the socioeconomic ladder and out of their current positions, which in Alemnesh's case involved migrating out of Ethiopia to work.

Thus even where there are no CHW labor associations or movements, there are still labor relations, with CHWs in some way rhetorically and collectively defining and defending their interests amid the competing interests and concerns of other, more powerful, actors. CHW labor relations, furthermore, are quickly evolving, as they have been influenced by a multitude of factors, including global economic conditions and the heightened interest in CHWs among many powerful global health institutions. On the one hand, community health workers are similar to workers in any industry, or to peasant farmers, who throughout history have often been dismissed as overly self-interested by capitalists and landlords seeking to de-legitimize their desires (Robertson 2001). On the other hand, the moral and political economies involved in labor relations in a humanitarian industry are distinct from those that exist in other industries, and need to be understood as such.

By comparing CHWs in Ethiopia, Pakistan, and Massachusetts, we see some of the more fundamental features that matter in CHW labor relations no matter the context, including forging collectives, building allies, and defending the legitimacy of CHW interests. We also see that CHW labor relations involve relationships and moral expressions that are context-specific. These evolving relationships and negotiations have major implications for the function of CHW programs and demand to be taken up as objects of study.

CHW Labor Relations and Policy-Relevant Research

The last several years have seen the publication of a rapidly growing number of studies of CHW motivations and behavior. Much of this research adopts what I call a human resources mentality—a research modality that responds primarily to the interests of CHW employers, donors, and policymakers, who tend to see worker retention and productivity as crucial cost-effectiveness issues. In this approach to research, CHWs are treated as individuals with certain motivations and levels of productivity shaped by various financial and nonfinancial incentives and other factors.[12] CHW behaviors thus become technical problems to be solved or managed by experts, through investigating and identifying the most cost-effective mix of incentives and organizational inputs. A dominant theory has circulated among higher-level actors in global public health to explain and guide efforts to shape the motivations and thus productivity and effectiveness of low-level health workers. This theory, adopted from western paradigms in psychology and economics, proposes a fundamental distinction between "intrinsic" and "extrinsic" motivations. Intrinsic motives are said to involve a sense of moral or community duty and sacrifice, aligning with empathy, altruism, and a desire for self-fulfillment through meaningful activities that are personally valued and that generate happiness and satisfaction. Extrinsic motivations are generated from external rewards or goals coming from outside the self: salary or opportunities for promotion, bicycles and umbrellas, and heightened social status and increased knowledge (Glenton et al. 2010; Greenspan et al. 2013; Palazuelos et al. 2013). Global health researchers and practitioners who invoke this theory of motivation often echo a 2001 USAID-commissioned report (Bhattacharyya et al. 2001) recommending the use of a combination of intrinsic and extrinsic motivators for CHWs. Some researchers have warned that extrinsic incentives—such as basic wages or salary—can "crowd out" a CHW's intrinsic motivations, turning her into a self-interested actor who no longer works out of a sense of duty, altruism, or desire for spiritual merit and self-fulfillment, echoing similar claims from CHW employers who are highly concerned with keeping costs down (e.g., Glenton et al. 2010). The research goal is generally to test and identify a cost-effective mix of intrinsic and extrinsic workforce incentives for a given time and place.

An interesting example of this kind of research is a recent study that addressed the relationship between CHW recruitment, incentivization, and productivity in Zambia through a randomized controlled trial (RCT), a methodology widely regarded as a gold standard in evidence-based public health (Ashraf et al. 2015). Conducted by development economists in partnership with the Zambian Ministry of Health, the RCT evaluated the differential impacts of alternative recruitment messages on CHW performance.[13] The results of the trial showed that public recruitment messages emphasizing the career ladder open to CHWs had a causal impact on CHW performance, leading to a community health workforce that held more household visits with intended beneficiaries and that conducted more community mobilization meetings. A comparison group of CHWs, who had been recruited with public messages emphasizing an opportunity to serve others in the community, held fewer community meetings and visited fewer houses. The study's authors suggest that these findings should "allay the concern that offering material rewards for public service delivery jobs displaces applicants with desirable social preferences and ultimately worsens the quality of services provided" (Ashraf et al. 2015: 25). In an online profile of the study, the authors are congratulated for "climbing down from the ivory tower" to "co-produce knowledge" with government health officials about how they can more efficiently and effectively manage community health workforces to improve indicators of population health and health-care coverage.[14]

Though the knowledge generated by this particular RCT and others like it is certainly of value to policy makers and other stakeholders, the cases of Alemnesh and Eskinder illustrate the limitations of research that adopts a human resources mentality and thus leaves out so much that matters to the processes and outcomes of CHW programs. Alemnesh was more than a high-performing CHW and a count for the "drop out" or attrition category, unhappy with her lack of pay and presented with another opportunity. She was also a moral and political actor within a hierarchy of supervisors, NGO and government officials, and international donors and policy makers. She was someone who had a heated recruitment interview with her supervisor-to-be, and a discussion—if a brief one—with her supervisor, as well as with her fellow CHWs, before she left the program. Likewise, Eskinder was more than a high-performing CHW and a count for the "retained" category. He was a person who, together with his fellow sisters, had collectively complained about lack of pay and material support, while "maintaining their love" for their patients. And he, along with his co-workers, listened to Sister Tsinkenesh as she tried to close the "information gap" that she perceived. These kinds of social and political facts are not easily quantifiable and are generally invisible to studies that adopt a human resources mentality. They are nevertheless important to individual CHWs and crucial to the functioning of CHW programs, and need to be understood.

It is almost certain that the near future will see more RCTs and other studies that aim to demonstrate the cost-effectiveness of different interventions aimed at maximizing CHW productivity and retention (Frymus et al. 2013). Pointing out the shortcomings of the Zambia CHW recruitment study, or of any RCT conducted in the context of development and social welfare, should not necessarily lead to a rejection of the RCT methodology and its power to identify policy-relevant causal processes. Though anthropologists have critiqued the rise of RCTs as a methodology considered to offer the hardest of evidence for public health and development policy makers (Adams 2013), it is hard to deny that the findings of such studies are of great interest to policy makers, donors, and payers, and that anthropologists can and should contribute their unique and powerful methodologies to enhance policy-relevant RCTs, particularly ones that test out meaningful and generous improvements in the living and working conditions of CHWs and of economically insecure and struggling people in general. As anthropologist Carolyn Smith-Morris and colleagues (2014) argue, ethnographers who collaborate to conduct "person-centered" and "contextually sensitive" RCTs in the health sector—RCTs that test out interventions that respond to the depth and complexity of poverty, health problems, and quality of life in specific contexts—can generate valuable but often overlooked knowledge concerning (1) the variable maintenance of RCT staff fidelity to principles of generously supporting employment and livelihoods; (2) the mechanisms and process through which RCT staff develop a shared focus—in other words, "the culture behind the RCT"—in order to carry out the RCT; (3) the roles and contributions of charismatic leader-champions, who create enthusiasm and use their influence to support the implementation of complex and novel intervention and experimentation strategies; and (4) the impacts of interventions on social, psychological, and economic variables *that matter to local actors* and which too often get overlooked in favor of variables that matter to payers, donors, and economists (Smith-Morris et al. 2014). If involved as collaborative partners in the process of studying CHW programs, ethnographers can offer crucial insights into the social-ecological workings of policy experiments; help develop better assessments and measures of the various social, psychological, and community health impacts of making CHW jobs more numerous, secure, well remunerated, and genuinely empowering; and help translate evidence into broader policy changes, through convincing governments, donors, and other actors to invest much more in CHWs (e.g., Ingram et al. 2015; Wiggins et al. 2014).

Research into CHW programs and outcomes of course does not have to involve a randomized trial in order to be valuable. As this book has demonstrated, whether or not a CHW program is undergoing a RCT, the outcomes of CHW programs depend upon much more than individual CHWs performing quantifiable tasks in response to a certain set of incentives and recruitment messages. Ethnographic and mixed methods research is needed to illuminate and explain the varied ways in which CHWs now and in the future pursue their desires to improve their own lives and job conditions, shape policies and the practices of other stakeholders, and address what they recognize as unfair and unjust—individually and through processes of collective organization and alliance formation. Ethnographic work will also be valuable if it shows how supervisors, programmers, and donors react to the efforts and attempts of CHWs and their allies to advocate for and pursue their interests. By making known the interests and tactics of CHWs and their hierarchies and webs of stakeholders, ethnographic work can ultimately contribute to the formation of better dialogical processes connecting these varied actors and thus to the establishment of stronger and more effective "therapeutic alliances" (Kohrt and Griffith 2015).

Taking an ethnographic rather than a narrow human resources approach to CHW research can and should also generate self-reflection on the part of all academic and professional researchers, about the ethics of "climbing down from the ivory tower" only to partner with relatively *high*-powered health policy makers and CHW employers. These actors tend to hold themselves accountable primarily to donors, do not necessarily share the interests of CHWs, and often aim to extract the labor of CHWs in more cost-effective ways. By ethnographically studying the entire hierarchy of workers, professionals, and donors—in other words, by "studying up, down, and sideways" (Nader 1972) in CHW programs—and by actively encouraging the participation of CHWs themselves in the entire research process, researchers can help reduce or at least avoid reinforcing problematic inequalities and relationships in the global health industry, between a class of laborers who are subordinated, disciplined, incentivized, directed, supervised, and researched, and a class of policy makers and experts who make key decisions, receive salaries not necessarily determined by cost-effectiveness analyses, and avoid becoming objects of study. Reducing such inequalities can further contribute to the establishment of stronger alliances between CHWs and other stakeholders in global health industry.

Conclusion

Recent pushes to finance expansion of paid CHW positions in sub-Saharan Africa and globally (e.g., Dahn et al. 2015; Earth Institute 2011) give hope for a future with more paid CHW jobs. Yet as I've argued here, there is more to do besides expanding the financial base for CHW investments. In eras of expanded, stagnant, and retrenched funding alike, there is a need for ethnographic work to answer questions about how labor relations and movements play out—in Ethiopia and around the world.

Events in Pakistan and Massachusetts show that, in the 21st century, some CHWs are working toward change in public policies through engaging in protest and pursuing specific legislative changes. Alemnesh and Eskinder were not able to raise their voices and self-advocate on a collective level, like CHWs in other parts of the world. They, like most Ethiopians at the time, were afraid to mobilize publicly for any cause. But their cases show that sometimes, carefully, CHWs in Addis Ababa's ARV center of excellence did form collectives and express their desires for employment and socioeconomic advancement. The comments of Eskinder and Alemenesh reflect that supervisors and health officials in Addis Ababa had encouraged them to feel a sense of commitment to patients, to believe that sacrifice was a central part of the position, and to seek primarily emotional and spiritual rewards for exercising their capacities. These examples thus drive home the challenging moral and political landscape facing CHWs in Ethiopia and many other places around the world where CHW associations and labor movements do not exist.

The efforts of CHWs in Ethiopia, Pakistan, and Massachusetts to achieve change in their job conditions and lives, the moral languages and rhetoric they employ, and the contexts in which they are embedded are obviously very different. What they have in common is that they aim to challenge and change certain policies and norms, in order to improve livelihoods and job conditions. Such changes will presumably have positive impacts on communities and support CHWs in doing their jobs well. These kinds of actions, furthermore, may reflect the potential of CHWs to achieve not only structural changes related to their job conditions but also changes that positively impact other social and ecological determinants of health in their communities. Indeed, it is difficult for CHWs and others to see improving their own livelihoods and ensuring health equity as separate goals.

Ethnographic and mixed methods research can provide a rich understanding of CHW retention, performance, and efforts to change the conditions of their work and lives, and illuminate how CHWs and various actors with higher levels of power interact to shape the functioning of programs and the distribution of responsibility, resources, and accountability in the hierarchies they inhabit. Such research can complement randomized experimental methods and reveal the multiple social, moral, and material considerations that go into worker productivity, retention, attrition, and other outcomes that matter to CHWs themselves. In addition, such research can contribute to a broader wave of methodological and conceptual advancement in global health scholarship and engagement, emerging through the efforts of ethnographers and who study up, down, and across the hierarchies of health systems, interventions, and experimental trials, setting their sights on the social realities of high-level decision makers, of people comprising the target populations of programs and projects, and of the midlevel actors on whom the burden of program implementation lies (Biehl 2011; Farmer 2008).

Notes

1. The relationships between workers, civil society, the state, and international donors in Ethiopia today have evolved markedly since the final years of Haile Selassie's reign. In early 1974, soon before the fall of Haile Selassie, Ethiopian military men seeking better pay and living conditions carried out a series of insubordinations. The aging Emperor gave in to several of their demands. These capitulations by a supposedly infallible and divine Emperor encouraged civilian unrest in Addis Ababa. In February, students demonstrated against a proposed educational reform. Less than a week later, teachers went on strike to oppose the same reform and to gain better pay. Taxi drivers simultaneously filled the streets to protest a 50% increase in fuel prices, a government policy decision precipitated by the influence of OPEC on global oil prices in the early 1970s (Donham 1999: 16). Labor unions then made their contribution: from early March to late May, Addis Ababa and other cities in Ethiopia were jolted by a series of workers' strikes. The unions were focused primarily on economic concerns. During the first quarter of 1974 alone, inflation had risen at a rate of 80% while wages remained stagnant (Donham 1999: 17). According to Ottaway and Ottaway (1978), the labor strikes of 1974 were unprecedented in modern Ethiopia. "For the first time in the empire's history, the normally mild-mannered Labor Confederation managed to organize a general strike that paralyzed all economic activity from March 7 to 9. The success of this action unleashed a wave of wildcat strikes . . . Practically every group from prostitutes to lay priests went out on strike for better wages and working conditions" (Ottaway and Ottaway 1978: 3–4; cited in Donham 1999: 17). The demise of Haile Selassie and the monarchy at the hands of the Derg in 1974 brought forth a new kind of politics. Though the Derg was influenced by class consciousness and Marxist-Leninist ideology, it was also a highly repressive regime that closely controlled the only legal party in the country, the Workers Party of Ethiopia (WPE). The WPE was eventually dissolved with the rise of the EPRDF. As mentioned in an earlier chapter, the EPRDF signed on to structural adjustment programs with the World Bank and IMF. One of the major outcomes, as elsewhere, was the laying off of a large number of government workers (Mains 2012). Of note, however, the EPRDF leadership was critical of structural adjustment policies and attempted to maintain strong state control over the economy and population, according to its "hybrid" style of government known as revolutionary democracy (de Waal 2012; Zenawi 2012). The EPRDF certainly has not repressed labor rights because of some underlying neoliberal ideology; instead, it has repressed labor unions to solidify its

own position as the undisputed champion of Ethiopia's economic, social, and cultural development (Feyissa 2011).

2. Established in 1961 during Haile Selassie's reign, the Ethiopian Medical Association (EMA) eventually came under the control of the Derg. When the EPRDF came to power, the Ministry of Health encouraged doctors in Addis Ababa to reestablish an autonomous association, and thus the EMA lives on today. See http://www.emaethi opia.org/index.php/about-ema/history.

3. There are no CHWs participating in any of the EPHA's committees or councils. There are no signs, furthermore, that the EPHA serves as a conduit for promoting Ethiopian CHWs' interests. See http://www.etpha.org/basic-facts/executive-board-and-staff.html. This is consistent with the historical marginalization of CHWs by health professionals in the medical establishment, a common feature of health system hierarchies in countries around the world (on Ethiopia, see Kloos 1998). As of 2016, CHWs in the Amhara State of Ethiopia have co-founded an association with other primary health care workers. This recent development underlines the call that this book makes for further research into the efforts of CHWs to freely associate, develop leadership, and advocate for policy changes.

4. While comparisons to Pakistan and Massachusetts are instructive, I choose to examine CHWs in these particular localities in part because CHW labor relations and movements in these places have simply been written about. It may be helpful to compare CHW labor relations across contexts that are more similar, as well. Comparative work in this area might also contribute to the forging of links between CHWs in different parts of the world, which could in turn lead to interesting developments in CHW labor movements.

5. The representative is Gloria Fox. Her son, Durell Fox, was an MACHW organizer—thus family ties can be important to CHW movements. In order to fend off any allegations of nepotism, Representative Fox demanded that MACHW leaders work extra hard to ensure the success of their attempts (Lisa Renee Holderby-Fox, personal communication). See http://www.machw.org/index.php?option=com_content&view=article&id=10&Itemid=110.

6. The proposed legislation essentially required the MDPH to develop evidence-based proposals "for building a sustainable program to promote employment of the state's approximately 3000 community health workers" (Mason et al. 2010: 2213–4). This legislation was moving forward in the state legislature at the same time as another important piece of legislation: the landmark Massachusetts health reform bill sometimes referred to as "RomneyCare," after then governor Mitt Romney. To the surprise of MACHW, legislators within the state House decided to incorporate the CHW bill into the larger health reform package, which passed in 2006. The CHW-focused legislation was signed into law as Section 110 of Chapter 58 of the Acts of 2006.

7. The new law would make certification an option for interested CHWs but not a requirement, and thus would avoid excluding any CHWs who would not or could not (due to lack of education, for example) seek certification. In cooperation with MDPH officials and the same House member who championed the 2006 CHW legislation, the bill was introduced in the 2009–2010 session. Although there was no organized opposition to the legislation, the bill required strong advocacy from constituents and legislators to gain attention during a legislative session "dominated by dramatic debates over revenue and budget cutting proposals" (Mason et al. 2010: 2214). MACHW rose to this challenge by keeping its CHW membership informed and engaged throughout the legislative campaign, through postcards, regional meetings, e-mail updates, and Web-based factsheets. More than 100 CHWs and other supporters assembled at MACHW's annual "CHW Day at the State House." According to Mason and colleagues (2010), the collective rally provided legislators and their staff with crucial information about CHWs and impressed upon many the need for

CHW certification. CHWs and other stakeholders also participated in bill hearings and smaller meetings with legislators.

8. MACHW continues to lobby legislators to, for example, allocate funds for public reimbursement of CHWs. MACHW is also pushing for fairer, more equitable wages for CHWs to ensure that payers do not expect CHWs to be satisfied with the minimum wage.

9. Pakistan's Lady Health Worker (LHW) program was founded in 1994, initially to provide primary health care targeting women and children in rural populations. LHWs have at least an eighth grade education and receive a few months of health-specific training. As a government-deployed community health workforce, they are similar in some ways to Ethiopia's HEWs, who are also all women. Since the 1990s, the number of LHWs in Pakistan has grown to over 100,000, targeting a population roughly twice that of Ethiopia. The LHW job description has also evolved to include more and more responsibilities, much like the plethora of preventive, promotive, and curative health "packages" for which HEWs are responsible (Global Health Workforce Alliance 2008b; Haines et al. 2007).

10. Anthropologists who study development and global health interventions are often compelled to look for and explain "resistance" among the intended beneficiaries of programs and the mid-level personnel who carry out programs. Resistance is useful to understand, as it points to power inequalities and other problems inherent in specific programs and in orthodoxies of policy and practice shared by many health-development interventions. Resistance is also compelling because it humanizes people and recognizes their inherent dignity. Resistance is thus an important window into moral economies and micropolitics that both facilitate and hinder certain programs and wider modes of global health and development practice.

11. An LHW who had participated in strikes in Karachi explained to Closser that the strikes were organized by a national committee and attended by LHWs, their children, and other family members, numbering in the thousands (Closser 2015).

12. For a critical analysis of how human resources management thinking has guided employee participation in the private sector and community participation in development in similar ways, see Taylor (2001).

13. The working paper is accessible at http://www.hbs.edu/faculty/Pages/item.aspx?num=46043 (accessed June 1, 2015).

14. The profile is available at http://hbswk.hbs.edu/item/7540.html (accessed June 1, 2015).

CONCLUSION

Listening to Community Health Workers: Recommendations for Action and Research

Whether in wealthy countries or some of the poorest, such as Ethiopia, so much of the pursuit of health equity and social well-being for impoverished and underserved people depends on the labor and lives of community health workers. And judging by the state of health and health-care inequalities in the world, and by recent trends in the global health industry, CHWs will likely maintain a crucial place in health systems for decades to come. With the passing of the Millennium Development Goals deadline and the establishment of new Sustainable Development Goals to be achieved in 2030, powerful global health and development leaders have called for the recruitment of more CHWs in order to universalize access to primary health care and achieve various demographic and population health goals.

In this book, I have examined the politics and acts of care in which urban Ethiopian volunteer CHWs participated in the first decade of the 21st century to begin answering the question of what it really means to become a CHW in the contemporary global health industry. Ethnographic research is crucial to building a solid understanding of how CHW programs work; how they are experienced by officials, supervisors, and CHWs themselves; and how they are embedded in broader social, political, and economic struggles. With an aim toward maximizing the impact of this work for those who seek positive change in CHW policy and practice, in this conclusion I provide some recommendations. My goal is not to provide an exhaustive discussion of or recommendations for every possible area of CHW policy and practice. Instead, I reflect on some of what most impressed me, both positively and negatively, in learning about the labors and lives of CHWs in Addis Ababa in order to raise a few key issues—and ways of intervening and acting—that I believe need greater consideration from those who seek to build better CHW programs and achieve goals of universal health care, health equity, poverty reduction, and social justice.

This concluding chapter also points to key considerations for scholars interested in studying CHW programs, with an aim toward raising the quantity and quality of policy-relevant research. CHWs cannot solve the world's problems on their own. Many of the problems they face are embedded in global politics that are difficult to change. Important changes are nevertheless happening within CHW programs and through coalitions of equity- and justice-seekers. Researchers need to study these processes and help apply their locally and globally derived knowledge in efforts to achieve global health equity.

Recruit Strong CHWs and Provide Supportive Supervision

Addis Ababa's antiretroviral center of excellence reminds us that programs can and should seek out compassionate, creative, and hardworking people to take on the role of CHWs and provide CHWs with supportive supervision—two programmatic components that are widely recognized as areas for improvement (e.g., Crigler et al. 2014; Jaskiewicz and Deussom 2014). As many analysts of CHW programs have discussed, CHW recruitment can sometimes be "corrupted" by the efforts of outsiders (often higher-level officials) to control recruitment processes and criteria (Perry et al. 2014). The way that the Hiwot and Medhin NGOs recruited CHWs did not exactly uphold the ideal of autonomous grassroots CHW recruitment and selection. Yet by cooperating with current and veteran CHWs, as well as with neighborhood *iddirs*, the NGOs arguably came close to this ideal. Cooperating with *iddirs* was prudent, given the interest in recruiting men and women who were morally acceptable and prepared to work hard in the service of others' well-being. NGO staff members rightly acknowledged that, generally speaking, the leaders of local *iddirs* best knew the backgrounds of people in their communities or were in positions to look into those backgrounds, and thus were well placed to judge whether recruits conformed to a widely shared model of a respectable and helpful citizen. The process thus depended on the perceptions and standards of locally embedded neighbors, many of whom had personal stakes in the potential failures and successes of the recruits. It was encouraging, furthermore, that identifiers like ethnicity, religion, gender, and age were not used to exclude potential recruits; the community health workforce thus ended up including diverse CHWs to serve a diverse population. It was also interesting to see some flexibility in the way CHWs were recruited, with Sister Nebyat (herself a compassionate person and local resident of the communities her organization served) personally inviting and persuading Birtukan, who otherwise was not interested and had not responded to any recruitment call.

I have described recruitment of CHWs in Addis as the beginning of a process of socialization, by which NGO and government health officials attempted to reinforce the recruits' willingness to work for free and make it known that they were not agents of social change, but instead subordinates to a hierarchy of decision makers that started with their supervisors. Recruitment processes in Addis Ababa can also be seen as successful for identifying large numbers of hardworking and well-intentioned CHWs, and as the beginnings of close and supportive relationships between CHWs and their supervisors. As I have shown, the people who directly supervised CHWs in the Hiwot and Medhin NGOs became very familiar with the lives of their CHWs and intended beneficiaries. They were also well intentioned and hardworking, and provided highly supportive supervision, even if they had their own grievances and faced their own constraints, including norms, policies, and resource allocations that were beyond their immediate control.

Emphasize the Humanity of Patients, Quality of Life, and Empathic Care

In Addis Ababa's ART center of excellence, a primary goal was getting thousands of new patients on antiretroviral drugs and adhering carefully to their pharmaceutical regimens. CHWs were thus expected to learn about several medical technologies, the impacts they had on bodies, and the importance of adherence. They were also expected to learn the bureaucratic system of which they were a part and to collect data and submit reports to their NGO supervisors and, ultimately, to the federal government, international NGOs, and international donors. While technical, biomedical, and bureaucratic forms of community health work may have been given more emphasis in Addis Ababa than they had before the rollout of ART, it was evident during the early rollout of these drugs at ALERT that CHW trainers and supervisors still placed a good deal of emphasis on empathic caregiving. CHWs in Addis Ababa's antiretroviral center of excellence were encouraged to assert the humanity of patients and the goal of improving their quality of life through empathic, supportive care, which involved confronting stigma and fear, building close relationships with patients, and mending relationships within their patients' families and networks.

Anthropologists and others have problematized the marginalization of empathic care within medical and specifically CHW fields (e.g., Kalofonos 2014; Nading 2013). Technical forms of care come to receive greater emphasis due in part to a failure to value empathic forms of care and to a converse tendency to attribute greater value to the power of biomedical technologies and quantitative monitoring of technical health-care deliverables. Maintaining a prominent role for empathic forms of care in CHW settings, therefore, depends upon conscious desires among CHWs, supervisors, program directors, policy makers, donors, and others to uphold the value of these forms of care, and to integrate empathic forms of care into CHW training, supervision, and assessment of performance. Anthropologist Arthur Kleinman (2008) asserts that it is possible to reform medical training to help health workers master the art of

> acknowledging and affirming the patient as a suffering human being; imagining alternative contexts and practices for responding to calamity;

and conversing with and supporting patients in desperate situations where the emphasis is on what really matters to the patient and his or her intimates.

This can be accomplished by incorporating social science and humanities perspectives into medical training, providing for plenty of hands-on experience in caregiving for "health catastrophes" in homes and institutions, and conveying social illness narratives that sensitize students "to the richness of the patient's life and interests" (Kleinman 2008: 23).

This is essentially what was happening in Addis. By carefully constructing warm, emotional ceremonies and training sessions that involved social dramas and community discussions centering on illness and stigma narratives, and by encouraging CHWs to physically and emotionally care for patients, trainers oriented the CHWs to the humanity of their patients and their deservingness of care and respect.[1] Through training and hands-on experience, furthermore, volunteer CHWs in Addis Ababa attempted to master the very arts to which Kleinman refers. CHWs in Addis often said that they felt happiness and a sense of fulfillment through caregiving and supporting people in need—particularly people who were marginalized and stigmatized. A sustained willingness to see community health and social well-being as a goal worthy of struggle as well as the genuine mental satisfaction that CHWs experienced though combating discrimination, caring for patients, and reconciling interpersonal conflicts appeared to depend in part on the efforts of NGO and government staff to ritually reinforce the significance of empathic care, anti-stigmatization, and equity; to culturally construct the CHW role as one that should be admired as morally upright; and to pump up CHWs with positive emotions. Thus ritual may be an important tool for upholding the value of empathic caregiving, building solidarity across social dividing lines, and ensuring that the CHW role is respected and enjoyed.

Certainly there was room for improvement in making forms of empathic care a focus of training, supervision, and assessment of CHW and program performance. I have argued that the emphasis on empathic care may have been partly instrumental in regards to the goal of enhancing the perceived connection between volunteering one's labor as a CHW and experiences of mental and spiritual satisfaction. Yet it was also clear to me that the emphasis on empathic forms of care partly resulted from the genuine value that multiple officials, supervisors, and trainers placed on the quality of life of patients, and not just high adherence rates, low viral loads, and lives saved. Many deeply understood, furthermore, that the quality of life of patients depended on secure access to employment and good housing and food, as well as efforts to fight HIV-related stigma, mend relationships between estranged relatives and lovers, and construct hope for future socioeconomic progress and greater well-being.

Build Solid Relationships across Social Dividing Lines

Health policy makers tend to envision CHWs as people who share the same background as the people they serve and thus enjoy positive and intimate relationships with all of them. Yet in many rural and especially urban communities there is great diversity and inequality in terms of socioeconomic status, ethnicity, religion, and gender, as well as varying levels of anonymity, leading to lack of social support and trust, and thus difficulties in forging relationships between CHWs and others (including intended beneficiaries). Several ethnographers have thus shown that CHWs sometimes face difficulties when attempting to serve intended clients, due in part to a lack of shared identity, respect, trust, and solidarity. Reporting on ethnographic research that targeted a national CHW program in Brazil in the mid-1990s, for instance, Wayland and Crowder (2002) showed that CHWs in the western city of Rio Branco were viewed by intended clients as "strangers" with whom they would never share intimate information, including information relevant to their health. More recently, Mumtaz and colleagues (2013) have shown that Lady Health Workers (LHWs) in the Pakistani Punjab avoid certain neighborhoods and houses in their assigned areas because of their status as low-caste women. Many also go about their daily work in pairs, to safeguard themselves and make it easier to access neighborhoods and houses which one LHW might feel uncomfortable visiting. Because of the social barriers they face, LHWs often end up focusing more of their time and services on poorer and traditionally underserved households—not a bad outcome exactly, but also not the intended outcome.

Through ethnographic work in South Africa's Khayelitsha township, Alison Swartz (2013) highlights that because different CHWs have distinctive experiences, perspectives on the world, and perceptions of each other, they do not always get along *with each other*. In Khayelitsha, a generational gap between older CHWs who lived as adolescents or young adults through the final years of apartheid and younger CHWs who came of age after the fall of apartheid, has led to a lack of mutual understanding and respect. Older, poorer CHWs claim to embody Ubuntu, a notion of shared humanity and mutual support, while younger, less poor volunteers are seen by the older CHWs as narrowly self-interested, ignorant about the past, and upwardly aspiring. Many older CHWs said that Ubuntu was being "killed off" by the younger generation, whereas younger CHWs described older women as being "jealous" of the training and employment opportunities that were offered to younger CHWs (Swartz 2013). This gap was shaped by South Africa's destructive legacy of apartheid, highlighting the importance of local histories of exclusion and violence in understanding the lack of solidarity that can exist within communities and within CHW ranks.

A lack of solidarity presents the practical challenge of recognizing and understanding strife, and building bridges of mutual understanding and respect between people who do not see themselves as members of the same in-group—in other words, a challenge to address an "illness of discrimination" that is not located inside the body but rather exists in the relationships between people in a social group (Barrett 2008). To put this in the language of social epidemiology and development economics, social animosities and disconnections present a need to create "bridging social capital"—the social capital that can exist between people of different socioeconomic and/or ethnic and religious identities, as opposed to bonding social capital, which exists between people of the same class, caste, religion, or ethnicity (Kim et al. 2006; UN-Habitat 2008).

Based on their research, Mumtaz and colleagues recommend that community members in Punjab, Pakistan be engaged to understand and address the social restrictions that LHWs face, which arise as a result of caste and socioeconomic inequalities. They also recommend actively challenging the stigma attached to the LHW role (Mumtaz et al. 2013: 56). Addis Ababa's antiretroviral center of excellence involved conscious desires and attempts to build solidarity across social dividing lines, including lines that create barriers between CHWs and patients as well as within CHW ranks. Supervisors and CHWs actively attempted to generate it, in part by promoting an ethos of shared humanity and anti-discrimination among people of various identities. Trainers and supervisors used recruitment and basic training of new recruits not only as venues for teaching CHWs about the forms of care they needed to provide but also as settings for encouraging and facilitating processes by which recruits respect the diversity of others' backgrounds, personalities, and resources, and build networks with one another. They encouraged CHW recruits to see each other, patients, and others in society as *wegen*, fellow people seeking similar goals of happiness, love, and spirituality—and deserving these aspects of individual and social well-being. They encouraged this ethos in various venues, including day-to-day interactions and in more ritually dense contexts like basic training, initiation ceremonies, and CHW celebrations.

In Addis Ababa, CHWs of different genders, ages, socioeconomic statuses, ethnicities, and religious affiliations thus worked together and cooperated. While there was evidence of some strife and animosities, many of their relationships were overwhelmingly positive. Many of the close relationships that existed between volunteer CHWs and patients bridged ethnic and religious differences, too. The survey we conducted showed that CHWs' close relationships bridged across ethnic and religious divisions 57% and 29% of the time, respectively. These rates are far higher than those that existed among the general population residing in a slum area of Addis Ababa, as measured by social epidemiologists working for the UN (see UNHABITAT 2008: 200), which suggests that CHWs can play important roles in building solidarity and support across social dividing lines.

Across CHW contexts, supervisors and trainers can often do more to question, encourage, and assess recruits' preparedness and success in building positive, respectful relationships with other CHWs and with patients of different ethnic, religious, and socioeconomic backgrounds. But one thing that my research in

Addis Ababa taught me is that CHW programs may not only expose animosities and lack of solidarity in urban communities; they may also provide working examples of how bridges can be built. There is a need to look for these existing strategies and successes, contribute to them, and amplify them.

Finance the Creation of Secure CHW Jobs

The CHWs I encountered did not receive a living wage or any substantial material benefits. Currently, there are tens of thousands of CHWs in Ethiopia who are either underpaid or unpaid, and there are countless others around the world. Despite all the accolades Ethiopia has received for creating roughly 35,000 salaried Health Extension Worker jobs, many of the women who have taken up these positions are unhappy with their pay and their workloads. The latter are often massive, due in part to the fact that the number of HEW jobs the Ethiopian government and its international donors have created is far too small relative to the large and impoverished Ethiopian population. This seems to be due, in turn, to the fact that the government and its donors have simply not raised and allocated enough money to create more HEW jobs (Maes et al. 2015).

Ethiopia's HEWs have only begun to autonomously organize their ranks, band together, and develop leaders of their own. They are beginning to participate in questioning their government, NGOs, or other more distant and powerful actors in the industry, to seek structural change in relation to their job and living conditions. They do not currently hold their own rallies and public events to get their perspectives and messages across. They do not systematically shape how recruitment and training happen, how data are collected, or what is measured. Instead, they are still largely expected to do what they're told by higher-level public health actors, held accountable for their performance and excluded from high-level policy tables and governing bodies. Meanwhile, their supervisors and health officials, who face serious budgetary constraints and directives to produce significant improvements in population health, attempt to rationalize a reliance on cheap and unpaid CHW labor through the use of moral rhetorics that are similar but in some ways distinct to the ones that could be heard in the context of Addis Ababa's antiretroviral center of excellence (Maes et al. 2015).

Lack of payment and participation in policy development and social change are problems that are evident in some form in many CHW contexts around the world, including low-, middle-, and high-income countries. In addressing these problems, the goal is not to see CHWs becoming antagonistic vis-à-vis governments, companies, non-profits, donors, and other powerful entities. Rather, the goal is to achieve greater health and economic equity, in part through recognizing, respecting, and promoting the social, economic, political, and health-care rights and capabilities of CHWs and their intended beneficiaries.

There are many things that readers can do to help reach these goals. One is to help raise money for CHW job creation and improvement. This does not have to mean only starting a new fundraising campaign and then donating the proceeds to a CHW employer or union—although it could, and web-based crowdfunding tools make it easier than ever to develop or contribute to a solid donation campaign to create more and better CHW jobs. It could mean advocating for reforms that raise the amounts of tax revenue and international aid that go into funding CHW jobs with good pay, benefits, and security. The last several years have continued to see growing levels of global health funding despite a slowdown caused by the global financial crisis of 2008 (Dieleman et al. 2014). Against this backdrop, the recently published Investment Case for CHWs (Dahn et al. 2015) is a solid call from powerful people to grow and sustain a financial base for creating and improving CHW jobs, along with guidelines and recommendations for developing context-specific pathways to sustainably financed CHW systems. This document builds on the work of the Clinton Foundation, Partners in Health, and the 1 Million CHW Campaign (Drobac et al. 2013; McCord et al. 2013). It is essential reading and ought to be widely circulated. One can also build on it, by identifying better ways to raise and allocate the resources needed to make CHW programs strong over the long term, and by advocating for wealthy nations and wealthy people in those nations to pay their fair share for global health.

In order to create more and better CHW jobs, it is necessary to be vigilant about the multiple barriers that exist along with lack of financing. I have argued in this book that moral sentiments of sacrifice, mental satisfaction, and related ideas can play a role in blocking progress toward these goals, by buttressing the exploitation of human capacities for empathy, solidarity, care, spirituality, and moral passion in pursuit of the goals of saving lives and extending health care. Both within and beyond Ethiopia, it is important to look for and question instances in which more powerful people use moral rhetoric to get less powerful workers to work for low wages or for free.

One common argument against paying CHWs is that doing so can ruin their pre-existing willingness to sacrifice to help others, receive divine merit, and experience mental satisfaction (e.g., Glenton et al. 2010). I have heard many government health and NGO officials make versions of this argument over the past ten years. This logic appears to be theory-driven and to respect the religious beliefs and social realities of CHWs in different parts of the world. If impoverished people are willing to volunteer their time, and find meaning or some other immaterial benefits in doing so, then why pay them and "crowd out" their intrinsic motivations? Wouldn't it be better to reinforce their intrinsic motivations and willingness to care for others or serve their community, and strengthen the community's sense of gratitude for the virtuous sacrifices made by CHWs?

This idea is flawed because it fails to grasp the full complexity of CHWs' social, moral, and economic worlds. Paying CHWs may have impacts on their psychosocial and spiritual experiences. But those impacts cannot be easily predicted.

Introducing wages and other forms of material remuneration need not be like flipping a switch changing the moral status of volunteers from positive to negative. If one were to begin paying wages to CHWs who previously served as volunteers, such an intervention would meet the ritual and symbolic environment and meanings already in place. The creation of well-paid CHW jobs therefore can and perhaps should be combined with ritual and other forms of interaction and communication designed to reinforce certain moral commitments and emotions in CHWs, foster their acceptance and respect by fellow community members, and encourage intimate forms of care and anti-discrimination crucial for improving the quality of life of marginalized people living with illness. By identifying and calling out instances in which the moral sentiments of the powerful are used to extract the labor of less powerful workers, and by accompanying the fair payment of CHWs with more socially and culturally thick rituals that generate positive emotional energy and new understandings, it may be possible to economically empower impoverished people while also reinforcing the pro-social, self-transcendent, and spiritual beliefs associated with community health work.

Strengthen CHW Participation in Processes of Social Change

There is a great need to enhance CHWs' participation in policy development, social change, and mechanisms aimed at holding more powerful health system actors accountable. Across contexts, more researchers, students, community members, and higher-level authorities should seek out or help generate open discussions involving CHWs about their daily work, including the struggles they face and their desires. For those who are not already connected to CHWs, the Internet makes it easy to reach out to nearby and even distant CHWs, and to start learning about their lives and work. For some, it may be possible to sign up for a CHW training program to learn more about local CHWs and become an advocate. Students seeking an internship with an NGO or public health institution could aim for one involving work alongside CHWs, keeping in mind that one does not have to go abroad to work with CHWs (there are likely several opportunities much closer to home).[2]

An important next step is to help raise awareness among powerful people and the general public about the challenges facing CHWs, their successes and value, and their desires. There are many ways to do this: writing letters and emails and making phone calls to legislators, representatives, potential donors and allies; co-organizing rallies or other events at schools, colleges, and universities; persuading local, national and international news agencies to do stories on CHWs; blogging on health-related websites; and using social media to rapidly distribute links, updates, and conversations on CHW-related events and publications.[3] With all of these efforts, it is important to make sure CHWs are not just sitting on the sidelines or in the audience. CHWs should serve as key sources of the effort, resources, and creativity needed to pull off public events and communications efforts. A diverse group of them should be speaking, writing, coming up with innovations, and evaluating them according to their goals and their understandings of what is useful and needed in meeting those goals.

Also important is nurturing new, emerging, and established CHW leaders, as well as building organizational strength and capacity among CHW ranks. Survey data collected from CHWs in the United States provide evidence that training in leadership and advocacy is associated with greater activity in processes of policy change, from identification of problems to organizing peers and pushing other higher-level actors to address them (Sabo et al. 2013; 2015).[4] Hence one of the primary activities of many community health-focused organizations and their academic partners in the United States is to provide CHWs with leadership and advocacy training through pedagogical forms adhering to principles of popular education and community-based participatory research (e.g., Ingram et al. 2015; Wiggins et al. 2013; 2014). These efforts deserve support where they already exist, and provide models—involving both successes and cautionary tales—for adaptation in other CHW contexts.

There are models in other parts of the world, too. In Nepal, for instance, a USAID-funded project implemented by CARE, a well-known international NGO, sought to help organize Female Community Health Volunteers (FCHVs) and empower them to self-mobilize and take collective action to improve health and health care in their communities. According to Gopinath (2007), the organized FCHVs not only succeeded in attaining specific goals like having separate toilets built for women in local health facilities; they also began playing an active role in the management of health facilities, vigorously voicing community concerns to various stakeholders at multiple levels, and leading equity-focused campaigns that resulted in an increase in participation in health-related activities among traditionally excluded castes. Qualitative data suggested that organized FCHVs were more likely to speak up about health issues and demand resources from health facilities, while unorganized FCHVs did not question the status quo and were afraid to speak about community health issues and other injustices for fear of losing their positions or access to resources, or of offending more powerful actors (Gopinath 2007).

A more recent pilot project in Nepal also aimed to enhance leadership within the FCHV workforce, raise the status of the workforce, and improve the quality and supportiveness of the supervision they received (Schwarz et al. 2014). The project, which involved collaboration between the Ministry of Health, an NGO, and a public hospital in the remote western district of Achham, was aimed at achieving greater health equity in the third poorest district in the country, home to a primarily agrarian population that has been heavily affected by civil conflict. Though the project, FCHV Leaders were nominated by local Mothers Groups and hospital staff, new weekly meetings between FCHV Leaders and hospital staff were instituted to provide for supportive supervision, and FCHVs began to receive financial compensation for their work. Observing that each of these innovations were well received by the various actors involved, Schwarz and colleagues (2014) called for testing the overall model in a large-scale effectiveness trial to better define its impacts and identify areas for improvement.[5]

Clearly some are already trying out new ways of organizing, empowering, training, and remunerating CHWs in various places around the globe. Each of these kinds of actions and interventions could help in achieving the goals that many CHWs and their allies seek, from CHW job creation and improvement of working conditions to health equity and social justice more broadly.[6] Importantly, many of the interventions mentioned above, which involved aligning with CHWs and nurturing their organization and leadership, depended upon people with deep knowledge of local political dynamics, including local risks and dangers involved in taking various kinds of political action. Mason and colleagues (2010) also note that leaders within the Massachusetts Association of CHWs required forms of nurturing and advocacy from allies who understood the political dynamics in which CHWs sought to engage. Thus the sooner would-be allies educate themselves on the issues, constraints, norms, and levers of change that exist within local and global social fields, the better. As Basilico and colleagues (2013: 340) assert, "moving from inspiration to action may be risky [and] fraught with unintended consequences," but it can still be done through long-term accompaniment of the intended beneficiaries and habitual critical self-reflection. In other words, allies should be prepared to be engaged over the long term; to anticipate, own up to, and carefully respond to unintended consequences; and to consistently question their motives, goals, and tactics.

Conduct Better Research and More of It

Clearly there are close links between pragmatic action, critical self-reflection, and in-depth research. One message of this book is that there is a big need for careful research into CHW programs. In various parts of the globe CHWs are now making movements toward organizing their own ranks; forging links with other CHWs, activists, and organizations, even across borders and transnationally; developing shared knowledge, skills, experiences, and goals; and seeking seats at policy tables and the power to hold government and transnational institutions accountable. CHW employers in many locales are variably aware, concerned, or excited about these potential movements.[7] The examples and experiences of organized and activist CHWs in other contexts may start to circulate and alter politics in other places. Globally, advocacy for more and better-supported positions for CHWs will evolve to take on new forms at local, national, and transnational levels. Across CHW programs, there will also be much variation and change in the specific capacities that CHWs exercise in caring for others. The values attributed to CHW labor and capacities, furthermore, are under negotiation and evolving. In so many different places around the world, new investments, innovations, and interventions in CHW programs are playing out now and will continue in the future, having both intended and unintended social, political, emotional, economic, and health consequences.

All of this flux and variation demands careful, multilevel ethnographic analysis by engaged scholars, to illuminate what is actually happening in the everyday operation of CHW programs. As Simon Lewin and Uta Lehmann put it in their contribution to the recently published CHW Reference Guide, there is a need to study not only CHW program impacts and productivity but also CHW program *governance*, or the set of processes, norms, structures, and relationships through which various individuals and groups exercise rights or other sorts of claims, resolve differences, and express interests in relation to CHW programs in specific political, economic, and cultural contexts. As I have put it, there is a need for research into the context-specific material, political, and moral economies of CHWs: the production, distribution, and circulation of community health workers themselves, and of the moral sentiments, emotions and values that various stakeholders use to limit, expand, improve, or exercise control over the labor and lives of CHWs. More research must study up and down the hierarchies of CHW programs and health systems, which extend from the CHW and her patients and fellow workers and community members, to transnational, high-level donors, officials, and professionals, taking the motivations, actions, and interactions of all of these people, no matter their place in the hierarchy, as objects of integrated study. The key is to move beyond the human resources mentality that reduces CHWs to a set of motivations and productivity levels to be scientifically manipulated according to rubrics of cost-effectiveness, and toward an ecological and more humanistic approach that documents the complex and challenging social, emotional, and economic lives of CHWs, including their various forms of care work and social change-directed efforts; and that explains how higher-level actors in specific contexts engage with key issues like CHW pay, performance, and freedom to organize and pursue policy and social change.

Of course, actors positioned near the top of global health hierarchies move about the world at a fast pace, following busy schedules. For researchers, they are often harder to access than CHWs and other local level actors. This points to a limitation of the research that I conducted in Addis Ababa: instead of further engaging higher-level actors and governing bodies, including the heads and directors of international donor and development agencies, I often relied on public documents to ascertain their intentions, beliefs, power, and constraints. This should encourage researchers to study further up, to see the connections between global-level decision making and local-level experience and interaction.

Anthropologists and the ethnographic and mixed methods they employ argu-ably should become a standard part of any community health program. For large national CHW programs such as Ethiopia's, ethnographic work should take place in multiple locales across ethnically and socio-politically diverse regions, while also engaging actors at higher and more central levels of power and decision making. To make this happen, funding agencies, governments, CHW employers, and NGOs and other institutions must take on a responsibility to help procure and provide the resources needed to fund high-quality and highly informative research—without impinging on researchers' freedom to address and explain the problems they identify.

Anthropologists and social scientists more generally have responsibilities, too—beyond simply doing the research. One is to write with clear language that is accessible to broader audiences. Extended theoretical discussions and use of esoteric jargon are intellectually satisfying and important for communication in some academic arenas, but they often hinder communication with CHWs, public health professionals, policy makers, and the public (Closser and Finley 2016). Likewise, in order to facilitate communication and the formation of mul-tidisciplinary research teams, social scientists have a responsibility to learn the language of other disciplines, including public health and biomedicine, statistics, economics, and more. In addition to pointing out the problems related to hold-ing up randomized controlled trials as a "gold standard" for evidence-based pub-lic health, anthropologists should be open to doing research within or as part of better multidisciplinary intervention-based studies, which demand critical and constructive analysis of both intended and unintended consequences (Adams 2013; Kohrt et al. 2015; Smith-Morris et al. 2014).

Researchers may also have a responsibility to produce timely research, and therefore to conduct research more rapidly. The dissertation-length study that I conducted in Addis Ababa is not the best model in this regard. I relied upon the advice, guidance, and assistance of multiple people, in particular several outstanding women and men who helped me conduct surveys and interviews, which helped me achieve my study objectives relatively smoothly and quickly. Going a step further, working with *teams* of ethnographers who systematically divide and integrate the work of data collection and analysis could be a much better way to go about producing rapid results that do not sacrifice accuracy and richness (see, for example, Bierschenk and Olivier de Sardan 1997). Team ethnography has also been used to produce relatively rapid comparative analyses of health, culture, and society across multiple contexts, which can be crucial in understanding the links between action and experiences at local and global levels (e.g., Closser et al. 2015; Hirsch et al. 2009).

While timely research and rapid production of results are desirable, there is also something to be said for longer-term engagement in order to build trust with research participants (Maes 2012; Maes and Kalofonos 2013). This can be crucial, for instance, in ensuring that CHWs and others with relatively little power are comfortable to express their true desires and opinions. Researchers certainly need to carefully consider the extent to which their respondents feel comfortable in speaking their minds openly, and make efforts to create that sense of comfort and safety. Longer-term engagement is also crucial in understanding change, and what drives change over the span of days, months, and years. Thus there is a need to balance rapid development and communication of results and long-term engagement.

Researchers can also make greater efforts to help publicize their work and the practical recommendations that come out of it. In addition to publishing articles in big public health journals, it can be helpful to write editorials in major newspapers, blog on websites, and circulate links and commentaries via social media. Researchers should consider leading or assisting in the production of documentary films—including both short YouTube formats and longer features—that accurately and fairly depict the realities facing CHWs. Although producing results rapidly and widely disseminating and publicizing those results are partly the responsibility of research funders and other sponsors, researchers can do much more in this arena.

Last but not least, research funders and researchers have shared responsibilities when it comes to breaking down inequalities in who is researched and who designs and does research. Simply put, CHWs should be more involved in the design and conduct of CHW-related research. The same goes for researchers from low- and middle-income countries, who often face rather limited opportunities and support to engage in global health research (Korht et al. 2015).

United, Spider Webs Can Tie Up a Lion

The problems facing CHWs in Ethiopia and throughout the world are the drivers of poverty, poor health, and poor health-care systems. As the Amharic proverb goes, these problems are lions: massive and threatening. They are also transnational and complex, involving economic imperialism, war and geopolitics, racism, sexism, and the complicity of rights-ignoring governments and corporations. Recall the caveat that CHW programs are more likely to uphold visions of grassroots empowerment and social change when embedded in contexts of popular movement or revolution—upheavals targeting the big problems of social inequality, structural violence, and injustice (Colvin and Swartz 2015; Lehmann and Sanders 2007; Wiggins 2012). If CHWs are to add value to health systems, they must be established on a secure foundation of greatly increased and sustained investments aimed at reducing poverty and strengthening health systems. Likewise, if CHWs are to contribute to lasting empowerment of marginalized communities and to engage successfully as activists and forces of social justice, their work must be embedded in broader social and political movements involving strategically aligned advocates, partners, and supporters who are prepared to recognize, question, and address inequalities and rights abuses. Health professionals, scholars, policymakers, and students should all be reminded to spin webs with CHWs and each other, to tie up these underlying problems, and bring about health equity and social justice.

Notes

1. On health-related "deservingness," see the work of anthropologist Sarah Willen (2012).
2. Many of these internships will be unpaid, as is often the case. If so, interns might think deeply about *why* their labor as an intern should or should not be unpaid: How is it different and similar to asking local CHWs to work for free or for low wages? During their internship, they could ask to take a look at the operational budget and ask about how and how much CHWs are getting paid and why.
3. There are many websites that focus on CHWs worldwide, including CHW Central (http://www.chwcentral.org/) and the 1 Million CHW Campaign (http://1millionhealth workers.org/). A Google search of "CHW association" brings up the websites of associations from multiple states, as well as the webpage of the CHW Section of the American Public Health Association.
4. Using data from a US-nationwide sample of CHWs (the National CHW Advocacy Survey or NCHWAS), researchers have produced estimates of the percentage of CHWs who engage in advocacy targeting, for example, a school board, city council, county board of supervisors, governor, business, clinic or hospital, law enforcement agency, health department, or the CHWs' own agency. Logistic regression analyses identified several statistically significant predictors of engagement in community and professional advocacy, including years of experience as a CHW, affiliation with a professional network, training in leadership and advocacy, and possession of various leadership qualities—e.g., feeling that one knows who to talk to about making changes, and feeling confident in public speaking (Sabo et al. 2013; 2015).
5. Social audits are another technique that could strengthen CHW participation in policy change and help instill greater accountability within states and other powerful institutions. A social audit is used to understand, measure, verify, report on, and improve the social performance, accountability, and transparency of organizations and state agencies, and to enhance the role of citizens—especially marginalized and poor groups whose voices are rarely heard—in the governance of said agencies (Jain and Polman 2003). The idea of the social audit was born in the early 1990s in India, as part of a larger struggle spearheaded by a grassroots organization based in Rajasthan (the Mazdoor Kisan Shakti Sangathan or MKSS), which aimed to ensure that subsidized food and other essential commodities were made available to the poorest, and that minimum wages were paid in drought relief works. An important innovation in this process was the "JanSunwai" or public hearing where details of the official records were read out to assembled villagers (Aiyar and Samji 2009). Aiyar and Samji (2009) describe how social audit interventions have been used successfully in India to hold the state accountable. They assert that while the social audit process was conceived in part to expose corruption, social audits can be a mechanism to strengthen democratic action more generally, by producing informed citizens, encouraging them to participate in local affairs, and helping to strengthen a respect for citizen's rights within institutions.
6. With the push to create CHW jobs and to uphold a CHW's right to fair payment for her or his work, there can still be room for unpaid volunteer community health labor.

Certainly there are many people who desire to and are economically and otherwise capable of volunteering their time, energy, and skills to the betterment of community health and social justice.

7. In Senegal, for instance, an NGO official told a reporter from the United States that it is simply unacceptable for CHWs to organize into "pressure groups" or a trade union, because if they did so, "then the government will have to find the money to pay them." See http://www.pri.org/stories/2013–12–19/thousands-health-workers-senegal-receive-no-pay-fair (accessed January 8, 2016).

REFERENCES

Abbink, J. 2006 Discomfiture of democracy? The 2005 election crisis in Ethiopia and its aftermath. *African Affairs* 105(419):173–199.

———— 2011a Ethnic-based federalism and ethnicity in Ethiopia: Reassessing the experiment after 20 years. *Journal of Eastern African Studies* 5(4):596–618.

———— 2011b Religion in public spaces: Emerging Muslim-Christian polemics in Ethiopia. *African Affairs* 110(439):253–274.

———— 2012 Dam controversies: Contested governance and developmental discourse on the Ethiopian Omo River dam. *Social Anthropology* 20(2):125–144.

Adams, Vincanne 2013 Evidence-based global public health. In *When people come first: Critical studies in global health.* J. Biehl and A. Petryna, eds. Pp. 54–90. Princeton, NJ: Princeton University Press.

Aiyar, Yamini, and Samji Salimah 2009 *Transparency and accountability in NREGA: A case study of Andhra Pradesh.* New Delhi: Accountability Initiative.

Akintola, Olagoke 2008 Unpaid HIV/AIDS care in southern Africa: Forms, context, and implications. *Feminist Economics* 14(4):117–147.

Alam, K., and E. Oliveras 2014 Retention of female volunteer community health workers in Dhaka urban slums: A prospective cohort study. *Human Resources for Health* 12. DOI: 10.1186/1478-4491-12-29.

Amare, Yared 1999 *Household resources, strategies and food security in Ethiopia: A study of Amhara households in Wogda, Northern Shewa.* Addis Ababa: Addis Ababa University Press.

———— 2010 Urban Food Insecurity and Coping Mechanisms: A Case Study of Lideta Sub-city in Addis Ababa. Forum for Social Studies Research Report No. 5.

Anbesse, Birke, Charlotte Hanlon, Atalay Alem, Samuel Packer, and Rob Whitley 2009 Migration and mental health: A study of low-income Ethiopian women working in Middle Eastern countries. *International Journal of Social Psychiatry* 55(6):557–568.

Arvey, Sarah R., and Maria E. Fernandez 2012 Identifying the core elements of effective community health worker programs: A research agenda. *American Journal of Public Health* 102(9):1633–1637.

Ashraf, Nava, Oriana Bandiera, and Scott S. Lee 2015 Do-gooders and go-getters: Career incentives, selection, and performance in public service delivery. Working paper. Cambridge: Harvard Business School. Available from http://www.hbs.edu/faculty/Pages/item.aspx?num=46043 (accessed June 1, 2015).

Bach, J. N. 2011 Abyotawi democracy: Neither revolutionary nor democratic, a critical review of EPRDF's conception of revolutionary democracy in post-1991 Ethiopia. *Journal of Eastern African Studies* 5(4):641–663.

Banteyerga, Hailom 2014 Boosting maternal health care seeking behavior in rural low income countries: A case study of West Gojam and South Wollo Zones in Amhara, Ethiopia. *American Journal of Health Research* 2(6):378–386.

Banteyerga, Hailom, Aklilu Kidanu, and Kate Stillman 2006 The System-Wide Effects of the Global Fund in Ethiopia: Final Study Report. Miz-Hasab Research Center and Abt Associates Inc.

Barnes, Cedric, and Harun Hassan 2007 The rise and fall of Mogadishu's Islamic Courts. *Journal of Eastern African Studies* 1(2)151–160.

Barrett, Ronald 2008 *Aghor medicine*. Berkeley: University of California Press.

Basilico, Matthew, Jonathan Weigel, Anjali Motgi, Jacob Bor, and Salmaan Keshavjee 2013 Health for all? Competing theories and geopolitics. In *Reimagining global health: An introduction*. P. Farmer, J. Y. Kim, A. Kleinman, and M. Basilico, eds. Pp. 74–110. Berkeley: University of California Press.

Berkman, Alan, Jonathan Garcia, Miguel Muñoz-Laboy, Vera Paiva, and Richard Parker 2005 A critical analysis of the Brazilian response to HIV/AIDS: Lessons learned for controlling and mitigating the epidemic in developing countries. *American Journal of Public Health* 95(7):1162–1172.

Berman, P. A., D. R. Gwatkin, and S. E. Burger 1987 Community-based health-workers— head-start or false start towards health for all? *Social Science & Medicine* 25(5):443–459.

Bhattacharyya, Karabi, Peter Winch, Karen LeBan, and Marie Tien 2001 *Community health worker incentives and disincentives: How they affect motivation, retention, and sustainability*. Arlington, VA: USAID.

Bhutta, Zulfiqar A., Zohra S. Lassi, George Pariyo, and Luis Huicho 2010 *Global experience of community health workers for delivery of health related millennium development goals*. Geneva: World Health Organization and the Global Health Workforce Alliance.

Bhutta, Zulfiqar A., Sajid Soofi, Simon Cousens, Shah Mohammad, Zahid A. Memon, Imran Ali, Asher Feroze, Farrukh Raza, Amanullah Khan, Steve Wall, and Jose Martines 2011 Improvement of perinatal and newborn care in rural pakistan through community-based strategies: A cluster-randomised effectiveness trial. *Lancet* 377(9763):403–412.

Biehl, João 2006 Pharmaceutical governance. In *Global pharmaceuticals: Ethics, markets, practices*. A. Petryna, A. Lakoff, and A. Kleinman, eds. Pp. 206–239. Durham, NC: Duke University Press.

———— 2007 *Will to live: AIDS therapies and the politics of survival*. Princeton: Princeton University Press.

———— 2011 When people come first: Beyond technical and theoretical quick-fixes in global health. In *Global political ecology*. R. Peet, P. Robbins, and M. Watts, eds. Pp. 100–130. London: Routledge.

Bierschenk, Thomas, and Jean-Pierre Olivier de Sardan 1997 ECRIS: Rapid collective inquiry for the identification of conflicts and strategic groups. *Human Organization* 56(2):238–244.

B-Lajoie, Marie-Renée, Jennifer Hulme, and Kirsten Johnson 2014 Payday, ponchos, and promotions: A qualitative analysis of perspectives from non-governmental organization programme managers on community health worker motivation and incentives. *Human Resources for Health* 12:66.

Borgonovi, Francesca 2008 Doing well by doing good: The relationship between formal volunteering and self-reported health and happiness. *Social Science & Medicine* 66(11):2321–2334.

Bornstein, Erica 2012 *Disquieting gifts: Humanitarianism in New Delhi.* Stanford: Stanford University Press.

Bornstein, Erica, and Peter Redfield 2011 *Forces of compassion: Humanitarianism between ethics and politics.* Santa Fe: School for Advanced Research Press.

Burgess, Gemma 2013 A hidden history: Women's activism in Ethiopia. *Journal of International Women's Studies* 14:96–107.

Campbell, Catherine, Andy Gibbs, Shongile Maimane, and Yugi Nair 2008 Hearing community voices: Grassroots perceptions of an intervention to support health volunteers in South Africa. *Sahara J-Journal of Social Aspects of HIV-AIDS* 5(4):162–177.

Closser, Svea 2010 *Chasing polio in Pakistan: Why the world's largest public health initiative may fail.* Nashville: Vanderbilt University Press.

——— 2015 Pakistan's lady health worker labor movement and the moral economy of heroism. *Annals of Anthropological Practice* 39(1):16–28.

Closser, Svea, and Erin Finley 2016 A new reflexivity: Why anthropology matters in contemporary health research and practice, and how to make it matter more. *American Anthropologist* 118(2):385–390. DOI: 10.1111/aman.12532.

Closser, Svea, Anat Rosenthal, Kenneth Maes, Judith Justice, Kelly Cox, Patricia A. Omidian, Ismalia Zango Mohammed, Aminu Mohammed Dukku, Adam D. Koon, and Laetitia Nyirazinyoye 2015 The global context of vaccine refusal: Insights from a systematic comparative ethnography of the global polio eradication initiative. *Medical Anthropology Quarterly* (Jun 18 2015).

CNHDE 2011 Evaluation of the health extension program implementation process and effect on health outcomes part III: Model-family and vCHP survey. Addis Ababa, Ethiopia: Center for National Health Development in Ethiopia, Columbia University, in collaboration with the FMOH of Ethiopia, UNICEF, and WHO.

Cohen, Jessica, and William Easterly 2009 *What works in development? Thinking big and thinking small.* Washington, DC: Brookings Institution Press.

Cole, S. M., and G. Tembo 2011 The effect of food insecurity on mental health: Panel evidence from rural Zambia. *Social Science & Medicine* 73(7):1071–1079.

Colvin, Christopher, and Alison Swartz 2015 Extension agents or agents of change? CHWs and the politics of carework in post-apartheid South Africa. *Annals of Anthropological Practice* 39(1):29–41.

Cometto, Giorgio, Kate Tulenko, Adamson S. Muula, and Ruediger Krech 2013 Health workforce brain drain: From denouncing the challenge to solving the problem. *PloS Medicine* 10(9):e1001514.

Crane, Johanna 2010 Unequal 'partners': AIDS, academia, and the rise of global health. *Behemoth: A Journal on Civilization* 3:78–97.

Crigler, Lauren, Jessica Gergen, and Henry Perry 2014 Supervision of community health workers. Chapter 10 in *Developing and strengthening community health worker programs at scale.* Henry Perry and Lauren Crigler, eds. Washington, DC: Jhpiego. Cueto, M.

Cueto, Marcos 2004 The origins of primary health care and selective primary health care. *American Journal of Public Health* 94(11):1864–1874.

———— 2013 A return to the magic bullet? In *When people come first: Critical studies in global health*. J. Biehl and A. Petryna, eds. Pp. 30–53. Princeton: Princeton University Press.

Dahn, Bernice, Addis Tamire Woldemariam, Henry Perry, Akiko Maeda, Drew von Glahn, Raj Panjabi, Na'im Merchant, Katy Vosburg, Daniel Palazuelos, Chunling Lu, John Simon, Jerome Pfaffmann, Daniel Brown, Austin Hearst, Phyllis Heydt, and Claire Qureshi 2015 Strengthening primary health care through community health workers: Investment case and financing recommendations. Geneva: Office of the U.N. Secretary-General's Special Envoy for Health in Agenda 2030 and for Malaria.

Daston, Lorraine 1995 The moral economy of science. *Osiris* 10:2–24.

Data Dea Barata 2012 Minority rights, culture, and Ethiopia's "Third Way" to governance. *African Studies Review* 55(3):61–80.

Dawe, David 2008 Have recent increases in international cereal prices been transmitted to domestic economies? The experience in seven large Asian countries. ESA Working Paper 08–03. Rome: Food and Agriculture Organization of the United Nations.

———— 2009 The unimportance of "low" world grain stocks for recent world price increases. ESA Working Paper 09–01. Rome: Food and Agriculture Organization of the United Nations.

de Waal, Alex 2012 The theory and practice of Meles Zenawi. *African Affairs* 112(446): 148–155.

Dieleman, Joseph L., Casey M. Graves, Tara Templin, Elizabeth Johnson, Ranju Baral, Katherine Leach-Kemon, Annie M. Haakenstad, and Christopher J. L. Murray 2014 Global health development assistance remained steady in 2013 but did not align with recipients' disease burden. *Health Affairs* 33(5):878–886.

Donham, Donald L. 1999 *Marxist modern: An ethnographic history of the Ethiopian revolution.* Berkeley: University of California Press.

Donnelly, John 2010 Ethiopia gears up for more major health reforms. *The Lancet* 377(9781):1907–1908.

Dräger, Sigrid, Gulin Gedik, and Mario Dal Poz 2006 Health workforce issues and the Global Fund to fight AIDS, Tuberculosis and Malaria: An analytical review. *Human Resources for Health* 4(1):23–34.

Drobac, Peter, Matthew Basilico, Luke Messac, David Walton, and Paul Farmer 2013 Building an effective rural health delivery model in Haiti and Rwanda. In *Reimagining global health: An introduction.* P. Farmer, A. Kleinman, J. Kim, and M. Basilico, eds. Pp. 133–183, Vol. 26. Berkeley: University of California Press.

Earth Institute 2011 *One million community health workers: technical task force report.* Pp. 1–104. New York: Earth Institute at Columbia University.

Endeshaw, Yoseph, Mebratu Gebeyehu, and Belete Reta 2010 Assessment of trafficking in women and children in and from Ethiopia. Addis Ababa: International Organization for Migration Mission in Addis Ababa.

Farmer, Paul 2008 Challenging orthodoxies: The road ahead for health and human rights. *Health and Human Rights* 10(1):5–19.

Farmer, Paul, Fernet Leandre, Joia S. Mukherjee, Marie Sidonise Claude, Patrice Nevil, Mary C. Smith-Fawzi, Serena P. Koenig, Arachu Castro, Mercedes C. Becerra, Jeffrey Sachs, Amir Attaran, and Jim Yong Kim 2001 Community-based approaches to HIV treatment in resource-poor settings. *The Lancet* 358(9279):404–409.

Fassin, Didier 2005 Compassion and repression: The moral economy of immigration policies in France. *Cultural Anthropology* 20(3):362–387.

———— 2008 The elementary forms of care: An empirical approach to ethics in a South African hospital. *Social Science and Medicine* 67(2):262-270.

———— 2012 *Humanitarian reason: A moral history of the present.* Berkeley: University of California Press.

———— 2013 The moral economy of childhood in the time of AIDS. In *When people come first: Critical studies in global health.* J. Biehl and A. Petryna, eds. Pp. 109–129. Princeton: Princeton University Press.

Feldman, Ilana, and Miriam Iris Ticktin 2010 *In the name of humanity: The government of threat and care.* Durham, NC: Duke University Press.

Ferguson, James 1994 The anti-politics machine: "Development" and bureaucratic power in Lesotho. *The Ecologist* 24(5):176–181.

———— 2010 The uses of neoliberalism. *Antipode* 41(S1):166–184.

Feyissa, D. 2011 Aid negotiation: The uneasy "partnership" between EPRDF and the donors. *Journal of Eastern African Studies* 5(4):788–817.

FMOH 2007 Health Extension Program in Ethiopia Profile. Addis Ababa: Federal Ministry of Health of the Federal Democratic Republic of Ethiopia.

———— 2010 Ethiopia's Fourth National Health Accounts, 2007/2008. Addis Ababa: Federal Ministry of Health of the Federal Democratic Republic of Ethiopia.

———— 2011 HSDP IV Annual Performance Report EFY 2003 (2010/2011). Addis Ababa: Federal Ministry of Health of the Federal Democratic Republic of Ethiopia.

FMOH/HAPCO 2006a AIDS in Ethiopia: Sixth Report. Addis Ababa: Federal Ministry of Health of the Federal Democratic Republic of Ethiopia.

———— 2006b Monthly HIV Care and ART Update—August 8, 2006. Addis Ababa: Federal Ministry of Health of the Federal Democratic Republic of Ethiopia.

Food and Agriculture Organization of the United Nations 2004 The state of food insecurity in the world. Rome: FAO.

Frymus, Diana, Maryse Kok, Korrie de Koning, and Estelle Quain 2013 *Community health workers and universal health coverage: Knowledge gaps and a need based global research agenda by 2015.* Geneva: Global Health Workforce Alliance and World Health Organization.

Gilson, Lucy, Gill Walt, Kris Heggenhougen, Lucas Owuor-Omondi, Myrtle Perera, David Ross, and Ligia Salazar 1989 National community health worker programs: How can they be strengthened? *Journal of Public Health Policy* 10(4):518–532.

Glenton, Claire, Inger B. Scheel, Sabina Pradhan, Simon Lewin, Stephen Hodgins, and Vijaya Shrestha 2010 The female community health volunteer programme in Nepal: Decision makers' perceptions of volunteerism, payment and other incentives. *Social Science & Medicine* 70(12):1920–1927.

Global Fund 2012 Annual Report 2012. Geneva: The Global Fund to Fight AIDS, Tuberculosis, and Malaria.

Global Health Workforce Alliance 2008a Country case study: Ethiopia's human resources for health programme. Geneva: Global Health Workforce Alliance and World Health Organization.

———— 2008b Pakistan's Lady Health Worker Programme. Geneva: Global Health Workforce Alliance and World Health Organization.

———— 2010a Case study: Scaling up education and training of human resources for health in Ethiopia. Geneva: Global Health Workforce Alliance and World Health Organization.

———— 2010b Global experience of community health workers for delivery of health related millennium development goals: A systematic review, country case studies, and recommendations for integration into national health systems. Geneva: Global Health Workforce Alliance and World Health Organization.

Goldsbrough, David 2007 Does the IMF constrain health spending in poor countries? Evidence and an agenda for action. Washington, D.C.: Center for Global Development.

Gopinath, Anjani 2007 Child Survival XIX Project Final Evaluation. Kathmandu: CARE Nepal.

Greenspan, Jesse, Shannon McMahon, Joy Chebet, Maurus Mpunga, David Urassa, and Peter Winch 2013 Sources of community health worker motivation: A qualitative study in Morogoro Region, Tanzania. *Human Resources for Health* 11(1):52.

Gurmu, Eshetu, and Ruth Mace 2008 Fertility decline driven by poverty: The case of Addis Ababa, Ethiopia. *Journal of Biosocial Science* 40(3):339–358.

Hadley, C., and D. L. Crooks 2012 Coping and the biosocial consequences of food insecurity in the 21st century. *American Journal of Physical Anthropology* 149:72–94.

Hadley, Craig, and Crystal L. Patil 2006 Food insecurity in rural Tanzania is associated with maternal anxiety and depression. *American Journal of Human Biology* 18(3): 359–368.

Hadley, Craig, Edward Geoffrey Jedediah Stevenson, Yemesrach Tadesse, and Tefera Belachew 2012 Rapidly rising food prices and the experience of food insecurity in urban Ethiopia: Impacts on health and well-being. *Social Science & Medicine* 75(12):2412–2419.

Hadley, Craig, A. Tegegn, F. Tessema, J.A. Cowan, M. Asefa, and S. Galea 2008 Food insecurity, stressful life events and symptoms of anxiety and depression in east Africa: Evidence from the Gilgel Gibe growth and development study. *Journal of Epidemiology and Community Health* 62(11):980–986.

Haidt, Jonathan 2003 Elevation and the positive psychology of morality. In *Flourishing: Positive psychology and the life well-lived.* 1st edition. C. L. M. Keyes and J. Haidt, eds. Pp. 275–289. Washington, DC: American Psychological Association.

——— 2007 The new synthesis in moral psychology. *Science* 316:998–1002.

Halpern, Orly 2007 In Ethiopia, elders dissolve a crisis the traditional way. The Christian Science Monitor. August 9, 2007. http://www.csmonitor.com/2007/0809/p01s02-woaf.html (acccessed September 13, 2016).

Han, Clara 2013 Labor instability and community mental health. In *When people come first: Critical studies in global health.* J. Biehl and A. Petryna, eds. Pp. 276–301. Princeton: Princeton University Press.

Hanlon, Charlotte, Girmay Medhin, Atalay Alem, Mesfin Araya, Abdulreshid Abdulahi, Mark Tomlinson, Marcus Hughes, Vikram Patel, Michael Dewey, and Martin Prince 2010 Sociocultural practices in Ethiopia: Association with onset and persistence of postnatal common mental disorders. *British Journal of Psychiatry* 197:468–475.

Hanlon, Charlotte, Rob Whitley, Dawit Wondimagegn, Atalay Alem, and Martin Prince 2009 Postnatal mental distress in relation to the sociocultural practices of childbirth: An exploratory qualitative study from Ethiopia. *Social Science & Medicine* 69(8):1211–1219.

HAPCO and World Bank 2008 HIV/AIDS in Ethiopia: An epidemiological synthesis. Washington, DC: The World Bank.

Headey, Derek, and Shenggen Fan 2008 Anatomy of a crisis: The causes and consequences of surging food prices. *Agricultural Economics* 39(s1):375–391.

Hirsch, Jennifer S., Holly Wardlow, Daniel Jordan Smith, Harriet M. Phinney, Shanti Parikh, and Constance A. Nathanson 2009 *The secret: Love, marriage, and HIV.* Nashville: Vanderbilt University Press.

Hussen, Sophia Ahmed, Mulugeta Tsegaye, Meron Gurji Argaw, Karen Andes, Danielle Gilliard, and Carlos del Rio 2014 Spirituality, social capital and service: Factors promoting resilience among expert patients living with HIV in Ethiopia. *Global Public Health* 9(3):286–298.

Iliffe, John 2006 *The African AIDS epidemic: A history.* Athens, Ohio: Ohio University Press.

Ingram, Maia, Kerstin M. Reinschmidt, Ken A. Schachter, Chris L. Davidson, Samantha J. Sabo, Jill Guernsey de Zapien, and Scott C. Carvajal 2012 Establishing a professional profile of community health workers: Results from a national study of roles, activities and training. *Journal of Community Health* 37(2):529–537.

Ingram, Maia, Samantha J. Sabo, Sofia Gomez, Rosalinda Piper, Jill Guernsey de Zapien, Kerstin M. Reinschmidt, Ken A. Schachter, and Scott C. Carvajal 2015 Taking a community-based participatory research approach in the development of methods to measure a community health worker community advocacy intervention. *Progress in Community Health Partnerships: Research, Education, and Action* 9(1):49–56.

Ingram, Maia, Ken A. Schachter, Samantha J. Sabo, Kerstin M. Reinschmidt, Sofia Gomez, Jill Guernsey de Zapien, and Scott Carvajal 2014 A community health worker intervention to address the social determinants of health through policy change. *Journal of Primary Prevention* 35:119–123.

International Monetary Fund 2008 The Federal Democratic Republic of Ethiopia: Selected Issues. 08/259. IMF Country Report No. 08/259. Washington, DC: International Monetary Fund (IMF).

Irwin, Alexander., and E. Scali 2007 Action on the social determinants of health: A historical perspective. *Global Public Health: An International Journal for Research, Policy and Practice* 2(3):235–256.

ITUC 2013 Countries at Risk: Violations of Trade Union Rights. Brussels: International Trade Union Confederation.

Ivanic, Maros, and Will Martin 2008 Implications of higher global food prices for poverty in low-income countries. *Agricultural Economics* 39(s1):405–416.

Jain, S. P., and Wim Polman 2003 *A handbook for trainers on participatory local development: The Panchayati Raj model in India.* Bangkok, Thailand: Food and Agriculture Organization of the United Nations FAO Regional Office for Asia and the Pacific, August 2003.

Jaskiewicz, Wanda, and Rachel Deussom 2014 Recruitment of community health workers. Chapter 8 in *Developing and strengthening community health worker programs at scale.* Henry Perry and Lauren Crigler, eds. Washington, DC: Jhpiego.

Kalofonos, Ippolytos Andreas. 2014 'All they do is pray': Community labour and the narrowing of 'care' during Mozambique's HIV scale-up. *Global Public Health* 9(1–2):7–24.

Kalofonos, Ippolytos Andreas 2010 "All I eat is ARVs": The paradox of AIDS treatment interventions in central Mozambique. *Medical Anthropology Quarterly* 24(3):363–380.

Kebede, D., A. Alem, and E. Rashid 1999 The prevalence and socio-deomographic correlates of mental distress in Addis Ababa, Ethiopia. *Acta Psychiatrica Scandinavica Supplementum* 397:95–101.

Kim, D., S. V. Subramanian, and I. Kawachi 2006 Bonding versus bridging social capital and their associations with self rated health: A multilevel analysis of 40 US communities. *Journal of Epidemiology and Community Health* 60(2):116–122.

Kim, J. Y., and P. Farmer 2006 AIDS in 2006 — Moving toward one world, one hope? *New England Journal of Medicine* 355(7):645–647.

Klaits, Frederick 2010 *Death in a church of life: Moral passion during Botswana's time of AIDS.* Berkeley: University of California Press.

Kleinman, A. 2008 Catastrophe and caregiving: The failure of medicine as an art. *The Lancet* 371(9606):22–23.

———— 2009 Caregiving: The odyssey of becoming more human. *The Lancet* 373(9660): 292–293.

Kleinman, Arthur 2006 *What really matters: Living a moral life amidst uncertainty and danger*. Oxford: Oxford University Press.

Kleinman, Arthur, and Bridget Hanna 2008 Catastrophe, caregiving and today's biomedicine. *BioSocieties* 3:287–301.

Kloos, Helmut 1998 Primary health care in Ethiopia under three political systems: Community participation in a war-torn society. *Social Science & Medicine* 46(4–5):505–522.

Kohrt, Brandon, and James Griffith 2015 Global mental health praxis: Perspectives from cultural psychiatry on research and intervention. In *Re-visioning psychiatry: Cultural phenomenology, critical neuroscience, and global mental health*. L. Kirmayer, R. Lemelson, and C. Cummings, eds. Pp. 575–612. New York: Cambridge University Press.

Korht, Brandon A., Emily Mendenhall, and Peter J. Brown 2015 A road map for anthropology and global mental health. In *Global mental health: Anthropological perspectives*. B. Kohrt and E. Mendenhall, eds. Pp. 341–361. Walnut Creek, CA: Left Coast Press.

LeBan, Karen, Henry Perry, Lauren Crigler, and Chris Colvin 2014 Community participation in large-scale community health worker programs. Chapter 13 in *Developing and strengthening community health worker programs at scale*. Henry Perry and Lauren Crigler, eds. Washington, DC: Jhpiego.

Leekassa, R., E. Bizuneh, and A. Alem 2004 Prevalence of mental distress in the outpatient clinic of a specialized leprosy hospital: Addis Ababa, 2002. *Leprosy Review* 75(4):367–375.

Lehmann, Uta, and David Sanders 2007 Community health workers: What do we know about them? The state of the evidence on programmes, activities, costs and impact on health outcomes of using community health workers. Geneva: Department of Human Resources for Health, Evidence and Information for Policy, World Health Organization.

Levine, Donald 1965 *Wax and gold: Tradition and innovation in Ethiopian culture*. Chicago: Chicago University Press.

Lewin, Simon, and Uta Lehmann 2014 Governing large-scale community health worker programs. Chapter 4 in *Developing and strengthening community health worker programs at scale*. Henry Perry and Lauren Crigler, eds. Washington, DC: Jhpiego.

Little, Peter D. 2014 "The government is always telling us what to think": Narratives of food aid dependence in rural Ethiopia. In *Economic and political reform in Africa: Anthropological perspectives*. P. Little, ed. Pp. 116–140. Bloomington: Indiana University Press.

Loening, Josef L., Dick Durevall, and Yohannes A. Birru 2009 Inflation dynamics and food prices in an agricultural economy: The case of Ethiopia. Washington, DC: The World Bank.

Lund, Crick, Alison Breen, Alan J. Fisher, Ritsuko Kakuma, Joanne Corrigall, John A. Joska, Leslie Swartz, and Vikram Patel 2010 Poverty and common mental disorders in low and middle income countries: A systematic review. *Social Science & Medicine* 71(3):517–528.

Maes, Kenneth C. 2012 Volunteerism or labor exploitation? Harnessing the volunteer spirit to sustain AIDS treatment programs in urban Ethiopia. *Human Organization* 71(1):54–64.

Maes, Kenneth, Svea Closser, Ethan Vorel, and Yihenew Tesfaye 2015 Using community health workers: Discipline and hierarchy in Ethiopia's Women's Development Army. *Annals of Anthropological Practice* 39(1):42–57.

Maes, Kenneth C., Craig Hadley, Fikru Tesfaye, and Selamawit Shifferaw 2010a Food insecurity and mental health: Surprising trends among community health volunteers in Addis Ababa, Ethiopia during the 2008 food crisis. *Social Science & Medicine* 70(9):1450–1457.

Maes, Kenneth C., Craig Hadley, Fikru Tesfaye, Selamawit Shifferaw, and Yihenew Alemu Tesfaye 2009 Food insecurity among volunteer AIDS caregivers in Addis Ababa, Ethiopia was highly prevalent but buffered from the 2008 food crisis. *Journal of Nutrition* 139(9):1758–1764.

Maes, Kenneth C., and Ippolytos Kalofonos 2013 Becoming and remaining community health workers: Perspectives from Ethiopia and Mozambique. *Social Science & Medicine* 87:52–59.

Maes, Kenneth C., Brandon A. Kohrt, and Svea Closser 2010b Culture, status, and context in community health worker pay: Pitfalls and opportunities for policy research. A commentary on Glenton et al. (2010). *Social Science & Medicine* 71(8):1375–1378.

Maes, Kenneth C., and Selamawit Shifferaw 2011 Cycles of poverty, food insecurity, and psychosocial stress among AIDS care volunteers in urban Ethiopia. *Annals of Anthropological Practice Thematic Issue: HIV/AIDS and Food Insecurity in Sub-Saharan Africa: Challenges and Solutions* 35(1):98–115.

Mains, Daniel 2012 *Hope is cut: Youth, unemployment, and the future in urban Ethiopia.* Philadelphia: Temple University Press.

Manchanda, Rishi 2015 Practice and power: Community health workers and the promise of moving health care upstream. *Journal of Ambulatory Care Manage* 38(3):219–224.

Mason, Terry, Geoffrey W. Wilkinson, Angela Nannini, Cindy Marti Martin, Durrell J. Fox, and Gail Hirsch 2010 Winning policy change to promote community health workers: Lessons from Massachusetts in the health reform era. *American Journal of Public Health* 101:2211–2216.

Matthews, Nathanial, Alan Nicol, and Wondwosen Michago Seide 2013 Constructing a new water future? An analysis of Ethiopia's current hydropower development. In *Handbook of land and water grabs in Africa.* T. Allan, M. Keulertz, S. Sojamo, and J. Warner, eds. Pp. 311–323. New York: Routledge.

Maupin, Jonathan N. 2011 Divergent models of community health workers in highland Guatemala. *Human Organization* 70(1):44–53.

———— 2015 Shifting identities: The transformation of community heath workers in highland Guatemala. *Annals of Anthropological Practice* 39(1):73–88.

McCord, G. C., A. Liu, and P. Singh 2013 Deployment of community health workers across rural sub-Saharan Africa: Financial considerations and operational assumptions. *Bulletin of the World Health Organization* 91(4):244–253.

Mendenhall, Emily, and Brandon Kohrt 2015 Anthropological methods in global mental health research. In *Global mental health: Anthropological perspectives.* B. Kohrt and E. Mendenhall, eds. Pp. 37–50. Walnut Creek, CA: Left Coast Press.

Messac, Luke, and Krishna Prabhu 2013 Redefining the possible: The global AIDS response. In *Reimagining global health: An introduction.* P. Farmer, J. Y. Kim, A. Kleinman, and M. Basilico, eds. Pp. 111–132. Berkeley: University of California Press.

Mogga, Souci, Martin Prince, Atalay Alem, Derege Kebede, Robert Stewart, Nick Glozier, and Matthew Hotopf 2006. Outcome of major depression in Ethiopia: Population-based study. *British Journal of Psychiatry* 189:241–246.

Morgan, Lynn 2001 Community participation in health: Perpetual allure, persistent challenge. *Health Policy & Planning* 16(3):221–230.

Muller, F. 1983 Contrasts in community participation: Case studies from Peru. In *Practising health for all*. D. Morley, J. E. Rohde, and G. Williams, eds. Pp. 190–207. Oxford: Oxford University Press.

Mumtaz, Zubia, Sarah Salway, Candace Nykiforuk, Afshan Bhatti, Anushka Ataullahjan, and Bharati Ayyalasomayajula 2013 The role of social geography on lady health workers' mobility and effectiveness in Pakistan. *Social Science & Medicine* 91:48–57.

Nader, Laura 1972 Up the anthropologist: Perspectives gained from studying up. In *Reinventing anthropology*. 1st edition. D. H. Hymes, ed. Pp. 284–311. New York: Pantheon Books.

Nading, Alex M. 2013 "Love isn't there in your stomach"—A moral economy of medical citizenship among Nicaraguan community health workers. *Medical Anthropology Quarterly* 27(1):84–102.

Nanama, Simeon, and Edward A. Frongillo 2012 Altered social cohesion and adverse psychological experiences with chronic food insecurity in the non-market economy and complex households of Burkina Faso. *Social Science & Medicine* 74(3):444–451.

Newell, Kenneth W., ed. 1975 *Health by the people*. Geneva: World Health Organization.

Nichter, Mark 1999 Project community diagnosis: Participatory research as a first step toward community involvement in primary health care. In *Anthropology in public health: Bridging differences in culture and society*. R. A. Hahn, ed. Pp. 300–324. New York: Oxford University Press.

Ooms, Gorik, Wim Van Damme, Brook K. Baker, Paul Zeitz, and Ted Schrecker 2008 The 'diagonal' approach to Global Fund financing: A cure for the broader malaise of health systems. *Globalization and Health* 4(6):e1–e7.

Ooms, Gorik, Wim Van Damme, and Marleen Temmerman 2007 Medicines without doctors: Why the Global Fund must fund salaries of health workers to expand AIDS treatment. *Plos Medicine* 4(4):605–608.

Ottaway, Marina, and David Ottaway 1978 *Ethiopia: Empire in revolution*. New York: Africana.

Palazuelos, Daniel, K. Ellis, D. DaEun Im, M. Peckarsky, D. Schwarz, D. Bertrand Farmer, R. Dhillon, A. Johnson, C. Orihuela, J. Hackett, J. Bazile, L. Berman, M. Ballard, R. Panjabi, R. Ternier, S. Slavin, S. Lee, S. Selinsky, and C.D. Mitnick 2013 5-SPICE: The application of an original framework for community health worker program design, quality improvement and research agenda setting. *Global Health Action* 6:1–12.

Pankhurst, Alula, and Damen Haile-Mariam 2000 The *Iddir* in Ethiopia: Historical development, social function, and potential role in HIV/AIDS prevention and control. *Northeast African Studies* 7(2):35–58.

Patel, Vikram, Ricardo Araya, Mauricio de Lima, Ana Ludermir, and Charles Todd 1999 Women, poverty and common mental disorders in four restructuring societies. *Social Science & Medicine* 49(11):1461–1471.

Pérez, Leda M., and Jacqueline Martinez 2008 Community health workers: Social justice and policy advocates for community health and well-being. *American Journal of Public Health* 98(1):11–14.

Perry, H. B., R. Zulliger, and M. M. Rogers 2014 Community health workers in low-, middle-, and high-income countries: An overview of their history, recent evolution, and current effectiveness. *Annual Review of Public Health* 35:399–421.

Perry, Henry, and Lauren Crigler, eds. 2014 *Developing and strengthening community health worker programs at scale*. Washington, DC: Jhpiego.

Pfeiffer, James 2013 The struggle for a public sector. In *When people come first: Critical studies in global health.* J. Biehl and A. Petryna, eds. Pp. 166–181. Princeton: Princeton University Press.

Pfeiffer, James, and Rachel Chapman 2010 Anthropological perspectives on structural adjustment and public health. *Annual Review of Anthropology* 39(1):149–165.

Pfeiffer, James, Wendy Johnson, Meredith Fort, Aaron Shakow, Amy Hagopian, Steve Gloyd, and Kenneth Gimbel-Sherr 2008 Strengthening health systems in poor countries: A code of conduct for nongovernmental organizations. *American Journal of Public Health* 98(12):2134–2140.

Piliavin, J. A., and E. Siegl 2007 Health benefits of volunteering in the Wisconsin Longitudinal Study. *Journal of Health and Social Behavior* 48(4):450–464.

Poluha, Eva 2004 *The power of continuity: Ethiopia through the eyes of its children.* Uppsala, Sweden: Nordiska Afrikainstitutet.

Rifkin, Susan 1996 Paradigms lost: Toward a new understanding of participation in public health programmes. *Acta Tropica* 61(2):79–92.

Robertson, Alexander F. 2001 *Greed: Gut feelings, growth, and history.* Cambridge: Polity Press.

Robles, Miguel, Maximo Torero, and Joachim von Braun 2009 When speculation matters. IFPRI Issue Brief 57. Washinton, DC: International Food Policy Research Institute (IFPRI).

Rowden, Rick 2009 *The deadly ideas of neoliberalism.* London: Zed Books.

Sabo, Samantha, Maia Ingram, Kerstin M. Reinschmidt, Kenneth Schachter, Laurel Jacobs, Jill Guernsey de Zapien, Laurie Robinson, and Scott Carvajal 2013 Predictors and a framework for fostering community advocacy as a community health worker core function to eliminate health disparities. *American Journal of Public Health* 103(7):e67–e73.

Sabo, Samantha, Ashley Wennerstrom, David Phillips, Catherine Haywoord, Floribella Redondo, Melanie L. Bell, and Maia Ingram. 2015 Community health worker professional advocacy: Voices of action from the 2014 national community health worker advocacy survey. *Journal of Ambulatory Care Manage* 38(3):225–235.

Schwarz, D., R. Sharma, C. Bashyal, R. Schwarz, A. Baruwal, G. Karelas, B. Basnet, N. Khadka, J. Brady, Z. Silver, J. Mukherjee, J. Andrews, and D. Smith-Rohrberg Maru 2014 Strengthening Nepal's female community health volunteer network: A qualitative study of experiences at two years. *BMC Health Services Research* 14(1):473.

Scott, James C. 1976 *The moral economy of the peasant: Rebellion and subsistence in Southeast Asia.* New Haven: Yale University Press.

———— 1985 *Weapons of the weak: Everyday forms of peasant resistance.* New Haven: Yale University Press.

———— 1990 *Domination and the arts of resistance: Hidden transcripts.* New Haven: Yale University Press.

Shweder, Richard A., Jonathan Haidt, Randall Horton, and Craig Joseph 2008 The cultural psychology of the emotions: Ancient and renewed. In *Handbook of emotions.* 3rd edition. M. Lewis, J. M. Haviland-Jones, and L. F. Barrett, eds. Pp. 409–427. New York: Guilford Press.

Shweder, Richard A., Nancy C. Much, Manamohan Mahapatra, and Lawrence Park 2003 The big three of morality (autonomy, community, divinity) and the "big three" explanations of suffering. In *Why do men barbeque?* R. A. Shweder, ed. Pp. 74–133. Cambridge, MA: Harvard University Press.

Siddiqi, Sameen, Tayyeb I. Masud, Sania Nishtar, David H. Peters, Belgacem Sabri, Khalif M. Bile, and Mohamed A. Jama 2009 Framework for assessing governance of the health system in developing countries: Gateway to good governance. *Health Policy* 90:13–25.

Singer, Merrill 1995 Beyond the ivory tower: Critical praxis in medical anthropology. *Medical Anthropology Quarterly* 9(1):80–106.

———— 2011 Toward a critical biosocial model of ecohealth in southern Africa: The HIV/AIDS and nutrition insecurity syndemic. *Annals of Anthropological Practice* 35(1):8–27.

Singer, Merrill, and Arachu Castro 2004 Introduction—Anthropology and health policy: A critical perspective. In *Unhealthy health policy: A critical anthropological examination.* A. Castro and M. Singer, eds. Pp. xi–xx. Walnut Creek, CA: AltaMira Press.

Singh, P., and D. A. Chokshi 2013 Community health workers—A local solution to a global problem. *New England Journal of Medicine* 369(10):894–896.

Singh, P., and J. D. Sachs 2013 1 million community health workers in sub-Saharan Africa by 2015. *The Lancet* 382(9889):363–365.

Smith, D. J. 2003 Patronage, per diems and the "workshop mentality": The practice of family planning programs in southeastern Nigeria. *World Development* 31(4):703–715.

Smith, Daniel Jordan 2014 *AIDS doesn't show its face.* Chicago: University of Chicago Press.

Smith-Morris, Carolyn, G. Lopez, L. Ottomanelli, L. Goetz, and K. Dixon-Lawson 2014 Ethnography, fidelity, and the evidence that anthropology adds: Supplementing the fidelity process in a clinical trial of supported employment. *Medical Anthropology Quarterly* 28(2):141–161.

Standing, H., A. Mushtaque, and R. Chowdhury 2008 Producing effective knowledge agents in a pluralistic environment: What future for community health workers? *Social Science & Medicine* 66:2096–2107.

Swartz, Alison 2013 Legacy, legitimacy, and possibility: An exploration of community health worker experience across the generations in Khayelitsha, South Africa. *Medical Anthropology Quarterly* 27(2):139–154.

Swidler, Ann, and Susan Cotts Watkins 2009 "Teach a man to fish": The sustainability doctrine and its social consequences. *World Development* 37(7):1182–1196.

Swindale, Anne, and Paula Bilinsky 2006 Development of a universally applicable household food insecurity measurement tool: Process, current status, and outstanding issues. *Journal of Nutrition* 136(5):1449–1452.

Taylor, Harry 2001 Insights into participation from critical management and labour process perspectives. In *Participation: The new tyranny?* Bill Cooke and Uma Gothari, eds. Pp. 122–138. London: Zed Books.

Teklehaimanot, Hailay, and Awash Teklehaimanot 2013 Human resource development for a community-based health extension program: A case study from Ethiopia. *Human Resources for Health* 11(1):39.

Terecha, Mesele 2005 *Leprosy, leprosaria and society in Ethiopia.* Addis Ababa: Armauer Hansen Research Institute.

Tesfaye, Markos, Charlotte Hanlon, Dawit Wondimagegn, and Atalay Alem 2010 Detecting postnatal common mental disorders in Addis Ababa, Ethiopia: Validation of the Edinburgh postnatal depression scale and Kessler scales. *Journal of Affective Disorders* 122(1–2):102–108.

Thompson, E. P. 1971 The moral economy of the English crowd in the eighteenth century. *Past & Present* 50:76–136.

Ticktin, Miriam Iris 2011 *Casualties of care: Immigration and the politics of humanitarianism in France.* Berkeley: University of California Press.

Ulimwengu, John M., Sindu Workneh, and Zelekawork Paulos 2009 Impact of soaring food price in Ethiopia. Discussion Paper 00846. Washington, D.C.: International Food Policy Research Institute (IFPRI).

United Nations Human Settlements Programme (UN-Habitat) 2008. *State of the world's cities 2008/2009.* UN-Habitat.

Vella, Stefano, and Lucia Palmisano 2005 The global status of resistance to antiretroviral drugs. *Clinical Infectious Diseases* 41:S239–S246.

Wainberg, Mark, Gerasimos Zaharatos, and Bluma Brenner 2011. Development of antiretroviral drug resistance. *New England Journal of Medicine* 365:637–646.

Wallerstein, N. 2002 Empowerment to reduce health disparities. *Scandinavian Journal of Public Health* 30(3):72–77.

Walt, G. 1988 CHWs: Are national programmes in crisis? *Health Policy and Planning* 3:1–21.

Watkins, S. C., and A. Swidler 2013 Working misunderstandings: Donors, brokers, and villagers in Africa's AIDS industry. *Population and Development Review* 38:197–218.

Watt, Patrick, Nouria Bricki, Lara Brearley, and Kathryn Rawe 2011 No child out of reach. London: Save the Children.

Wayland, C., and J. Crowder 2002 Disparate views of community in primary health care: Understanding how perceptions influence success. *Medical Anthropology Quarterly* 16(2):230–247.

Werner, David 1981 The village health worker: Lackey or liberator? *World Health Forum* 2(1):46–68.

Whitfield, L., and A. Fraser 2010 Negotiating aid: The structural conditions shaping the negotiating strategies of African governments. *International Negotiation* 15:341–366.

WHO 1978 Declaration of Alma-Ata. Geneva: World Health Organization.

———— 1989 Strengthening the performance of community health workers in primary health care. Geneva: World Health Organization.

———— 2002 Community home-based care in resource-limited settings: A framework for action. Geneva: World Health Organization.

———— 2006 The world health report 2006: Working together for health. Geneva: World Health Organization.

———— 2008 Task shifting: Rational redistribution of tasks among health workforce teams—Global recommendations and guidelines. Geneva: World Health Organization.

———— 2009 Ethiopia extends health to its people: An interview with Dr. Tedros A. Ghebreyesus. *Bulletin of the World Health Organization* 87(7):495–496.

———— 2015 Global strategy on human resources for health: Workforce 2030 (Draft for consultation). Geneva: World Health Organization.

Wiggins, Noelle 2012 Popular education for health promotion and community empowerment: A review of the literature. *Health Promotion International* 27(3):356–371.

Wiggins, Noelle, Adele Hughes, Adriana Rodriguez, Catherine Potter, and Teresa Rios-Campos 2014 La Palabra es Salud (The Word Is Health): Combining mixed methods and CBPR to understand the comparative effectiveness of popular and conventional education. *Journal of Mixed Methods Research* 8(3):278–298. DOI: 10.1177/1558689813510.

Wiggins, Noelle, Samantha Kaan, Teresa Rios-Campos, Rujuta Gaonkar, Elizabeth Rees Morgan, and Jamaica Robinson 2013 Preparing community health workers for their role as agents of social change: Experience of the Community Capacitation Center. *Journal of Community Practice* 21(3):186–202.

Willen, Sarah 2012 How is health-related "deservingness" reckoned? Perspectives from unauthorized im/migrants in Tel Aviv. *Social Science & Medicine* 74(6):812–821.

Yohannes, Paulos 1988 Filsata: The Feast of the Assumption of the Virgin Mary and the Mariological tradition of the Ethiopian Orthodox Tewahedo Church. Thesis (Ph D), Princeton Theological Seminary, 1988.

Zenawi, Meles 2012 States and markets: Neolliberal limitations and the case for a developmental state. In *Good growth and governance in Africa: Rethinking development strategies*. A. Noman, K. Botchwey, H. Stein, and J. E. Stiglitz, eds. Pp. 140–174. Oxford: Oxford University Press.

Zezza, Alberto, et al. 2008 The impact of rising food prices on the poor. ESA Working Paper 08-07. Rome: Food and Agriculture Organization.

Zilber, Nelly, et al. 2004 Development of a culturally sensitive psychiatric screening instrument for Ethiopian populations. Amsterdam: Royal Tropical Institute and KIT Publishers.

INDEX

Note: Italicized page numbers indicate photographs.

Taylor & Francis eBooks

Helping you to choose the right eBooks for your Library

Add Routledge titles to your library's digital collection today. Taylor and Francis ebooks contains over 50,000 titles in the Humanities, Social Sciences, Behavioural Sciences, Built Environment and Law.

Choose from a range of subject packages or create your own!

Benefits for you

>> Free MARC records
>> COUNTER-compliant usage statistics
>> Flexible purchase and pricing options
>> All titles DRM-free.

REQUEST YOUR FREE INSTITUTIONAL TRIAL TODAY

Free Trials Available
We offer free trials to qualifying academic, corporate and government customers.

Benefits for your user

>> Off-site, anytime access via Athens or referring URL
>> Print or copy pages or chapters
>> Full content search
>> Bookmark, highlight and annotate text
>> Access to thousands of pages of quality research at the click of a button.

eCollections – Choose from over 30 subject eCollections, including:

Archaeology	Language Learning
Architecture	Law
Asian Studies	Literature
Business & Management	Media & Communication
Classical Studies	Middle East Studies
Construction	Music
Creative & Media Arts	Philosophy
Criminology & Criminal Justice	Planning
Economics	Politics
Education	Psychology & Mental Health
Energy	Religion
Engineering	Security
English Language & Linguistics	Social Work
Environment & Sustainability	Sociology
Geography	Sport
Health Studies	Theatre & Performance
History	Tourism, Hospitality & Events

For more information, pricing enquiries or to order a free trial, please contact your local sales team:
www.tandfebooks.com/page/sales

Routledge
Taylor & Francis Group

The home of
Routledge books

www.tandfebooks.com

CPSIA information can be obtained
at www.ICGtesting.com
Printed in the USA
BVHW01s1459091217
502352BV00006B/29/P